DIAGHILEFF

HIS ARTISTIC AND PRIVATE LIFE

A DA CAPO PRESS REPRINT SERIES

The Lyric Stage

GENERAL EDITOR: DALE HARRIS
SARAH LAWRENCE COLLEGE

DIAGHILEFF
HIS ARTISTIC AND PRIVATE LIFE

BY ARNOLD L. HASKELL

In collaboration with
WALTER NOUVEL

DA CAPO PRESS · NEW YORK · 1977

Library of Congress Cataloging in Publication Data

Haskell, Arnold Lionel, 1903-
  Diaghileff, his artistic and private life.

  (The Lyric stage)
  Reprint of the 1935 ed. published by Simon and
Schuster, New York.
  1. Diagilev, Sergei Pavlovich, 1872-1929.
2. Impresarios—Biography. I. Nouvel, Walter, joint
author. II. Title.
GV1785.D5H3 1977 792.8'092'4 [B] 77-23180
ISBN 0-306-70869-8

This Da Capo Press edition of *Diaghileff, His Artistic and Private Life* is an unabridged republication of the first edition published in New York in 1935.

Published by Da Capo Press, Inc.
A Subsidiary of Plenum Publishing Corporation
227 West 17th Street, New York, N. Y. 10011

Manufactured in the United States of America

Diaghileff and Serge Lifar, 1927

DIAGHILEFF

HIS ARTISTIC AND PRIVATE LIFE

BY ARNOLD L. HASKELL
In collaboration with
WALTER NOUVEL

SIMON AND SCHUSTER · NEW YORK

1935

DEDICATION

Diaghileff's lifework was threefold:

> Painting
> Music
> The Stage

This Biography is therefore dedicated
to
ALEXANDRE BENOIS
IGOR STRAVINSKY
SERGE GRIGORIEFF

for reasons that its readers will appreciate.

A. L. H.

CONTENTS

CONTENTS

——ILLUSTRATIONS——

xiii

ILLUSTRATIONS

xiv

ILLUSTRATIONS

xv

At one time the writing of this book seemed an impossibility. I knew Diaghileff casually over a number of years. I knew his ballet well, and that is all I had to go upon. It was clear from the first that his early years, through war and revolution buried in a now remote historic past, were the important ones in any attempt to discover the man himself. The Diaghileff that I knew could not be separated at any point from his work. His adventures were artistic ones—of the mind. I admired him greatly; and although that was an impetus, it was not enough in itself, and even those who knew him intimately during the latter part of his life could tell me little and spoke in formulæ. He was never given to talking about himself; few people received his confidences; and he had an intense dislike for personal publicity. No man in his position ever left fewer letters to guide a biographer.

I travelled widely in search of information. Diaghileff dead aroused as much controversy, gave rise to as many contradictory and conflicting views, as Diaghileff alive. I found myself, at first, almost compelled to be friendly with one group to the exclusion of another. Many of his collaborators feared that I would not do justice to their claims. They even saw in Diaghileff's growing fame a menace, for had he not become famous through their work? Many who had made the journey with him could not in all sincerity understand what the fuss was about: "Diaghileff never created. He gave me the chance to do all my work. He was understanding and sympathetic." They were too close to him to understand just how he worked, too much a part of his creation.

Then came another conflict. Many had such decided ideas about his life and character that they decided they must write their own biographies of Diaghileff. To each associate he appeared in a totally different light. These books remain to be written; they will be extremely valuable, but I have wished to give something more nearly complete, because more impersonal.

I went to Serge Grigorieff first. He knew most things, and remembered them too, but he was too busy with ballet in the present to sit down and talk of the past. My first really productive encounter was with Alexandre Benois. As Diaghileff had formed countless artists, so did Benois play the chief rôle in forming Diaghileff. With the greatest kindness he gave me much valuable early information and set me on the right track. Visit after visit to people who had worked with him for months or for years filled in small gaps, and gave me many pages of unrelated material.

§ 2

Some of my material was given to me by my good friend Valerian Svetloff, *doyen* of ballet critics. He was keenly interested in the progress of this book, eager to help in every way possible. Alas, that he could never see it completed!

Svetloff lived through the whole life of the Russian Ballet, from the day that it truly became Russian and the supremacy of the Italians was overthrown, to the period of the little *émigré* dancers, pupils of his great heroines. It was he who wrote that a certain *débutante*, Mlle Pavlova, was destined for great things, and who recorded those great things in a monumental volume devoted to her art. He watched that glorious career from the beginning to the Swan's final flutter at The Hague.

Svetloff knew more than any man about ballet, because he lived it and it was all a part of his own experience. To the end of his life he resisted the temptation of damning the new in the name of the old. He was the first to acclaim Fokine, and to see in him not a rabid revolutionary, but a creative mind who could lead the ballet back to Noverre's principles.

His *Ballet Contemporain,* evidence of that faith, became a classic shortly after its publication.

As a man he was kindly and generous, ever ready to serve the cause of ballet, with no jealousies or interested motives. I shall ever be grateful for his helpful encouragement. He assisted me at a time when impression was crowding in upon impression. We had a common enthusiasm for the genius of Trefilova that I was then struggling to put into words. That enthusiasm bridged the years. He never laughed at me, never patronized me, but accepted me from the first as an ally. His praise, the letters and articles I received from him, are infinitely precious.

He knew Diaghileff and understood him. He was from the first in his inner circle. His notes have helped me; his advice would have helped me more.

I can only wish for him what I wish one day for myself : that he is in a place where Pavlova is forever young; that he can see Taglioni and her peers in the famous *pas de quatre,* and assist in a conversation between Diaghileff and Noverre.

§ 3

My last visit was to Walter Nouvel, whom I had not known previously. He alone had lived through nearly all the periods. He had worked with Diaghileff, quarrelled with Diaghileff, admired and loved him, and could yet talk of him with a refreshing detachment.

He was one of the rare people with no axe to grind, no pet

theory to prove. He was not seeking a special place in the sun. Because of that, no doubt, his many achievements will go unacknowledged here. He was as desperately keen as I was to prepare some fitting memorial to his friend—a work that by telling everything frankly would defend his memory against unjustified attacks. It was a pleasure to talk to him; and almost immediately we decided on a collaboration, in the belief that the intimate view and the distant view together would give a trustworthy picture of the man, true in perspective. We were both of us aware of his faults; Nouvel had suffered at times from his difficult character; we decided to be entirely honest in telling everything that we knew.

Nouvel has provided me with a mass of carefully compiled notes, and without his help the task would have been an impossibility. I have often interpreted that material in my own manner, but the resulting portrait seems to us both a good and complete likeness.

Diaghileff's life was not one of active adventure. It was a life of artistic adventure, rich in its variety of human contacts. It has been necessary, therefore, to give an adequate background to many artistic struggles without losing sight of the central character. If many of his collaborators, who have been sketched in here, have not had justice done them, the fault is not consciously ours. So few documents exist, so many important decisions took place during dinner-table conversations, that it is generally impossible to pin down an idea to an individual. For the same reason some who did fine work may have been omitted altogether.

The Diaghileff period abounded in interesting men and interesting ideas; he was in close contact with them all, but so far the literature on the subject is scanty. No doubt it will be amplified bit by bit through personal memoirs.

This is not the story of the Diaghileff Ballet, but of the man himself; and the ballet, though it occupied the greater part of his active life, was but one manifestation of his creative ability. So great a friend and a judge as Alexandre Benois even grudges it the monopoly of those twenty years. Diaghileff himself was greater than his Ballet, and he can only be discovered through a careful study of those early years in Russia. If we begin at any later period, we lose sight of him and fail to follow the amazing consistency of his artistic life—a consistency that totally escaped the writer till he began to delve into the past. From Perm to the founding of the Ballet, and from then to Venice, is one direct evolution along the lines mentioned in his Palais Tauride speech —an investigation of the past, and then an adventure into the future in search of a new æsthetic, a continual reconciliation of classicism and modernity.[1]

No memoirs that will come in the future can detract from Diaghileff's own rôle. From 1909 to 1929 was the Diaghileff era in European Art.

ARNOLD L. HASKELL

London—Paris—Monte Carlo
   1934–1935

---

[1] The actual story of the gradual changes in ballet, brought about by Diaghileff, apart from the details of production, is told in three separate chapters (VIII, XIII, XVIII), in order not to confuse the main current of the story.

──ACKNOWLEDGMENTS──

There are many whom I must thank for the invaluable help they have given me, either through conversations, notes, and letters, or their published work. Had any one of them failed me, this story would have been incomplete.

I must thank Mrs. Williams for her account of the Diaghileff family taken from her delightful biography of Anna Pavlovna Filosofova; Mrs. Gabrielle Enthoven for the use of her unique collection of programmes and photographs at the Victoria and Albert Museum; the Baroness d'Erlanger for her account of Diaghileff's death; Tamara Karsavina for much invaluable information; also Princess Krasinska, Mesdames Vera Trefilova, Lydia Lopokova, Lydia Sokolova, Lubov Tchernicheva; His Imperial Highness the Grand Duke André of Russia for many conversations; Professor McColl for his loan of an interesting letter; Mr. Albert W. King for the same reason, and for much information; Mr. Eric Wollheim for an interesting interview; Mr. Edwin Evans, perhaps the only Englishman to understand Diaghileff as a compatriot; Miss Netta Lacey for delving into his archives; Messieurs Serge Lifar, Anton Dolin, Serge Grigorieff, Leonide Massine, Georges Balanchine, Michel Fokine, Ian Hoyer, and other members of the company; Monsieur Alexandre Benois, who knows everything and is generous with his information; Monsieur Igor Stravinsky for the rich material in his fine biography, *Chroniques de ma vie*; and Mr. W. A. Propert, friend of Diaghileff and great historian of his ballet. The Prince

ACKNOWLEDGEMENTS

Serge Wolkonsky for a long account of affairs during his directorate of the Imperial Theatres and Mr. Montagu Nathan for the loan of many books and much information. Lastly, Mr. Walter Nouvel for his many pages of illuminating notes, for his patience, for his consistently un-Russian punctuality. His friendship is not the least reward for this work.

A. L. H.

THE SHADE OF DIAGHILEFF

Monte Carlo—Five years after—1934.

"He was a remarkable man," began Grigorieff, and Lubov Tchernicheva, his wife, beautiful Cleopatra of the great days, superb Zobeide of to-day, nods in agreement . . . "*mais tout à fait remarquable, alors.*"

"I know, Sergei Leoniditch, I know, but that is really no great help. They all begin like that, when talking of Diaghileff, unless they are French, and then they say, *Ce prodigieux animateur*. In what was he remarkable, how and why? You have lived the whole story, and now you have had full time to pause and look back on it. Give me some illuminating definition that will set me on the right track."

He sat, drumming with his fingers on the café table.

"You knew both the man and his work. You must realize, therefore, how difficult it is to separate them, to describe so long a period of movement, experiment, and achievement in a phrase or two . . . but wait. Here is a vivid instance that struck me only this morning. Nijinsky's wife has written a book about her husband from her own intensely personal angle. I disagree with the accuracy of many of her facts, and of most of her interpretations and conclusions. Of course she knew Diaghileff only slightly, and it was inevitable in the situation that she should tend to belittle him, or, more accurately, to increase Nijinsky's stature at his expense. Well, after reading the book with all its special pleading, what remains? *Diaghileff*. One is left with the impression of a truly colossal Diaghileff, and her hero Nijinsky remains vague, a somewhat unconvincing puppet. Obviously anyone who knew Diaghileff, even superficially, will realize that he had more profitable and constructive things to do with his time than fritter it away in a cruel and senseless vendetta; he was altogether too big a man; yet, in spite of all her hostility, Romola Nijinska was clearly so impressed by his size, so obsessed by it, that she could not detract from it by an inch. He is both the hero and the villain of her book."

We are sitting at the Café de Paris, Monte Carlo. Where could it be more natural to begin a quest for the real Diaghileff, to separate man from legend, than here, his home and headquarters for so many years? To whom should one go first for guidance and a blessing, if not to Serge Grigorieff, his trusted lieutenant from the beginning of the adventure? Grigorieff is the only name to be found both in the Châtelet programme of 1909 and the Covent Garden programme of 1929.[1] That stretch of time means poise and knowledge. Grigorieff almost alone among the collaborators has no axe to grind, no theory to prove. He saw the happenings of those days in such close and practical detail that he is the last man to indulge in dreams or in the luxury of hero-worship—that refuge of the inactive. If anyone realized and suffered from Diaghileff's faults, it was Grigorieff.

"No one ever quite knows what Sergei Leoniditch is thinking," they say in the Ballet, such is his reserve and his habitual lack of enthusiasm in a world of easy enthusiasm. Success that intoxicates a theatre and a whole capital leaves him unmoved, magnificently calm to confront the next great difficulty that is sure to arise.

"*Oui* . . ." dragging the word, as if in serious doubt, "*c'était*

[1] "No one is indispensable; Grigorieff almost." Diaghileff to A. L. H.

un bon spectacle ce soir . . . pas mal dansé . . . et un bon public surtout."

It is his job to estimate the faults, not praise the virtues.

That is the attitude of the man I have watched at work in so many countries over so many years.

Once someone in an article dared to call him "a stage director of genius." When I translated it to him, thinking to give him pleasure, he smiled feebly out of politeness, and then, as he repeated the words, took on a pained expression.

"Genius, h'm, that is the word I always use about those who try to be too clever."

Yet I think it must have required something very near genius to have understood Diaghileff for twenty years, something much more than tact, for Sergei Pavlovitch, unlike a film Tsar, did not always wish for tacit agreement; only one had to know just when to advance an opinion, and Grigorieff always knew.

I have started wisely: names, addresses, dates—he has them all.

"It will be difficult, but very, very interesting. It is good that you do it." That is the blessing.

We are joined by Vsevolod Grigorieff, the son of Sergei Leoniditch, and his bride of that week, Tamara [Sidorenko], beauty and dancer of talent, who knew not Diaghileff. Vsevolod joins in our conversation. He remembers the great man well, especially here in Monte Carlo. He tries to explain him to his lovely young Tamara.

"He was a remarkable man," begins Vsevolod—and then pauses. We are all agreed upon that point, and I find myself echoing the phrase and nodding vigorously to Tamara in an effort to make her understand.

•　　᛫　　᛫　　᛫　　᛫　　᛫　　᛫　　▪

Just a season ago, one night, a young girl from the new gen-

eration of dancers ran terrified, down the long dark corridor
leading from the tomb-like rehearsal-room, towards the reassur-
ing light of a lantern. Up the slope she ran, breathless. Was it
following her? She had heard footsteps, had seen some vague
white shadow advancing down the corridor, filling it so that she
could not pass. Deeply moved, and, of course, a little proud, she
told her friends. Who or what could it be? They decided that it
must be the spirit of Diaghileff, haunting the rehearsal-room
that in life he had so strongly dominated—that same rehearsal-
room in which he had on one memorable occasion flown into
such a rage, stamping and beating on the floor with his stick,
that a group of frightened rats bolted out from the wainscoting.

And so a story of haunting has grown, as it was bound to; yet
another chapter added to the legend, soon doubtless to be embel-
lished with ornament and detail, until fact and fiction are one
and inseparable.

Yet I cannot be surprised. For me, too, Monte Carlo is Diag-
hileff-haunted, in full sunshine as in shadow. I can see and feel
him everywhere, not as some vague white shade that frightens,
but as a positive fact, seated at this Café de Paris, where we, who
knew him, are talking of a past that is suddenly so much the
present; standing on the Hôtel de Paris steps across the way,
dwarfed and paled by the uniformed negro giant, turning
slightly to talk to an elfin Picasso, followed by the burly bearded
Evans and others. Now he is shielding his eyes from the glare,
as he waits for his favourite carriage. I can see him, also, by that
historic seat outside the rehearsal-room, overlooking railway
line and sea—a seat that is itself haunted by the shades of countless dancers who have sat there—weeping at the loss of a rôle, or
at his brusque reprimand, "*On ne danse pas ainsi dans les Ballets
Russes. Je ne l'admets pas.*" The tears are an exception: more
often they are gossiping and laughing, handing round press-cut-
tings and photographs. It is here that they ask Grigorieff for ad-

vances and plead their poverty, and he answers them at times gruffly, lest they break the bank by their importunities. Cecchetti joins Diaghileff at the door, talks to him as no one else dare, mocking at the new choreography in the picturesque language of his own devising, true souvenir of world triumphs. Just now they are discussing the progress of a certain young Serge Lifar, who is shortly to make his début in an important rôle. "Will he be a new Nijinsky, *maestro?*"

For me all of that is in the air of Monte Carlo and will always be, far more exciting and definite than those gaming-rooms that are for the *balletomane*, gloriously crazy in his own manner, merely an incident between *Les Sylphides* and *Le Train Bleu*.

It is natural, when beginning the biography of someone whom one has known, to re-create for oneself a definite physical image. In the case of Diaghileff it is indispensable. The man has given his name to a whole epoch, and in doing so has been lost as an individual, so that now his memory has become the easy prey of every modern romantic. Is it to be wondered at? It is so painfully easy to add Nijinsky's Trilby to Diaghileff's Svengali, and so to make up a pretty story. It is far more difficult to probe into the mind of a master painter who never painted, a master musician who never wrote or played, the master dancer who never danced or devised the steps of a ballet. Yet, in a sense, he was all these things at times.

It is necessary from the very start to cling on to his physical image, or the white shade of legend might intrude and come between us and reality. That is why I look for him now in the sunshine of Monte Carlo, or try to see him once again in the mistiness of London, waiting to take his satellites and "geniuses" to the Savoy grill.

The first fleeting glance is that of a dandy in the general allure, of someone intensely interested in his person, the actual physical rather than the adornment. One can divine the careful *toilette* from the very first moment, and it is that that gives the sense of smartness, in spite of a dinner-jacket that may be sadly frayed, or of boots that are much worn. Then comes the sense of poise—his whole stance shows his knowledge of his absolute superiority. It is the easy poise of the man who has been born to command, and not the restless, arrogant truculent manner of the self-made man who has his doubts. Diaghileff has not the slightest doubts, and never has had, and with him the strength is accompanied by that grace and charm which are the prerogative of the born leader.

Next comes the feeling of weight. The head is too large for the body, a fact that is usually hidden by a wide nutria collar that adds bulk to the shoulders. The hair is brown, growing back high on the forehead, thick, carefully brushed, with a distinguishing white mesh high up on the right-hand side. There is a magnificent expanse of noble forehead. The eyes are of great depth, brown, luminous, penetrating, beautiful. One of them is brought into relief by an eye-glass firmly wedged in, suspended on a black cord. There are pouches under them—baggy when he is overwrought or tired. The nose is a snub, with wide nostrils; a thin circumflex-shaped moustache, very much cultivated and almost a line high up on the lip, accentuates its length and the heavy fleshy mouth. In repose it is determined, in animation, with its projecting animal teeth, almost brutal. The chin juts out.

It is a face almost without lines. There is there the mixture of the healthy, apple-cheeked boy that was, and the cynical highly experienced man of the world, a contradiction that is arresting, and that is stressed all the more vividly by the chinchilla mesh.

Then, finally, one's glance settles on the characteristic that is the most memorable of all—the hands, fat and flabby with fingers pointing backwards to an unusual degree, yet, for all their flabbiness, quick and capable. One can sense the form and framework under the fat.

xxx

It is very tempting, when one knows the whole story and is working backwards, to endow the physical portrait of a man with certain dramatic characteristics, to play the theatrical producer and to cast the type from the script, but such need not be the case here. Never did anyone look more like the great animator and the determined man of action that he was than Sergei Pavlovitch Diaghileff.

In later life, when a man has achieved, his manner and expression alter to suit his new relationship to the world around him. This was not so with Diaghileff, and it is an important point in estimating his early years. Benois has shown me a photograph of him as a youth; there he stands, a little slimmer, his hair in a military crop and minus the distinguishing white mesh —that is the only difference. It is the great Diaghileff, conscious of power, but in schoolboy uniform.

＊　＊　＊　＊　＊　＊　＊　・

My interest in this man began through my passion for his work. It was not enough to watch *Les Sylphides* and to be enraptured. What was the formula? Who were its creators? Chopin, Fokine, Benois, and Diaghileff? The first three I could understand, but this Diaghileff, of what did his share consist? On the programme his name was simply down as organizer, and that might mean anything. After watching my first rehearsal, I could begin to understand. I was deeply impressed, and went out of my way to smuggle myself into the rehearsal-room, to avoid his eyes and to watch him or hear him talk. I noted every phrase, and went over its meaning many times. Yet my attitude was never that of hero-worship. I was far too interested to accept him at once and as a whole. Sometimes, in the theatre, I would forsake the dream to visit the dreamer, creeping up behind a pillar that would allow me a full view of the figure seated in the semi-dusk of the back stalls. The action on the stage would be reflected in his face, now impassive, now satisfied, then critical and disapproving, as he turns to whisper a questioning observation to Boris Kochno, his neighbour and aide-de-camp. Occasionally he reacted more strongly, with pleasure and then with pain, as a black-tunicked figure in white tights leaped through the air to the closing bars of the music, bringing back to him the momentary image of that greatest creation who was for a time his greatest friend.

The tender beckoning . . . the leap; once again *Les Sylphides* is finished. The applause jars as we are awakened too brusquely from the dream—Diaghileff gets up, and we pass in the narrow aisle.

"My favourite ballet. It would hurt me to miss a single performance of it. The style of dressing the hair was not quite right to-night. They must be more careful. A few such slips and the work is lost; it is fragile. Style is an essential in *Les Sylphides*," and he walks away to greet several friends.

Surely the majority of the audience, who now brush past him into the *foyer*, do not know who is this man. There is no photograph in the programme, no kind of personal publicity to guide them. *Diaghileff*, the name, is a brand of ballet, a hallmark. Even those of us who know him slightly, who see him season after season, continually ask ourselves the questions: What is his true relationship to the beauty we have just been watching? Diaghileff absent, would the sylphs remain hidden in their park? Could we, then, only find Alarcón's story of the Miller, his Wife and the Governor, between the covers of a book?

The answers to these questions give the story of Diaghileff in his long voyage of exploration from the little town of Perm to the great capitals of Western Europe.

PART I

IN RUSSIA
1872–1905

CHAPTER I

ANCESTRY AND CHILDHOOD
1872–1890

Diaghileff's grandfather—The family at home—Schooldays.

"When one wants to, one always can."
DIAGHILEFF'S *lesson from his* STEPMOTHER

In tracing the ancestry of the central character of a biography it is not always easy to decide just what is relevant. Even in the case of an entirely self-made man, if such a thing exists, it is of importance to show the roots from which he sprang, or the *milieu* from which he made a successful revolt. With a nature such as Diaghileff's it is vital, and selection shows no such difficulties. His ancestry and early surroundings play a large and easily recognizable part throughout his whole career. Although in a sense Diaghileff made himself, through inventing his occupation in life, it is never a question of just examining the raw material from which he was made—a material that is to become completely altered and disguised with education and experience —but of recognizing at once the core that has always existed, that was a solid foundation, added to, perfected, but never altered. The direction of his life is straightforward and consistent from his birth in Perm to his death in Venice.

The first essential conception is that of Diaghileff as coming from a family that was both well born and wealthy. That conception provides the key to the man's whole outlook.

Very superficially, if asked to describe his profession in a word one would say *impresario*, and that would be grossly inaccurate.

3

An *impresario*, although he may be a man of exquisite taste and judgement, is a business man promoting entertainment for gain. To be an *impresario* is to have a definite profession. That was not the case with Diaghileff. Whether he gained or whether he lost, his aims and outlook were totally different. He made for himself an occupation that did not exist previously, carving it out of his character and tastes. "We always danced for Diaghileff," said a prominent member of his company, "and his approval alone mattered. If he were absent even for a performance or two it became immediately noticeable." That is true, for Diaghileff was always the aristocrat, organizing and creating work for his own satisfaction and that of his friends, and graciously allowing the public to participate. He was the host at his own performances, the descendant of those who had held serfs, and it is significant that the Russian theatre proper had its origin in the companies of serf actors, promoted by their wealthy and aristocratic owners for their own satisfaction and that of their friends. He enjoyed his performances whether they were a box-office success or not, though he felt hurt, as a good host might, if the public did not echo his own enthusiasm.

Another important lesson to be learned from his ancestry is his attachment to Russia. Although he left his country behind him at an early date, and played so prominent a rôle in the development and launching of the *école de Paris*, wandering from capital to capital, he was always essentially a Russian, with the background of a spacious and cultured Russian household that interested itself actively in the arts, because from such people any other attitude would have been impossible.

As will be seen, his whole motive in exiling himself abroad was as much to show the rest of Europe what Russia could produce by way of art as to learn new methods from them. There are many who hold—the present writers among them—that Diaghileff was at his most inspired when the link with his native country was the strongest. The view of Diaghileff as a true cosmopolitan, a citizen of all Europe, is inaccurate. He carried something of Russia around with him wherever he was—something not only of St. Petersburg, but of his first country home in the province of Perm.

§ 2

His grandfather, Pavel Dmitrivitch, was born in 1808, of the country aristocracy, or, as we might say, of a county family. They possessed serfs, but, an indication of their liberal Western outlook, the house servants were paid for their work. At the age of eighteen he finished at the military engineering school and took up a government post, where he rapidly made himself noticed. But he was restless and unable to settle down, and soon had himself transferred to the Ministry of Finance, from which he retired in 1850. He was too great an individualist to feel completely happy in the service of others.

Handsome and wealthy, he had contracted a love match with Anna Ivanovna Sulmeneva, and the first years of their marriage were ideally happy. Pavel Dmitrivitch inherited an estate in the Perm government, where he settled down, on his retirement, to begin work on his own account. There was a distillery attached, which he enlarged, and he made a considerable fortune with no great effort, selling methylated spirits to the government.

Then came a cloud that destroyed the happiness of their domestic life. His wife was a pious woman, who fulfilled admirably all the precepts laid down by her Church, though as a realist she never allowed religion to interfere with the amenities of life. Pavel Dmitrivitch was sceptical on religious matters, and even treated them with a certain irony, as belonging definitely to the province of women, together with childbearing and household duties. She argued with him, upbraided him for his lack of religious faith and, alas for their happiness, ended by succeeding only too well—a fact for which she bitterly reproached herself in later years. Pavel Diaghileff passed from the extremes of scepticism to an acute form of religious mania. He neglected his business, and began to worry that the source of his money was tainted, since the peasants on occasion intoxicated themselves with the harsh spirits; but, fortunately for his family, so sound was the business that it continued to run itself in spite of his vagaries. Then his symptoms took on a more alarming turn. He would throw himself on the floor in an ecstasy and remain rigid for hours, arms spread out in the attitude of crucifixion, while his house became the hopeful and crowded gathering ground of endowment-seeking monks and pilgrims.

Part of the time they spent in a large villa at Peterhof, very much *en famille*, surrounded by their nine children, the eldest just about to be married, while the youngest was still at the breast; and besides their own family, there were many cousins and adopted children. Anna Ivanovna's responsibilities can be well imagined. In that one respect, at any rate, they had both adhered closely to biblical teaching.

One day, during a stay at Peterhof, Pavel Diaghileff went to St. Petersburg, to the Ministry of Finance, to draw some money, and for a fortnight not a word was heard from him—he had completely disappeared. His wife was terrified, going over in her imagination scenes of robbery and violence. Then he returned, penniless, haggard, dazed, and depressed. He would tell no one where he had been, or what had befallen him, and from this period begins a new epoch in their married life.

Pavel Dmitrivitch suffered a complete nervous breakdown, locked himself in his room, and refused to see anyone but his wife. There were moments of violence too, when he tried to swallow some holy crosses. When he had slightly recovered from the more violent symptoms, the two of them went to St. Petersburg to try to find some way out, but with no success. By day he tramped the streets, visiting church after church in quest of peace, by night he paced feverishly up and down his room. It was a new Pavel Dmitrivitch who returned to the country. The brainstorm had burned itself out, leaving behind it a permanent change. The man who had been a keen theatre-goer, an *abonné* at the opera, passionately fond of music and all the good things that life had to offer, was dead. In his place there lived an ascetic. His wife was religious in an orthodox manner—she might even pass for a very pious woman—but this new state of things she could not comprehend. This was not the man she had married, and to the end of her days she could not accustom or reconcile herself to the change. They were strangers now, and there was constant friction too, chiefly over money matters. With so large a family to feed, it cannot be wondered at that Anna Ivanovna was a realist, fighting grimly for her children's life and inheritance. The clergy, whom she had formerly venerated, became veritable nightmares, as she saw her husband endow monastery after monastery in his restless quest for salvation.

On one occasion he deposited 1,000 roubles (£100) in the plate at church, which the thrifty housewife promptly picked up, when it came to her turn to contribute, substituting the more ordinary rouble; and such scenes, comical to the outsider, tragic for the wife, were only too frequent.

All these episodes we know from the lively letters of Serge Diaghileff's stepmother, to her married sister-in-law Anna Pavlovna Filosofova.

But with these nightmares and extravagances in the background, or even with the old ascetic, who had brusquely turned his back on the pleasures of his youth, ever hovering about the house, it must not be imagined that the place was a place of gloom. Those grievous troubles that were the mother's could not greatly affect a large company of children and grandchildren of varying ages. The very house itself was cheerful in aspect, with huge balconies entirely surrounding it and looking out on large terraces of brightly coloured flower-beds. In the summer meals would be taken on the balcony, and not infrequently as many as fifty sat down at table, not for a party, but for an informal family gathering. From the house a path led straight to the village church, which was hidden by a clump of trees, and, when for a moment there was a hush in the childish talk and laughter, the low chanting of the priests could be distinctly heard.

For a stranger to come suddenly in upon one of these large family gatherings must have been a bewildering experience. He would immediately notice certain family traits that they had in common: the thick-set build inclining to plumpness, the deep sad eyes, and the protruding jaw with the heavy fleshy underlip. If the stranger were at all musical, he would soon feel himself completely at home. Piano, violin, and chamber music were listened to with interest and respect even by the youngest child present. And the old ascetic himself could become quite human on the occasion of such gatherings: delighted with the biblical rôle of a patriarch, taking real pleasure in being thus surrounded by youth. After dinner there would often be an impromptu performance of opera—Glinka for preference, with everyone knowing the score by heart—and then late tea on the balcony, romping and laughing, chasing the bats that flitted in and out under the eaves.

The children were strictly brought up, and never spoilt. There were too many for any one to receive much individual attention, and each had to play his part in the smooth running of the household.

Besides their strong physical resemblance there were many points of character that the Diaghileffs shared: vitality, exuberance, strong stubborn wills, and the capacity for intense infectious enthusiasm. In the case of the grandfather these qualities had become exaggerated to the point of mania; with his daughter Anna Pavlovna (Filosofova) his religious ecstasies had been transformed into charitable works, the cause of woman, and political propaganda of the Left, that was also perhaps exaggerated at times in its expression; with his grandson Sergei Pavlovitch into the artistic manifestations that he carried like a missionary throughout the world.

It was never easy for a Diaghileff to keep any interest to himself—an interest instantly became an enthusiasm. They were all strongly imbued with the missionary spirit, vitally interested in the reactions of others. Many years later, to go to a museum with Diaghileff was an exhausting experience, a vivid illustration of this trait. He would stop in front of some particular object, look at his companion, and then wait, eager to see what the immediate reaction would be, irritated and disappointed, all his pleasure gone, if it did not elicit a reply that he could echo. His companion would soon be exhausted, but Diaghileff could continue endlessly, waiting, listening, and guiding. The Diaghileff character may have been self-centred, but it was always intensely interested in others, eager and well able to shine in a large company, and as popular as it wished to be at any given moment. This genuine interest in others gave it a charm that all could feel, which, together with this strong inherited will, was Diaghileff's chief weapon in later years.

§ 3

One of these family reunions at Perm, or more likely, perhaps, at Peterhof, might be especially festive, for Pavel Pavlovitch Diaghileff, father of Sergei Pavlovitch, had come home on leave from his regiment.

Pavel Pavlovitch was a great favourite—handsome, jovial, able with no great effort to charm everyone with his high spirits and his love of joking. No exception to the rest of the family, he was genuinely fond of music, and sang to admiring drawing-rooms in an agreeable tenor voice. But there the resemblance ceased. His father, his sister, Anna Pavlovna, and his son, Sergei, were passionately interested in certain fixed objects to the exclusion of all else, while Pavel Pavlovitch was in every way undistinguished, a good-natured *bon vivant*, with no ambitions, who took the line of least resistance, and lived only for the easy, pleasant things of life.

After his studies in the cavalry school he had been for many years an officer in the *Chevaliers-Gardes*, the first cavalry regiment of the Guards, the most elegant and exclusive of all. In Russia an officer could only remain in the regiment up to the rank of colonel, after which to gain promotion he was compelled to leave the capital and command a regiment of the line in the provinces. Only after such service did a few favoured ones obtain command of a regiment of the Guards.

Diaghileff *père* passed the next period of his life in a succession of provincial towns, and only rarely did he come home on leave.

Many years later he was promcted major-general of a brigade at Peterhof, and it was there that he spent his last years with his family, dying in retirement with the rank of lieutenant-general. A worthy, agreeable, and altogether unspectacular career.

Father and son had fundamentally but little in common, and their attitude towards one another, while cordial enough, was one of indifference. Pavel Pavlovitch was limited in culture, a typical officer of the guard.

He plays but an unimportant rôle in his son's development, and from the time that Sergei Pavlovitch went to St. Petersburg they very rarely had any opportunity of meeting. His first wife, Diaghileff's mother, died in 1872 when giving him birth. She was born Evreinova, of a noble and well-known family. "All I remember of her," says a relative, "was her really beautiful eyes, that she passed on to her son." Diaghileff rarely saw his relatives on his mother's side, and what else she gave him but life, and a useful legacy when he came of age, we cannot say.

A strong contrast to the care-free officer was his second wife, Helen Valerianova Panaïeva, Diaghileff's stepmother, and the person who had the greatest influence on his life. She was a woman of both rare moral outlook and rare intellect. Her whole life was devoted to the happiness of her husband and children, and she was for them an object not only of love, but of veneration. She made no discrimination between her stepson Serge and her own children. On the contrary, unlike the stepmothers of fiction, her love for him was still further increased by admiration for his extraordinary gifts, which she soon recognized and fostered. She had brought him up from his infancy, and with incomparable tact she had found the way to tame his impulsive stormy nature, to discipline him, and to teach him to discipline himself. She was never severe or nagging, and she guided him as no one else could, with gentle and loving firmness.

His vast ability was inborn, but the fact that in after-life he could harness it, and turn it to practical account, is due to the early principles she taught him. She always remained for him the highest moral authority—his living conscience—and when, in his active after-life, some difficult moral problem perplexed him, he always turned to her for guidance, help, and sympathy.

It was undoubtedly Diaghileff's stepmother who contributed largely to the development of that extraordinary will-power and tenacity of purpose which was his dominant characteristic, and which turned ideas into actions. He often told Nouvel that his mother, and he never called her otherwise, had taught him never to use the phrase "I cannot."

"It is a phrase which you must forget; when one wants to, one always can."

11

She had been beautiful in her youth. Small in build, she had grown fat with increasing age, but till late in life her face conserved its fine regular features, and her eyes were remarkable for their expression of active kindliness, which attracted all who knew her. At the same time her whole manner was one of nobility and dignity.

Her family, the Panaïefs, was exceedingly musical. Her sister, a pupil of Pauline Viardot, was an accomplished singer, as famous for her grace and beauty as for her artistic gifts. She was a celebrity in the world of St. Petersburg, and magnificently connected. She was especially friendly with the family of Count Alexandre Adlerberg, Minister of the Imperial Court under Alexander II, who left to her his famous musical library. This she promised in her turn to leave to Diaghileff, but, alas! he died, and no one seems to know what has happened to the library.

The father Panaïef, from whom his daughters had inherited the love of music, played an active rôle in its propagation. In the wave of nationalism that heralded the reign of Alexander III, with the rapid development of Russian music, the Imperial Italian Opera had been closed down. Panaïef, who was an ardent *Italianomane*, rapidly came to the rescue, and built with his own fortune, which he lost in the enterprise, a private theatre where Italian opera was carried on with the finest singers of the day, and among them his own daughter.

It is not surprising that the word *intelligentzia* is Russian in its origin. Professional men of all kinds, in those spacious days before the war, took an interest in matters far removed from their everyday occupations—an interest that was neither unusual nor patronizing. They were amateurs in the arts, *dilettanti* if you will, but they were ready to give up their leisure and often their fortunes in the pursuit of some ideal. Golf, the crossword puzzle, and the detective story had not yet come to monopolize their interests. Because of the liberal attitude that usually accompanied an artistic education, and the particular fact that so many noteworthy artists were not well born, the word has come down to us in a somewhat distorted sense, as meaning those engaged in political propaganda of the Left.

Intelligentzia can bear no relationship to our own word "highbrows," which has in it a strong flavour of disapproval and of amazement that things of the mind can possibly interest normal persons. Nobody looked askance at the successful Russian engineer or wealthy merchant, who gave up his leisure to painting and music, sponsored some artistic movement, or frequented the society of artists. His colleagues did not tap their foreheads significantly, nor did his credit and reputation for business acumen suffer.

Serge Diaghileff truly came from the Russian *intelligentzia* of his time—he was a militant member of it. Where others made a hobby of such things, he passed a lifetime in their service. He was no "highbrow," astonishing his friends. His interest in the arts was perfectly natural to his station in life—was hereditary even. His individual genius, the thing that differentiated him from a mere *dilettante*, lay in his will to discover and to create.

§ 4

It is not to be wondered at that with this environment the young Diaghileff started life with an ardent love of music and the theatre. We know more of the atmosphere of his home than we do of his own early life and thoughts, for Diaghileff was never given to talking of the past or of himself at all. He had not the time, and his active mind was always turned towards the future.

"I am not interesting to anyone," he told persistent interviewers, who asked him for biographical detail, "but my work is. Ask me about that, and I will tell you as much as you like."

This was not modesty, or even the assumption of it; on the contrary, it was conscious superiority. Diaghileff always knew his true value too well to insist.

All that we know of his schooldays comes, therefore, from his schoolfellows, and those with whom he was truly intimate. A schoolfellow, Vasilieff by name, gives an interesting picture:

"The school was old-fashioned, patriarchal even. The head-master was eighty years of age, and walked along the corridors in his dressing-gown. Whenever a boy got in his way, his invariable custom was to seize his hair and pull it, but no one was in the least frightened of 'Grandpa,' as he was called.

"Soon after Diaghileff entered the school this master was replaced by a younger man, who was ambitious, and, like a new broom, swept everything very clean. I remember Diaghileff well. Physically he was far bigger than the average boy . . ." and then follows in miniature the description of him that we know, minus white mesh and eye-glass.

"Diaghileff was superior to us in every way, and the description 'young master' [1] fitted him admirably. He was far better grounded in general knowledge, and we all looked up to him. I remember an engaging habit he had of snapping his fingers to emphasize some point in the conversation, a fascinating trick doubtless borrowed from an elder. Even the masters treated him with special deference."

All the same, he cannot have been a very satisfactory pupil, not because he was lacking in ability, but because the whole school world was too far removed from his especial interests, which were all centred at home—round the piano, and the many interesting people who visited his parents. He never did his homework, but was crammed at the last moment by the best pupils, who not only never refused him help, but who were proud to be of service to him. If he broke down in the middle of *viva*

[1] Russian: *barin.*

voce, there was always a chorus of eager voices ready to prompt him, and, in a written examination, when he seemed lost or uneasy, his schoolfellows would shoot over to him slips of paper with the answers. Diaghileff throughout his life came well out of all such critical situations.

His masters, too, were especially eager not to plough him. It was a great honour for them to be entertained at the "big house" by his parents. In this way he often received advance information of the questions to be set. "To-day I am going to be put on to construe such and such a passage." "How on earth do you know?" "Oh, the master dined with us last night."

This aroused a certain jealousy, but never any real unpopularity. Diaghileff assumed a superiority that was tacitly admitted.

His schooldays were neither happy nor unhappy. They were an episode that had to be gone through—a bore and an interruption in the midst of an interesting and adventurous home life. In character he had outgrown school before ever he started it. Even then he was the Diaghileff of the later years, the leader who sought the collaboration of others, only now it was with a Latin exercise instead of a work of art.

This is not the picture of a spoilt child, but of an unusual one. Thanks to the atmosphere of his home, it is there that he received his true discipline and education; it is there that he received the ability to digest the mass of artistic knowledge that he was to receive during his first years in St. Petersburg.

With his home studies it was different—he was all eagerness, learning imperceptibly with no effort or drudgery. He was given elementary piano lessons, showing a natural finger agility, which made it easy for him to surmount technical difficulties. As a schoolboy he had even played in public the first part of the Schumann concerto. He was especially fond of reading music, which he did with the greatest facility. It was this foundation

15

that gave him so invaluable a grounding in musical literature, both classical and modern, and it was in Perm also, that he made his first attempts at original composition.

Everything that Diaghileff did was carrying him rapidly forward to follow the career of his own devising. The home is not merely a prelude, but the first definite step in his education. It must be greatly amplified, but nothing that he learned there will need discarding. It is, indeed, the solid foundation both in character and knowledge that made his future achievements possible.

─────CHAPTER II─────

DIAGHILEFF COMES TO TOWN
1890–1895

Meeting his future collaborators; Benois, Nouvel, Filosofov—
The Filosofovs—Revelation of Diaghileff as a fighter—First
contact with ballet—Leon Bakst—the old nyanya—*Coming*
of age and travels—His attitude towards sex.

"This early Diaghileff was a wild enthusiast without the faculty of discrimination."

A. BENOIS

"There was about him something definitely provincial."

W. NOUVEL

In 1890, when this apple-cheeked young country bumpkin came
to the capital, he began the second phase of the education that
was to enable him within a few years to lead the artistic opinion
of the world. The whole course of this magnificent apprenticeship was haphazard. All that could be foreseen at the time was
that it would make him into a man of the world, able to occupy
the position for which his wealth and family fitted him; yet
from his very first day in St. Petersburg, without his realizing
it, his whole future life was mapped out, not by the law school
faculty at the university, but by the little group into which he so
providentially fell, his ready-made friends, who were kind to
him because he was "Dima" Filosofov's country cousin and
might feel lonely at first.

Early that summer, as soon as he had passed his final examinations at the Perm gymnasium, Diaghileff went to stay in the
country with his cousin, Dmitri Filosofov, whom he had not yet

17

met, but who was already almost familiar through innumerable family conversations.

Filosofov had just completed his studies at the private May *gymnasium*, St. Petersburg, together with Alexandre Benois and Walter Nouvel, nucleus of the small group whose influence, at the contact with the irresistible driving force that was Diaghileff, was to be felt throughout the world.

Individually these men merit the closest study, for not only are they remarkable in themselves, but Diaghileff carried something of them in all his work long after he had left Russia behind him for good; something concrete in their active collaboration at various periods, and something more powerful still—his outlook and the whole manner of thinking that he had developed in their constantly stimulating society. His whole career follows definite lines according to his proximity to them, a point that is especially noticeable during the war and the early years of the revolution, when intercourse with Russia was interrupted and his work in consequence took on an entirely new orientation. They think, study, discuss; Diaghileff it is who turns their thoughts into action, transforms them with his genius, weds music to the plastic arts, and so creates. His is always the will, the driving force that saves discussion from becoming purely academic, that takes the picture from the museum on to the stage. His individual contribution is that of giving life.

During their last years at school, a common desire for a knowledge of the many exciting things outside the ordinary curriculum had bound together the trio, Benois, Filosofov and Nouvel, in a close and harmonious friendship, and the very trend of their studies made them complementary one to another. Filosofov was interested in political and social science, in philosophy and literature; Nouvel in music, history, and *belles-lettres*; while Benois, the most thorough and deeply cultured of all, with a knowledge far beyond his years, was interested in everything.

He specialized in the history, the appreciation, and the practice of the plastic arts. He was a little older than his companions, and they were deeply impressed by his knowledge and felt his authority. He rapidly became their mentor, president of their small academy, explaining and lecturing to them on the history and principles of art with extraordinary charm and skill, a gift that has made him the foremost of Russian critics as well as a leading painter and decorative artist.

After a short stay in the country Diaghileff arrived at the capital for the first time in his life, alone, for his cousin was to join him shortly afterwards for their first trip abroad. Since Benois was already travelling, it was Nouvel who first made him welcome as "Dima's" friend, and who undertook to show him round. They were only separated by a flight of stairs, as Diaghileff was staying with the Filosofovs in the same building as Nouvel.

This whole conception of Diaghileff arriving for the first time in a big city, lost and wide-eyed with amazement, seems to-day so contradictory to everything that we know of him, that I have asked Nouvel for a picture of that first meeting. It brings Diaghileff nearer to us to see him, not always as a superman, guiding and directing, surrounded by a group, but very much isolated and a little bewildered.

"My first impression was that of a strong, handsome boy, young and in flourishing health, a trifle inclined to fatness. He had wide shoulders, upon which was planted an enormous head out of all proportion to the rest of the body. His hair was thick, and stuck up in bristles like a brush. He had very beautiful large dark brown eyes, that were extraordinarily animated, and a small snub nose very ordinary in shape. His mouth was large, and it became cavernous when he laughed, showing a row of fine teeth. He had fleshy lips, a low forehead, a prognathous jaw,

19

and a wide chin, that revealed a stubborn will. His complexion was magnificent.

"His constant animation, his volubility, and the facility with which he expressed himself, his deep booming voice—all denoted a vitality that was infectious. At the same time there was about him something definitely provincial. He lacked that ease and *aplomb* that distinguished the young man from town.

"From the very beginning we found a common interest in music. I was then under the charm of the French, especially of Bizet and Delibes. He scarcely knew them, and spoke of Glinka and Serov, the father of the painter, a fine musical critic and one of our first Wagnerians, but a second-rate composer, whose operas were more akin to Meyerbeer than to Wagner. At that period our tastes were still very far from being formed. We were enthusiastic about so many things: life was beautiful, so full of thrilling new discoveries, that we could not afford the time to stop and criticize, even had we known how. We were eager to soak in still more and more impressions, to seize upon everything that promised us some beauty.

"So from that very first interview our friendship began, and in spite of many quarrels it lasted until his death."

A few days later Filosofov returned, and the cousins went off on their journey.

§ 2

In August, when they returned, all four entered the university, to study law, not with any real conviction, but because it was one of those things a young man of wealth and position could do—if he were not going into the army—without wasting his energies upon too much academic work.

Diaghileff shared a room with his cousin at the Filosofovs'. "Dima's" mother, Anna Pavlovna, the sister of Diaghileff's father, was a remarkable woman, both as an individual and as a type of the Russian liberal intellectual of the period. She was as celebrated for her beauty and grace as for the important rôle she had played in the liberal movement of the reign of Alexander II, especially in the question of female emancipation and superior education for women. She was a beauty and a blue-stocking combined, a sought-after, smartly dressed society hostess, and a labour agitator—altogether a character from some novel by Turgenev. Her liberal ideas and her untiring activity linked her to the subversive elements of the *intelligentzia*, and so compromised her in the eyes of the government and the Emperor himself that, in spite of her husband's high position, she was exiled for a certain period and forced to leave with her children for a long stay abroad. It is said that this punishment was inflicted on her for having given refuge to Vera Zassulitch, the famous Social Revolutionary terrorist, who had shot at General Trepov, the head of the St. Petersburg police. Anna Pavlovna did more than this—she actively assisted in her escape by hiding her in her husband's fur coat. Curiously enough, they were living at the time in a sumptuous state apartment in the very house of the military tribunal itself, of which her husband was *procureur*.

Filosofov presented a sharp contrast to his wife, whom he adored. Twenty years older, he was at the time that Diaghileff came to St. Petersburg a big old man with a grey beard, cold, austere, and dignified, who, in spite of his exquisite politeness on all occasions, inspired not only respect, but fear. That was only his exterior. Inwardly he was good, sensitive, and even a little weak, especially towards his wife, who could twist him around her little finger, and to whom he readily forgave all the many actions that were so compromising to his situation and career.

Filosofov had acquired a high position under Alexander II, who loved him as much as he detested his wife. He became secretary of state, and at one time almost Minister of Justice. He was the type of official who took part in the liberal reforms of the first part of Alexander II's reign, especially in the great emancipation of the serfs. His father had held serfs, and, in marked contrast with the Diaghileffs, had treated them with a certain brutality, living the self-indulgent life of an Eastern potentate. Anna Pavlovna has left us an account of the atmosphere in this home, and the austere son was the opposite of his father, each of them centuries removed from the other in his ideas—a situation that could only have happened in the Russia of those days. With the advent of Alexander III and the new so-called reactionary tendencies, actually, as we now can realize, by contrast with what followed a prudent conservatism, his career came to an abrupt end. He was named a privy councillor, the highest step in the ladder of a bureaucratic official, but actually an empty honour that meant retirement.

The assassination of Alexander II had produced a profound impression on the whole of St. Petersburg society. It had subdued those *milieux* that dabbled in advanced ideas, and had made them realize something of the explosive nature of the material they were handling. Anna Pavlovna was greatly upset by the event, abandoned the extreme expression of her views, and moderated her reforming zeal, while always faithful to her fine liberal ideals. She remained in silent opposition, a *frondeuse* to the end.

There were many traits of character that Diaghileff and his aunt possessed in common—ambition, vivacity, the capacity for feverish activity—but their conception of life was entirely different, even poles apart. She loved him and admired his gifts, but the generations that separated them in so rapidly developing a period in Russian social history made it impossible for her to follow his aims. She belonged definitely to the 1860's, when the arts were neglected in favour of political activity, or made to serve and illustrate that activity, and when the more intelligent young men went about dishevelled and in peasant blouses, very unlike the dandified Sergei Pavlovitch. The friends rather made fun of her, while at the same time showing her their esteem and appreciating her great kindness to them. Much disposed to talk, she welcomed lengthy discussion, defended her views with passion and, when outwitted by the younger minds, finished up by bursting into tears.

This was the *milieu* into which Diaghileff had fallen. The house was a hospitable one, as were all Russian houses at that time. Every Wednesday and Sunday all the Diaghileff and Filosofov relatives came to dine, bringing with them their friends, and many others would drop in unannounced. It was an enormous assembly, and the dinners were gay and entertaining. Everything was discussed there, the current life of the capital passed under review; there were quarrels, too, at times, and the young people laughed and joked. Even old Filosofov himself was on occasions known to smile at some risky anecdote.

The two cousins were close friends, inseparables for fifteen years. Two fine young men of eighteen, they offered a sharp contrast both in physique and in character. Filosofov was taller than Diaghileff, slender and delicate, a truly aristocratic type of beauty that showed up Diaghileff's country robustness. Blond, with a fine clean-cut face, good features, and large cold grey-blue eyes, he had long tapering fingers *à la* Van Dyck, with almond-shaped nails, while Diaghileff's were square-nailed and stubby. The mental contrast was even more striking. Filosofov was neither expansive nor exuberant. He was calm, reserved or even cold, with a keen intelligence and a wit that was biting, caustic, and at times malicious. As in the case of his father this harsh exterior hid a great sensibility—a sentimentality, even, which he tried hard to subdue. He was easily influenced by a more dominating character.

The four friends met daily at the university, and for a time they followed some of the particularly brilliant lecturers with real interest, especially Filosofov, who alone had ambitions for an academic career. Diaghileff was the first to become unutterably bored. He had not the slightest interest in the law; life outside the university walls was proving irresistibly attractive; and there were those many years in the country to be made up for.

That year the friends formed a little club that was to continue and formalize their schoolboy discussions. They met weekly at Benois', where each one in turn lectured or read papers on some subject of interest; Benois on the plastic arts, Filosofov on sociology, and Nouvel on music. They were also confirmed bookworms, devouring fiction as well as history and biography. Diaghileff never attended these meetings, and, unlike his friends, was seldom seen with a book in his hands. That did not mean that he was not well grounded, only that his reading was narrowly restricted, and never became a passion with him. He knew well and loved Pouchkine, Tolstoi, Dostoievski, and Turgenev; but actuality, continual movement, people, and discussion meant more to him than any passive sedentary occupation. Music was then his greatest interest—singing, opera, and especially the theatre.

"We thought him inferior to us in general culture," says Nouvel, "and we treated him with a certain marked superiority that greatly irritated him, poking fun at his provincialism. He had, in fact, compared to us who had always lived in the capital, very little general knowledge then, especially of the plastic arts, which did not even seem to interest him."

But Diaghileff was gaining knowledge feverishly: argumentative when he felt his inferiority, eager to make up for his years in the country, a difficult companion at times.

Benois, also, has given me a vivid picture of him during that early period of adjustment.

"His general artistic culture was small and unformed in the extreme. It was the same in literature. This early Diaghileff was a wild enthusiast without the faculty of discrimination. I doubt, in fact, whether I would ever call him a connoisseur in a wide sense of the term, even later when his critical powers were so splendidly awake. *Flair* he had in plenty, almost from the start. He could, and did, become an expert in any one subject when his interest was aroused. Yes, Diaghileff, strange as it seems, could spend hours among dusty archives in quest of information about some specific subject, and then he would study it to the full, only to drop it when the next enthusiasm came along.

"As I remember him then, he was the dandy of our little group. We thought ourselves rather above such things as dress, and even prided ourselves on a sort of picturesque untidiness, but Serioja was known for his shining top hat, his monocle, his taste in fancy waistcoats, and his fur coat. I suppose he was always something of a snob, and he had a *penchant* for snobs, which was a continual subject of dispute amongst us. It had its æsthetic justification in his case—this love for the elegant and decorative sides of life. He and Bakst, the other dandy of our group, were always shocked at our raggedness.

"His education was slow and normal. He did not come to us as a leader, and, in fact, was not definitely one of us for some time. He imposed his will only gradually. Diaghileff was difficult in this formative stage, often arrogant in argument, supporting the most fantastic assertions with fire, and denying them with equal vehemence at the next opportunity. He easily offended people, and, if he respected them, quite as easily made the peace, leaving no trace of offence or rancour behind, but his frequent *crises de vanité* made him insupportable at times. I suppose that it is only fair to say that all of us were conceited and had strong notions of our 'missions' in life, which we made abundantly evident to others less fortunate than ourselves. It was just the period of the Nietzschean superman, and we were all supermen in our own estimation, though, there was generally something of irony in our attitude as well—at any rate amongst ourselves."

Benois has related a trivial early episode which is important, as it first gave him the clue to Diaghileff's real character and thus altered his point of view.

"One day Diaghileff and I went to visit Nouvel at Pargolovo, a country place some fifteen miles from St. Petersburg. As we did not find him at home I proposed a small excursion in the picturesque hills round about Finland. But it was hot, muggy weather, and as we were soon tired we lay down and stretched ourselves out under the trees. Not yet having enough in common to sustain a long and reasoned conversation, I thought it a good chance to put my young friend through a sort of examination as to his general knowledge and sentiments—a common pastime amongst us. I was eager, too, to penetrate a little further into Serioja's *fond mysterieux*, and to find out if he would really suit us, or whether his views might not be too far removed from ours. After some hesitation he fell in with my suggestion and told me that he intended, while at the university, to make a serious study of music; that he wanted to become a composer and at the same time to go on with his singing. There were certain things in his profession of faith that shocked me a little. If he had a veritable cult for Glinka (and that was a family tradition, his father knowing the whole of *Rousslan* by heart), if he showed a great admiration for Borodin (*Igor* had just been put on at the St. Petersburg opera), as a contrast he had a pronounced weakness for the *mélodies larges* of the Italian operas, did not dislike Rubinstein, and did not yet show sufficient admiration for our god—Wagner.

"Then suddenly this somewhat pedantic conversation was interrupted in the most unexpected manner. I was lying on my back, watching the clouds go by, and could not see what was happening beside me. Serge profited by this and, sidling up to me, suddenly threw himself on me, punching and pummelling me, roaring with laughter all the while. Never had such an abomination taken place in our group before. We were serious, well-brought-up boys, real 'mother's darlings,' and we professed, well in accordance with the ideas of our time, a hearty contempt for anything that savoured of what was later called physical culture. Also after a few moments I soon realized that Serge, the big Serge, was very much the stronger, and that although the older I was risking a most humiliating defeat. I then had recourse to a ruse, letting out a piercing yell and assuring my opponent that he had put out my arm. Serge, thoroughly worked up, let me go, regretting not having carried his victory further, and helped me to get up, which I did, groaning and rubbing my arm energetically.

"This stupidly childish scene remained fixed in my memory with extraordinary precision, and I think that the reason was that then for the first time I had a revelation of the real nature of Diaghileff, his outstanding character of a fighter. Though we were to become intimate friends long before becoming collaborators, extremely fond of one another, there was always an undercurrent of struggle mixed with our relationship, and it was this struggle that gave our friendship its special savour."

Perhaps of all the friends Nouvel was nearest to him through their common passion—music.

"Because of our great love for music we soon became fast friends, meeting daily at the Filosofovs' to play duets or sing through entire operas. He had a strong baritone voice, rather harsh and guttural in timbre, while mine was thin and often rather hoarse. We played anything we could get hold of, especially the moderns, without the slightest discrimination. Diaghileff loved Tchaikovsky, Glinka, Borodin; among the Italians,

27

Verdi and even Puccini; and Gounod, Massenet, and Delibes among the French. Power was the essential thing that he admired in music and singing—power, passion, and temperament. Soon Wagner became his idol. During his trip abroad with Filosofov, their first visit was to Vienna, and there he heard for the first time a really great opera, *Lohengrin*, and the effect staggered him."

During that first winter in the capital Diaghileff became literally obsessed with music. Nightly he went to the concert hall or the theatre, while by day he haunted the music shops, buying any score that he did not know so that he and Nouvel could go over it together. They did not always agree in their tastes. Nouvel was in love with the eighteenth century, while Diaghileff was not yet conscious of anything containing subtlety, delicacy, or charm. He wanted strength, force, even brutality—something grandiose and pathetic. He was passing through a phase of romanticism in his development. For him Tamagno was the greatest of all singers.

The previous year Tchaikovsky's *Sleeping Princess* had been mounted at the Théâtre Marie in lavish fashion. Benois and Nouvel, both confirmed *balletomanes*, as became true sons of St. Petersburg, went time and time again, and were enraptured. Diaghileff saw it, but was not greatly impressed. It was his first real experience of ballet, and choreography was still very much a sealed book to him. He went rather because it was the fashionable thing to do. He could be seen there, and there was ample opportunity for greeting the right people in the long *entr'actes*. He definitely preferred opera, and two new works that year made a marked impression on him, Borodin's *Prince Igor*, completed by Rimsky-Korsakov and Glazounov, and Tchaikovsky's *Dame de Pique*. From the first he was a passionate admirer of Tchaikovsky, and more particularly of his symphonic works.

Diaghileff's first contact with ballet is interesting, especially since it was caused through what later became a favourite work, and one of his own most popular revivals. Whereas his friends had known ballet all their lives and could argue, analyse, and compare, he came upon it late, and at a time when music meant so much more to him than any visual impression.

Benois tells of his own initiation as a *balletomane*:

"I danced myself as a child, improvising to my brother Albert's brilliant piano improvisations, and that gave me a feeling for movement. Then when I was fourteen I first saw La Zucchi, and was completely captivated. I thought of nothing else, and for three years scarcely missed a performance. I need not explain to you of all people the strength and meaning of such an obsession. My school work obviously suffered, and by the end of that period I was a complete *balletomane*. Much that I saw irritated me. I dreamed of better things in this wonderful plastic medium, and enjoyed the work of certain individual artists."

This was the man whom Diaghileff had as a cicerone at his first ballets, and the two of them had many a heated argument. For several years Diaghileff held firmly to his opinion, heard the music, and did not see the action. He only finally capitulated at about the time of Glazounov's *Raymonda*, the year before his theatre service, and began to realize what could be accomplished in the medium; but it required many more years of contact with plastic art, music, and the drama before he could conceive of their perfect union in ballet, and realize that with the group of artists he now dominated such perfection could be attained.

Diaghileff's original approach to ballet was through music, and what supplied a still greater bond between Nouvel and himself was a common desire to compose. They had not yet begun to study seriously, but criticized one another's compositions. Though Diaghileff was never to create original work, this early practical training gave him a sound knowledge of composition. The only fragment of opera that he had composed that year in imitation of Moussorgsky, whom he had just discovered, met with no success among his friends. A failure as a composer, he was never a mere *dilettante* in music, and his later discoveries were a rare combination of *flair* and actual knowledge. This thwarted desire to compose turned his creative energy into a new channel and made his ballet into an instrument for self-expression.

"When, much later," says Benois, "the moment for our collective creation had arrived, Diaghileff showed himself in everything regarding music much the best equipped, which fact manifested itself at times with a lack of consideration, amounting even to brutality."

A year again passed for Diaghileff in continual movement. He wished to hear, see, and know everything. He went everywhere, and everywhere he gathered a vast circle of acquaintances. People interested him, and were as much a subject for close study as were the arts.

That summer vacation he passed, as usual, with the Filosofovs in their estate of Bogdanovskoïë.

Back once again in St. Petersburg he took a small flat, which he shared that winter with a university friend, Michael Andreiev. He had engaged an excellent cook, his friends visited him, and it was his pleasure to entertain them at lunch. How many schemes were to be started with Diaghileff sitting at the head of a table entertaining his friends, here in St. Petersburg, in Paris, Monte Carlo, at the Savoy grill! Good food invariably—he had a healthy voracious appetite—copious wine to wash down every course, and the conversation of the elect, with ideas so abundant and guests so receptive that it was impossible afterwards to say with whom the various schemes had orginated. Here in his modest flat started the habit of a lifetime—food, talk, and then action.

The second winter was even more animated than the first.

The country bumpkin was taking to the town, and it was no longer so easy to discover his provincialisms and to laugh at them. Sometimes the friends visited the Filosofovs, more often still Benois, who lived with his father. This was a true artist's *milieu*, Benois *père* being architect of the Imperial Court, and there Diaghileff began to learn something about painting.

§ 3

The centre and very heart of the group was Alexandre Benois. Already then a storehouse of systematized knowledge in almost every branch of art, contact with him and his family started both Diaghileff and Leon Bakst on their spectacular courses. His whole background was admirable for the purpose, and gave him that detached outlook which, combined with his rare knowledge, could impress others.

The Benois family was descended from French emigrants—artists, painters, and architects—who, while they brought to Russia the art of the West with all its technical resources, found there space and leisure in which to develop to the full and became themselves Russians, but always a little detached. They were related to the great Venetian family of Cavos, and Alexandre inherited from them an immense feeling for the theatre. His maternal grandfather was a composer of parts, his uncle a distinguished theatrical architect. No Benois was ever a nonentity.

One met painters in that house, sculptors and architects, and the talk always turned on artistic events. It was there that the friends first met Leon Bakst, then still known as Rosenberg. It was Albert, Alexandre's elder by twenty years, already famous as an architect and water-colourist, who had brought him into the circle while he was still a student at the Académie des Beaux Arts. He struck them as being shy and timid, and Albert protected him. It was only later that he really became one of them, first friendly with Benois and Nouvel, and then with Diaghileff, who was to play the greatest rôle in his life, and to carry his visions of pure colour throughout the world, till every fashion fell under his influence and he had created an epoch of decorative art.

Leon Bakst, the last arrival in that intimate inner circle, had been neither to the *gymnasium* nor to the university with his friends; indeed, what was rare for a cultivated Russian then, he never qualified for his Bachelor's degree. His true matriculation turned out to be his association with Benois, and later with Diaghileff. It is astonishing to realize that two young undergraduates could so powerfully influence their whole period.

Bakst, still called Rosenberg, was the only Jew in the group, his surroundings and his heritage were different from theirs. He lived in the lively narrow commercial Sadovia Street, near the busy market, but a stone's-throw away from where Raskolnikov had failed and suffered in his attempt to be a superman.

His grandfather, with whom he had the most in common, was something of a dandy of the French Second Empire, while his parents were respectable and respected commercial folk. His first contact with anything more exciting than the dull round of school life was in the construction of toy theatres, a substitute for the real thing, and in the excitement of family play-acting and charades. Not till he was over twelve years old did his thoughts turn towards painting, and then almost by the accidental discovery of his talent, just as later he himself was more surprised than anyone by his mastery of stage design. In the school a prize was to be awarded for the copied drawing of the poet Joukovsky, whose centenary was being celebrated. Surprisingly enough Leon won it, and from then on, his self-confidence being established, his thoughts turned seriously towards painting. The very notion that plastic art could be a serious vocation did not enter the minds of the Russian *intelligentzia* at the time, and his par-

Diaghileff with his old nurse by Leon Bakst, 1903

Diaghileff and Bakst—Caricature by Jean Cocteau

Diaghileff and Nijinsky—Caricature by Jean Cocteau

ents were not pleased, especially as his school work suffered considerably. So Leon had to do his "scribbling" at night, by can-
dlelight, when the family was abed. This opposition made the
desire to be a painter seem all the more wonderful, and gave it
the heroic glamour of something romantic that had to be won
through suffering.

In the usual way that parents have, the Rosenbergs thought
of the one established artist that they knew, and relied on him to
pour cold water on the scheme in the way that established artists
invariably do. This artist was Antokolsky, their co-religionist,
idolized sculptor, heroic monumental mason of that day, but
now forgotten, swept aside in that gigantic spring cleaning that
Diaghileff, Benois, and Bakst himself were to lead with the *Mir
Isskustva*. On principle Antokolsky, who had had a bitter struggle, was not encouraging.

"Better find the boy a good profession. There is not much of
a living in art these days; but you might let me see some of his
drawings, in case . . ." He saw, and was completely, even en-
thusiastically, convinced. When we think of this artist to-day, if
we ever do, let us count that in his favour.

His preliminary caution, coupled doubtless with the fact that
he was "one of them" and unlikely to have any crazy unpractical notions, overcame all family resistance, and at the age of
sixteen Bakst was "officially engaged" to painting with the Académie des Beaux Arts as his first goal. He failed in his initial
exam, and spent a year practising his drawing, being received
only the following year. The academy was in a bad state at the
time, well behind the popular taste even, that had already capitulated before the *Ambuiants*, and, as anti-Semitism was officially
encouraged, he had by no means an easy passage.

The artistic life and education of nearly all great artists who
have left their mark on an epoch follow almost an identical pattern that has become a novelist's formula: academy, revolt,

struggle, success. In many respects Hollywood and the writers of popular serials are the most successful of all in depicting life as it really is, and once again Bakst's example proved the essential service that can be performed by the out-of-date academy in giving the exceptional pupil something to revolt against. Without the academies the history of art would be a dull one indeed.

If the academy could do no more than attempt to turn Bakst towards sculpture, reprimand him for his bold use of colour, or praise him ironically by calling him "the newly found Rubens," contact with his fellow students had its effect, especially his friendship with the far older Serov, son of the composer of *Judith*, who was already making a considerable name.

Bakst's life at the academy, however, only lasted for a year and a half. The subject set for a medal examination was "The Madonna Weeping over Christ." Bakst decided to strike out on a new line, and to interpret it in a manner that he could feel and understand, rather than in the polite *pastiche* of the old masters that was, of course, expected of him. He drew freely from the life of the ghetto, accentuated the Jewish types almost into caricature, and depicted an elderly, dishevelled, hysterical madonna, an unidealized woman of the markets, who had lost her son. Doubtless it was a crude and mediocre work, but it showed original thought. When the adjudication came his work was struck out, he was publicly reprimanded, and he walked out of the building, a revolutionary. The academy once again had started a great career.

The novelist's formula is closely followed through with the traditional trip to Paris, even though Bakst was too much a dandy for life *à la* Murger. There he came into contact with the Finnish painter Edelfelt, an uninspired follower of Bastien-Lepage, but an able and conscientious guide, who could show him the groundwork, and with him Bakst painted landscape in the open air, studying light and form. Through his protector, Benckendorff, he was entrusted by the Russian government with the painting of a heroic canvas on the inconceivably dull subject of the arrival of Admiral Avellan in Paris, one of the gestures in connection with the recently established Russo-French *entente*. Then he became drawing-master to the family of the Grand Duke Vladimir and began to paint society beauties. That is where this particular story varies a trifle from the formula, but ever so slightly, for temptation is also a favoured motive. Yesterday's rebel was well on the way to becoming an official artist, an Antokolsky in paint, who would be forgiven his little backsliding as canvas succeeded canvas, glorifying the official policy, until one day he went to just such another grand tea-party to hear the "wonderfuls" and "charmings" of his society admirers. There he met Benois again, who did not join in the chorus of praise, but told him very bluntly, without sparing his feelings, the exact reasons why. Benois' reasons must have been so convincing that they offset the rudeness of his manner, and made a deep impression. They turned Bakst's mind in the direction which subsequently made him famous.

In the Benois *milieu*, and through the new contact with Leon Bakst, Diaghileff began bit by bit to realize the meaning of the plastic arts, but very much as a *dilettante*. It was still music that absorbed him, and it was at this time that he began to take singing lessons with Cotogni, the fine baritone at the Italian opera.

St. Petersburg in the 'nineties was rich in music and the theatre, and it was possible to see and hear the very best that Russia and Europe could provide. At the Maryinsky Theatre yearly new works and revivals were put on in an impeccable manner: *premières* of Tchaikovsky, Rimsky-Korsakov, and Borodin; Wagner, with the finest German singers of the day as well as the De Reszkés, Melba, and Litvinne; French opera, with Van Dyck and Sybil Sanderson. In addition, for several months of the year there was the private Italian opera, with such celebrities as Caruso, Tamagno, Battistini, and Sembrich. The symphonic concerts given by the Imperial Society of Music had as guests the greatest conductors and virtuosos of the day.

The ballet was just then beginning to produce its finest exponents—great artists and personalities who avoided the acrobatic antics into which the Italian school was degenerating, and who were to carry dancing to the point the furthest removed from the circus. They were Russians now—Kchesinska, Preobrajenska, and later Pavlova, Trefilova—this was the true dawn of Russian Ballet, Diaghileff's medium in the years to come.

The much-boasted theatrical activity of the new régime is no innovation, but just a continuation of what St. Petersburg had always known, understood, and loved.

Diaghileff again spent the summer with Filosofov at Bogdanovskoïë, and the following winter moved into a larger flat, always with his friend Andreiev, and here his two half-brothers, Valentin and Georges (Youri), pupils in the Alexandrovsky cadet corps, came to stay with him.

He had a great affection for both of them, but especially for Youri. When, during that winter, Youri fell dangerously ill with diphtheria Diaghileff nursed him with all the tenderness and devotion of a mother; a particularly heroic action in one who had a morbid and exaggerated fear of contagion, a fear that was so deep that it habitually led him into taking the most ridiculous precautions—such as driving in a closed carriage in summer-time in order not to catch glanders from the horses! Benois has told me how this thought of illness and infection was ever present in his mind.

"Diaghileff would rush in to his friends full of some new idea. 'How are you? Well? How are the children? What, you say your small son has a cold! Why did you shake hands with me? Now perhaps I shall catch it. You know how terrified I am of such things. It is too bad.' And for the rest of the evening he would sit in seclusion, as far away as possible from the reckless carrier of germs. Unreasoning fear balanced by acts of genuine heroism are opposites that are characteristic of Diaghileff."

It was at this time that Diaghileff installed in his flat his old *nyanya*, who had served his mother, and who had assisted at his birth. There is a painting of him, by Bakst, done just then, at the very beginning of his journey, and it shows him with this old grey-haired *nyanya* in the background. That is typical. Bakst knew him well, and there is a conscious symbolism there. He is looking ahead, right out of the canvas, but the background is significant—an important part of him, a portion of his inheritance. Diaghileff was in many respects sentimental, and of all the little group of friends it was he who was most closely attached to his country, most competent to reconcile the past with the present and the future—old Russia with the *école de Paris*.

This *nyanya* was a great character; a peasant, whose age was unpredictable, but who certainly appeared far older than she really was. She had the narrow outlook of the rustic, and was always ready to grumble at any "new-fangled nonsense." She had lived through the emancipation of the serfs, and had never ceased to disapprove this reform, though through it she herself had been freed. Since she, as a "house" serf, had passed all her life in her master's house, she was devoted to the family, and upheld their privileges more jealously than they did themselves. She had but small respect for either the morality or the intelligence of the peasants, and the very notion that they should be considered worthy of freedom revolted her. Whenever she heard of any crime committed anywhere: "That's what comes of this liberty," she would say, using a word that denoted "licence." She adored her Serioja, though he worried her, teased her, and took the greatest pleasure in shocking her; soon placating her with a kiss or a caress, for he too loved her, and his teasings only endeared him to her the more.

This old serf did scarcely any regular work, all the household duties being accomplished by Vassily, the *valet de chambre*. Her whole task lay in the ritual of preparing the tea, afternoon and evening, and in pouring it out. She took up her post standing, a diminutive figure, at the top of the table by the samovar. She also looked after the jam—an essential attribute of Russian tea. She held resolutely to these self-chosen responsibilities, which she regarded as a sacred trust, and she fulfilled them well.

She lived thus fifteen years, dusty and worn, like a piece of old furniture, and without her the room seemed incomplete. When Diaghileff began to travel she went to live with his parents in Peterhof, and there she died.

During the winter 1892–3 Diaghileff continued his feverish existence, entertaining with joy a larger circle of acquaintances than before, and music was always a feature of these entertainments: duets with Nouvel, chamber music, and singing. Tchaikovsky's trio, dedicated to the memory of Nicholas Rubinstein, was an especial favourite, and never failed to find a place in the programme. There were in the big world that season many artistic events of the greatest importance, including the first performance of Tchaikovsky's *Casse-Noisette* ballet, and Rimsky-Korsakov's opera-ballet *Mlada*, the music of which, for the Egyptian scene, was later to be inserted by Diaghileff in *Cléopâtre*.

And so all the time this haphazard education was going on, now with a rapidly increasing pace. During the summers passed at Bogdanovskoië, Filosofov had been at great pains to develop the general culture of his country cousin, and to pass on to him some of the worldly knowledge that the true sons of the capital had already acquired. In Diaghileff he found a pupil with a truly remarkable gift of "appropriating" knowledge, using it as if it had originated with him. Diaghileff seized upon things with rapidity, never, perhaps, going very deeply into them, but easily grasping the essentials with an unusual *flair*.

Almost overnight during this third winter in the capital it became impossible for his friends to mock any longer at his country ways. Bit by bit he was becoming their equal, and his opinions were listened to with a new-found respect. These opinions grew more and more decided, and he could now back them up with concrete reasons where previously passion had sufficed.

This marked development was greatly accelerated when Diaghileff came of age and inherited a small fortune from his mother instead of having to rely on a parental allowance. He was meeting painters, and now had the means to buy their paintings and to be a Mæcenas on a small scale. This ability to back his judgement greatly enhanced it. At twenty-one the pupil was gradually giving way to the man of action.

"It was in 1893," says Benois, "when he came of age, that Serioja began to acquire real confidence in himself, and so to conquer our esteem. We no longer looked on him as the country cousin who needed our protection. In that year he inherited a small fortune from his mother, and launched himself on furnishings for his flat, which he decorated with taste. His first important purchases were some pictures by Kramskoi, and we looked at him with different eyes after that.

"Then, two years later, he made a long voyage abroad and really grew up. In Munich I gave him an introduction to a connection of mine, Hans von Bartels, who showed him round. It was his first flight. He went to Bayreuth, bought works by Lenbach, was profoundly moved by Böcklin, a normal development of the period. There was, of course, no kind of method in his studies. He picked up just what he needed at the time. He came to the Impressionists much later than we did, and began to worship them before he really knew much about them, though in the end he went very much further than any of us."

Diaghileff's foreign journey was a regular grand tour in the old spacious manner. He had a passion for celebrities and no qualms about visiting them. He would ring the bell, see the great man, and come away with a dedicated portrait, which he treasured. In this way he visited Zola, Gounod, and Verdi, whose *Otello* he so greatly admired. The pleasure was not one-sided, for the great men were charmed and interested by him. They drew him out, and listened to his ideas. To them he showed no trace of that arrogance that at times made him such a difficult companion. He could respect greatness in others, and was always prepared to worship whole-heartedly, though with understanding. Here again, unconsciously, he was preparing himself for a career where the handling of great and generally difficult people was to play so large a part. Much of the charm of Diaghileff lay in the fact that he could listen as well as direct. On his return to Russia he made the indispensable visit to Tolstoi at Yasnaya Poliana. There is no record of what occurred, but it made a deep impression on him, and he harangued his friends for hours upon the theories that he had gathered there.

§ 4

The most difficult problem confronting the biographer, and one that must be dealt with at this early stage, is that of Diaghileff's particular attitude towards questions of sex. It is impossible to omit all reference to it without giving an entirely distorted and inaccurate picture of the man, but at the same time this is still a subject that shocks and savours of the sensational, so that the smallest reference to it may well take on an importance in the mind of the reader out of all proportion to the truth. It should be seen, therefore, in its proper perspective, and accepted from the first as a part of this man. It is not for us here to moralize, but only to consider it in so far as it affected him personally, and, through that, his life as an artist. We cannot judge—but we must try to understand.

I think that just because of the sensationalism of the subject people have always exaggerated the part that it played, at any rate in so far as Diaghileff's artistic life is concerned. It may have given him a certain motive power, have lent force to many of his enthusiasms; but when we examine his creations carefully we find that sex is altogether swamped by many other considerations that are essentially artistic. It is absurd, in fact, to think of a man like Diaghileff as being blindly controlled by sex. Those who attracted him were almost without exception first-class material for the purposes of a creative artist. He may have loved them, but he selected them primarily for their mental gifts, formed them, developed them, gave them creative opportunities, and so they became for the time being the instruments of this artistic will, though only until they had fully found themselves. That is the simple fact.

He did not raise weaklings to the first positions because of any blind unreasoning passion. His mind was always in full control, and, however great his will, he could never have made the second rate into the first rate.

He was attracted by the virile, so that he never made the atmosphere of his company precious or effeminate, and the fact that his later audiences tended to become so was not his fault. It disgusted him; he loathed that type of man, and said so forcibly on many occasions.

His love for the virile normal man doomed him to constant unhappiness and disappointment. It was obvious that as soon as his loved one had fully developed, he would leave Diaghileff for the first attractive woman who crossed his path. Diaghileff was no philanderer. Had he been a man of normal outlook he would have made a husband of great fidelity. He was not capricious in his affections—invariably it was the others who abandoned him.

41

Always he was saddened, surprised—and felt himself betrayed. In all these unions the mental aspect predominated. Later in life his friendships were more paternal in spirit than anything else.

This search for the true permanent companion was perhaps the personal tragedy of Diaghileff's life.

During his whole period, what did he alter or modify in ballet that can be directly attributed to his tastes? There is singularly little that we can find. Purely on account of his reputation an amazing amount of rubbish has been spoken, quite out of accordance with the facts.

The male choreographer had always existed, and it was Diaghileff who gave opportunities to the first woman choreographer in the Russian Ballet, Bronislava Nijinska, for whom his admiration was so great that he said, "If I had a daughter, I would like one with such gifts."

To what extent did he stress the male rôle in ballet?

It is certain that the emergence of the man from the background, and from the indignity of acting as *porteur*, developed enormously with the Russian Ballet of 1909, but not to the extent that one might think, and in any case it was not at this period directly due to Diaghileff. The male dancer in Russia had always been a marked feature of the ballet, and the very first enthusiastic notices in the Paris Press stress that fact; Russia had never known the absurd *travesti* that was the custom in France. "We, too, have our great *ballerinas*, but what is exceptional in these Russians is the fine virile dancing of the males, which has proved a revelation to us, and which enhances a hundredfold the grace and charm of their *ballerinas*." It was the virile Bolm, in *Prince Igor*, who especially delighted Paris.

The majority of the leading male dancers who came to Western Europe in no sense shared Diaghileff's tastes.

In the early days the stressing of the male rôle was one of Fokine's logical developments in his evolution from Petipa, who rarely set an attractive dance for a man, and Fokine, an essentially normal man, was not influenced by any other considerations than those of art. He realized that in the orchestration of dancing—that is, choreography—the strong male note is highly effective as a contrast, and that it can be used in giving character, light, and shade to a work, and that, dramatically, the *pas de deux* is a love duet. He also realized that this use of the male as a dancer instead of merely as a "lifter" removed the art from the province of acrobatics, which was Diaghileff's essential aim, and the object of the whole group that was led by him.

Historically the male was always prominent in ballet, making his appearance many years before the *ballerina*, and it was only with the outstanding popularity of Taglioni, followed later by Elssler, Grahn, Grisi, and Cerrito that the man took an entirely subordinate rôle—a fortuitous distortion that Fokine righted.

I have myself heard Diaghileff explain to a dancer the interpretation of *Le Spectre de la Rose* in a perfectly normal manner, carefully, deliberately suppressing in the man any desire to shine at the expense of the woman. And, whatever his feelings towards the particular man may have been, it was his pleasure in the work, his reason and artistic taste alone that guided him.

It is only when Nijinsky comes to the fore as a choreographer, and on that account the experienced Fokine is thrust aside, that Diaghileff can truly be said to be in sole charge. The fact of Nijinsky's selection may be due to Diaghileff's tastes as well as to his vision, but the works produced through their collaboration, especially the most important *Le Sacre du Printemps*, show not the slightest traces of any abnormality, and so it is throughout.

He, because of these private feelings, may have developed certain collaborators rather than others, though by far the greatest majority of them were never his intimate friends, but the resulting work was not affected by that, and who can say, judging by

43

the results that have delighted us, that he did not always select the best man available for the work in hand?

At the most the male may have received a greater share of Press publicity than would otherwise have been the case, but the private life of Diaghileff affected on the whole his artistic results less than happens in the more ordinary case of the *entrepreneur* who has a mistress in the company.

The negative results of Diaghileff's views are perhaps more important. Had he been a runner after women, he might have influenced the future of ballet in an entirely different manner. His views gave him an extraordinarily detached judgement and understanding of women. He could see the mind as well as the body, talk to them, and appreciate their problems. Many of his most devoted friends were women, who understood him, helped him in his task, and made it easier for him at times; and these women were among the most brilliant of their day.

In his actual choice of women dancers it gave him a taste for the slimmer and more boyishly built. He disliked the severely classical *tutu* that revealed a large expanse of thigh, a taste that has now become general from ballet proper to cabaret, films, and music-hall.

At the early period of which I am writing, his university friends, the little group that was to travel so far with him, did not suspect his tastes. At times he would boast to them, as any student might, of his many feminine conquests, and, if the subject were ever brought up in the course of conversation, he would speak of it with disgust and abhorrence.

When later they suspected something of the truth it was talked of jocularly, and Diaghileff himself made a joke of it, admitting nothing. It was not in any way the fashion in student circles in Russia, and was very badly regarded. In the reign of Alexander III, important public men had been ruined on the mere suspicion of such things, so that such questions were never publicly discussed.

It was only many years later, when Diaghileff had finished with Russia, that it became "official" and was openly admitted by him, though everyone knew it by then, and it had already become an open scandal that had even reached the columns of the less respectable boulevard papers, and had been hinted at in more than one caricature. His own intimate circle did not share in his tastes, so that, however strong a hold it may already have had on him, there can be no question of its ever absorbing him and colouring all his artistic views.

It is in vain that one asks the question—how did this taste originate? It is a question that his friends of that time have repeatedly asked themselves and cannot answer. I know, however, of one confidence that he made to a close friend, "*Si Madame —— avait voulu de moi je n'aurai jamais regardé un homme de ma vie.*" Disappointment in love, however, does not cause such an outlook, and Diaghileff's own statements are a particularly unreliable form of evidence.

His first and only experience of normal intercourse with a woman was unfortunate in the extreme. It gave him a horror almost amounting to a phobia, and to the end of his life he mentioned it with extreme disgust.

At the age of seventeen his father thought that it might be an excellent and enlightened thing to urge the lad to sow his wild oats, and to indicate to him where this might be done with the minimum of trouble and risk. Small as the risk was, the young boy fell a victim to a small infection, which was rapidly cured, and the supposition is perhaps not too far fetched that this incident may have influenced his attitude towards the matter throughout his whole life.

If I have dealt at some length with this wholly unpleasant subject, even at the risk of causing offence, it is because by doing so, by putting it down in black and white, it can be considered as a part of this man and then dismissed from the mind, except in so far as it explains certain situations. To hint at it, to let slip a phrase here and there would be to distort and make the whole picture an unpleasant one. I have only acted thus after great thought and consultation with those who truly honour his memory and wish to safeguard it from the many imputations to which an absolute lack of frankness might lead.

Let us bear carefully in mind, however great our natural repugnance, that Diaghileff was not ruled by his passions, that he was in no sense a philanderer or a seducer, and that the mental aspect, the quest for an artistically creative companionship, was always the paramount consideration.

PRELUDE TO ADVENTURE
1895–1899

*The death of Tchaikovsky—Musical studies, and a rebuff
from Rimsky-Korsakov—Growing interest in painting—
Meeting with Mamontoff—French influences—Princess Ten-
ischeff—Diaghileff as financier—A revealing letter—
Schemes and letters—His first activities—Founding* The
World of Art—*The artistic situation in Russia.*

"I think I have just found my true vocation—being a Mæcenas."

DIAGHILEFF *in a letter*

Life was full and worth the living to Diaghileff now that he had
travelled, shed his provincialisms, and knew enough to be
thoroughly *dans le mouvement*—always a great pre-occupation
with him. Music and social contacts took up his entire time. He
had of necessity almost completely dropped his university work,
and, anyway, the study of law was right outside his interests.
His friends, equally indifferent to it, had already graduated, but
Diaghileff postponed the day of reckoning from term to term,
till the little he knew was entirely forgotten, and he felt incapable of passing without a period of intensive cramming. It was
impossible—in those days, an unheard-of thing—for a man in
his social position to leave the university without a degree; so he
crammed, finally scraping through the examinations in 1896,
six years after graduation. That was his final contact with juris-
prudence.

In the meantime an event had occurred that plunged the
friends into a profound melancholy—the unexpected death of

47

Tchaikovsky at the early age of fifty-three. This composer, who is looked upon by all foreigners as being the least national and representative of the Russian school, and by the Russians as perhaps the most significant of all, was an object of veneration with the music-loving public of the period, and a veritable cult for the friends, who had not only a profound admiration for his work, but a real affection for his truly charming person. Diaghileff knew him slightly, and a fact in which he took great pride and pleasure was the distant connection between the Tchaikovskys and the Diaghileffs. Characteristically he never referred to him otherwise than as "Uncle Peter."

"As with all the works of this great composer," says Nouvel, "we waited with impatience the first performance of his latest symphony, *The Pathetic*, which he was to conduct himself at the symphonic concert of the Imperial Music Society.

"The day before, at nine in the morning, Diaghileff and I went to the *répétition générale*. With what eager attention did we listen to his rehearsal of the symphony, and to his piano concerto. We drank in each note. I remember, also, that in the same programme were Mozart's *Danses d'Idoménée*. I shall never forget the expression of beatitude on Tchaikovsky's face while he played the work of the composer for whom he had an admiration amounting almost to worship.

"The following night the performance took place before a packed and enthusiastic house. We were all especially impressed by the fact that the symphony was concluded by a melancholy *adagio*, whose last bars diminished like a dying breath. Who could have thought that night that this would be the funeral song of the composer himself?

"A few days later Diaghileff came to me in a great state of agitation. Tchaikovsky was seriously ill—cholera, most likely. There had been a serious epidemic the previous year, but now it was abating, only mild cases remained, and deaths were few and

48

far between. We had great hopes for his recovery. Diaghileff was living near the composer, and went several times a day to find out the latest news, which he communicated to me. On the eve of October 25th,[1] he told me that his state was desperate, and the following morning I received a note from him, announcing the death of the great composer.

"From the earliest hour Diaghileff was in the house of death, and he it was who brought the first wreath. At one o'clock I went thither to pray with my brother. The news had not yet been publicly announced, and there were few people there save relations and close friends. All were weeping.

"The funeral was an imposing one. By the orders of Alexander III, who had greatly appreciated him, it was paid for by the ministry, and the service was held in the great cathedral of the Virgin of Kazan. Dense crowds paid their final tribute."

This cult for Tchaikovsky remained with Diaghileff till the end of his life. Many years later his production of *The Sleeping Princess* was a concrete proof of it, and its failure as much a blow to his feelings as to his purse. Tchaikovsky had been declared old-fashioned in favour of those very composers whom Diaghileff had launched, and who were the first to agree with him. Snobbery, so often his ally, had failed him for once.

His own desire to become a composer now suffered a severe setback, and his pride as well.

Nouvel and Diaghileff felt that it was time to consult a competent authority for some guidance as to their progress. Rimsky-Korsakov's eldest son had been a schoolfellow of Nouvel's at the May *gymnasium*, and through him he arranged for an interview with the composer.

Nouvel went to the audition in fear and trembling, as he knew that the old man was severe and uncompromising in his judgements, and that he never hesitated to discourage the young

[1] Old style.

49

should he consider them unworthy to follow a musical career. The ordeal passed off well. Rimsky-Korsakov was highly critical, did not hold out any great hopes, but nevertheless advised the young man to continue his studies, and even recommended him to his pupil, N. Sokoloff, later one of the greatest professors of the Conservatoire.

Excited at the news of his friend's good fortune, Diaghileff immediately decided to follow suit, but in his case the outcome was entirely different. Nouvel never knew exactly what had happened at the interview, but Diaghileff was certainly turned down, and roughly so. In all probability Rimsky-Korsakov was shocked from the first by Diaghileff's arrogant attitude, and by his good opinion of himself as a composer, which results did not justify. The old musician spared him so little that Diaghileff left slamming the door, shouting out as he went: "The future will show which of us two is considered the greater in history." A phrase that he soon after regretted.

Rimsky-Korsakov, though usually very touchy, bore him no real grudge for this, which he correctly attributed to youthful impetuosity, and their subsequent relations were pleasant enough.[1]

In spite of this severe rebuff Diaghileff continued his composition, going that autumn to Sokoloff with his friend. While Nouvel persisted for several years, Diaghileff soon grew tired of systematic work, and, after making several changes of professor, finally abandoned composition.

This decision came about through a still more damning check, not the adverse opinion of one man this time, but something much more final—public opinion as represented by his friends and acquaintances.

[1] In 1907 Diaghileff wrote to him: "I prefer to put my point of view in writing, for when we meet your charm, your authority and your 'godliness' obscure so much the human in you that I know I shall be frightened of you and not say half I think." This tone must have gone a long way to obliterate the unfortunate words.

He had composed a *duo* for soprano and baritone to the words of Pouchkine's *Boris Godounov*, the scene by the fountain, where the false Dmitri makes love to Marina. He had worked at this seriously for some time, greatly believed in it, and decided to give it a hearing in his home before a large number of his friends. His aunt, Madame Panaïeva Kartseva, had kindly undertaken to sing the soprano rôle, while he himself took the part of Dmitri.

The result was a bitter disappointment. The work made not the slightest impression. His friends had pronounced judgement.

He never composed anything further. This completed his practical musical education, but the knowledge, unlike that connected with the law, was not wasted. He did not abandon his interest in music, he still remained the same avid concert-goer, being at this particular moment an extreme Wagnerian. That year he joined the Imperial Music Society as a paying member, and made every effort to have some element of youth introduced into the programmes, but the pundits would not listen to him. As he could not reform or mould existing institutions, the time was soon at hand for him to create his own.

§ 2

The essence of these men was their wide horizon. They were amateurs of all the arts, and the relationship between the arts lay in them, and was obvious to them. They represent completely the whole cultural movement of their period.

Diaghileff had been living for a considerable time now among painters, and in the atmosphere of painting. The *métier* was no more a mystery to him, but hitherto he had watched and listened without showing any marked personal reaction. His tastes were far less universal than those of his friends. Certainly he was interested in all things artistic, and it was well to know something of what is going on in the world of painting—to follow the activities of Bakst and Benois—but music was to be his life's work. Then came these two set-backs, and his consequent lack of faith in his own creative ability.

Diaghileff turned more decisively to painting—contemporary painting—because it was his nature to be interested in the people themselves who were doing things. He had a *flair* for the discovery of talent, and in the exercise of this gift he found his greatest joy. He was as much an amateur of people as of works of art, and often he was able to discover the work of art through the person.

Now he began to visit exhibitions with regularity, and this new interest threw him into closer contact with Benois and Bakst, under whose guidance he began to collect on a small scale, and to take up art criticism in a series of highly polemical articles in which he outlined his artistic beliefs.

He was now beginning the second—the plastic—phase of his artistic education.

This *fin de siècle* was an exciting period in European painting—a time of feverish activity that called for real discrimination on the part of the amateur, who was often, in the morning, thoroughly ashamed of his enthusiasm of the night before. It had its repercussions in Russia also, and the two great capitals St. Petersburg and Moscow reacted in manners entirely different one from the other. The city of Peter was naturally for Europeanization, while Moscow was solidly nationalist, believing in the rejuvenation of Russian art itself. The attitude of each city to the ikon was typical and revealing. St. Petersburg looked upon it as a valuable and interesting antiquity—a relic of history; Moscow as something living—an inspiration for the contemporary artist. If St. Petersburg looked to France, it was mainly the eighteenth century that held her interest; while Moscow was more venturesome and speculative, and her merchant collectors bought contemporary works for their galleries which are now the basis of the Soviet museums of modern art. This differing outlook of the two great cities was marked almost to the point of hostility.

Diaghileff made frequent visits to Moscow, though he showed no marked preference for either tendency. There he met a remarkable man, in many ways a pioneer in the direction that he himself was to take, and the understanding between them must have had its influence on him.

Sava Mamontoff was a Moscow merchant patron of the arts, but something more than the wealthy man who just signs cheques, and then sits back to await results. He had started as a backer of the private Italian opera, and had then come under the influence of the strong nationalist feeling that was going through Moscow; Stanislavsky had just started his Art Theatre, and was showing Tchekov according to entirely new principles. Everywhere was the desire to express Russian themes in a new manner. Mamontoff turned his mind to Russian opera. He had surrounded himself by a group of young painters, and it was to them that he entrusted the decorative side. This was a bold innovation in the direction that Diaghileff himself was to follow— a landmark in the history of the theatre. For the first time scenic and costume designing was entrusted to easel artists, who were within a short time to sweep away the specialists with their stereotyped ideas and their heavy built-up sets, and to substitute youth, colour, and freshness. Painting took its place in the theatre, and the scene with its costumes, carefully graduated patches of colour, became a living canvas. The opera convention, handled by such a master producer as Sanine, was no longer ridiculous—it was given a truth of its own that has persisted to-day in well-produced Russian opera, in marked contrast to the Italian or the German. The painters took a pride in finding the exact tone for their costumes, often searching the junk shops for antique fabrics that would give them their values, as exactly as if they were mixing paint on their palettes.

It is thanks to Mamontoff that such works as *Boris Godounov*, *Khovantchina*, *La Pskovitaine*, *Sadko*, and *Snegouroutchka* were recreated, and it is here for the first time that the genius of Chaliapine was revealed. He had previously made his début at the Imperial Theatres, but with no great success, the type of rôle assigned to him being quite unsuitable. Mamontoff was the first to point out to him the right direction. His interpretation of the rôle of Ivan the Terrible in Rimsky-Korsakov's *Pskovitaine*, which later Diaghileff was to give on the Continent, wisely renamed *Ivan the Terrible*, was the beginning of his triumphs as a singer-actor.

Diaghileff soon made friends with the artists surrounding Mamontoff, notably Serov, Korovin, the brothers Vasnetzoff, Maliutine, Vroubel, and others. Of these artists, M. A. Vroubel was the special pride of Moscow, the most versatile artist that Russia has yet produced—painter, sculptor, architect, book illustrator, and scenic artist. His *décors* for the Mamontoff opera were pioneer works in the direction that Bakst was to take. Almost unknown in Western Europe, his tragic story has given him in Russia the romantic glamour of a Van Gogh or a Gauguin, and this glamour has obscured one's view of him as an artist. He had high ideals. "Is there anything," he wrote in his youth, "more tragic than to feel the infinite beauty around one, to see God everywhere, and yet to be conscious of one's own incapacity to express the great things?" He struggled in this atmosphere of doubt; was crude, harsh, powerful, and at times poetical—a queer tormented visionary. Diaghileff knew him well, and appreciated him. His first attack of madness occurred during the fourth *Mir Isskustva* exhibition of 1902. All night he remained in the gallery, with a bottle of champagne for company, repainting his huge canvas of the "Demon." The morning of the private view he was found, a gibbering, incoherent being. He remained in an asylum for two years. His last public appearance was at the great Palais Tauride exhibition, where he struck everybody by his volubility and incoherence. He died soon afterwards in an asylum.

Diaghileff's comprehension of Moscow must have given him a strong urge in a practical direction. He was full of admiration for Mamontoff, both because of his theatrical activities, and of his movement for the propagation of popular art. On his side Mamontoff appreciated Diaghileff from the first for his *flair*, his enthusiasm, and his understanding of artistic problems.

§ 3

Diaghileff had found the happy medium between Moscow and St. Petersburg—what yet remained for him to find was a true understanding of French art.

In St. Petersburg, Benois, Bakst, and Nouvel had made an important friendship that, together with their travels, added French thought and culture to their knowledge.

Charles Bırlé was a young attaché at the French consulate, an amateur painter of advanced tendencies, and a fervent admirer of contemporary French literature, and he it was who first initiated them into what was going on in Paris, and made them love Baudelaire, Verlaine, the Parnassians, and the Symbolists. Through him they now followed carefully the *Mercure de France*, *La Plume*, and, later, *L'Ermitage*, which were received in his name to avoid the rigid censorship. Up till then they had gone no further than the naturalism of Zola, than Flaubert and Maupassant. Just at the time, too, there was an exhibition of French painting, and they saw the Impressionists for the first time, not through reproductions, in the right mood for enthusiasm and for understanding.

Paris immediately became for them the Promised Land.

This evolution of taste took place also in Diaghileff, but less directly. He was at that time still pre-occupied with music, and it came to him at first superficially, through the conversation of his friends. It was impossible to foretell that five years later he would be ready to edit the *Mir Isskustva*, which was to revolutionize the trend of Russian art, and lead it from Munich to Paris.

It was also at this time that he met his first "backer"—a woman, as so many were to be—and this meeting was of capital importance in his career, completing the chain of preparation that had been forged with so much chance system.

When Princess Tenischeva first appeared in St. Petersburg in 1890, it was as Madame Nicolaeva, but, divorced shortly after, she married the millionaire Prince Tenischeff. She was at first little known in St. Petersburg society, and the only person to be met with in her house was her inseparable companion, Princess Sviatopolk-Tchetvertinsky, who lived with her. This isolation was due, perhaps, to Prince Tenischeff's divorce, as his first wife, a Zamiatin, belonged to one of the leading families.

At that time the Princess was a handsome woman in her early thirties. She was a lover of painting, and herself painted as an amateur. Both she and her husband were musicians. She had a fine voice and sang with a certain artistry, while he played the 'cello and often organized evenings of chamber music.

Our whole story at this epoch abounds in people who were amateur musicians and painters, and there is much to be said for an education that found such things important and that made no sharp dividing line between those who bought and those who created. The decay in amateurism at the present day leads inevitably to a decay in appreciation.

While still Madame Nicolaeva, she visited all the art exhibitions with zest, constantly buying pictures, especially water-colours. Her entry at a *vernissage*, accompanied by her inevitable companion, was the signal for a large crowd to gather round her. Her purchases were somewhat haphazard, and her collection, in consequence, though large, was mixed. Having struck up a friendship with Benois, she chose him to guide her in her purchases, and to organize and weed out her collection. Benois educated her artistically, and developed her love of art.

It was through Benois that Diaghileff got to know her, though as a child he remembered to have seen her in the country.

As Princess Tenischeva she led a life of luxury, with houses in St. Petersburg and Paris, and a country estate at Talashkino, where she had installed her studios for the development of peasant art. She was surrounded by artists, from whom she commissioned works, had her portrait painted on innumerable occasions by the most celebrated portraitists, and entertained in lavish fashion.

She was thus clearly the predestined helper of Diaghileff and his friends when their schemes had reached a more concrete stage.

§ 4

In 1895 Diaghileff was looking about for some concrete manner of employing his vast energies. He was a learner still, and so he was still groping, even though his tastes were more developed, and though he had ideas of his own which he was in process of working out.

For a time he tried his hand at certain business ventures, and Filosofov, writing to Benois, says:

"Serge is drawn to the financial centre of things like a moth to the flames."

Financial matters, however, could never fully satisfy such a mind as Diaghileff's, though one may for a moment let one's

imagination wander and think of what would have happened
had he adopted such a career.

He had in essence all necessary gifts for one of the most
romantic careers—the floating of large spectacular companies,
an existence *à la* Monte Cristo. He could have founded vast
enterprises out of nothing; he had the personality and driving
power to appeal to the imagination both of the financier and of
the public, but once the enterprise was actually in being he
would have tired of the result and grown weary of the company
into which such things threw him, and then he would have
begun to doubt.

Shrewd and keen in driving a bargain, because that meant a
fight and an adventure, the details of business administration
only wearied him. No books of any kind were kept. For a time
Svetloff inaugurated a system of bookkeeping. Diaghileff was
amused and delighted, but soon dropped it. Later, when there
was some talk of making the ballet into a limited company, the
scheme had to be abandoned because of this lack of accounts. In
spite of the difficulties Diaghileff was delighted at this narrow
escape from restraint, which would have destroyed the personal
character of his enterprise.

Money and possessions meant little to him, and throughout
his life, with its endless possibilities, he kept but little for himself—just a few cases filled with rare editions, which he had
begun to collect at the latter end of his life. His pictures, which
represented a considerable value, he gave to others. He spent
money freely only in entertaining, and in satisfying his dreams
on the stage. Himself scrupulously honest, and, like many honest
men, incapable of peculation, he had a sneaking admiration for
those who could be dishonest on a grand scale—for the Kreugers
of this world. The thing itself was so very far removed from
him. One of his *boutades* was, "I like dishonest people; you do
not have to be particular in your dealings with them," but he

himself always was. On the rare occasions he was cheated he bore not the slightest malice, but dismissed the matter with a, *"Il se défend comme il peut—voilà tout."* He took an immense pride in paying his company well, and was indignant on one occasion when he heard that a well-known café was giving them food at what he considered was an excessively reduced rate.

"They are not paupers, but well-paid artists of the Russian Ballet."

In big money matters Diaghileff would act in a big way. Many of those artists who took a risk with him in the early days, when he formed his own company away from the Imperial Theatres, received a considerable sum at the bank, as a voluntary gesture. It was in the small things that he was petty and niggling.

"When I came to him," says Grigorieff, "to go over accounts, he would sign the large items without a moment's hesitation, but he would need lengthy arguments to agree to sixteen francs for some ribbon, and then he only signed the account with great unwillingness."

Throughout his whole life he dealt with immense sums, but never diverted any to his own use. He never possessed a car, often his boots were worn and his trousers sadly frayed. "All that I gain by way of profit," he said, and it was literally true, "is my keep in the best hotels, and the great privilege of a seat at the Russian Ballet." His rooms in those "best hotels" were always modest. Many of his artists, notably Nijinsky, ended up with far more money at their disposal than he ever had.

Diaghileff as a financier might have been a success, but for him the amassing of money could never have been an end in itself. Had he wished to run his ballet as a commercial enterprise, he could have laid by a considerable fortune through selling to an eager public *Sheherazade* and the early works for which they clamoured. To do such a thing he would have regarded as sacrilege. All the money from one successful venture was put into the next, which invariably entailed a whole system of education to make it acceptable. When, at times, that system was a failure, he remained without funds, and had to resume the fight all over again. Diaghileff as a business man was creating several new businesses a year, deserting the proved success as soon as it began to weary him. He had artistic wares to sell, but he only sold those that he thought the public ought to have. Call it idealism, the love of adventure, or, perhaps most truly of all, the fear of growing old and settled. By constant changes he sought to postpone old age and to cheat death itself.

§ 5

That year he wrote a letter to his stepmother, his greatest *confidante*, taking stock of himself. It is typical of his manner, half serious, half jesting, and it indicates the career that he was about to create.

"I am firstly a great charlatan, though with *brio;* secondly a great *charmeur;* thirdly, I have any amount of cheek; fourthly, I am a man with a great quantity of logic, but with very few principles; fifthly, I think I have no real gifts. All the same, I think I have just found my true vocation—being a Mæcenas. I have all that is necessary save the money—*mais ça viendra.*"

He was wrong about himself; a charlatan of no gifts or principles, in spite of all the charm in the world, would never have performed so gigantic a task for over twenty years.

§ 6

Such a devouring energy as Diaghileff's, now that music had failed him, could not be content with occasional art criticism for any length of time. It was but a step from criticizing to proving how things should be done. It was essential for him to do something positive that would bring his organizing abilities into play. The scene was set, and everything that was to follow now in such rapid succession was the result of the contacts he had made at home and abroad during the last few years. There was a method, if an unconscious one, in this running from person to person, this collecting of endless contacts, social and artistic. Now truly begins the second period of his life: the reaping of the harvest sown during the first and positive achievement, that at the start is non-creative, the period in which he is prepared to back his own judgement of pictures already painted. From that to influencing the painters themselves, and bringing them into contact with other artistic tendencies, is but a short step. From 1895 to 1905 is the prelude to adventure.

Diaghileff was always singularly averse from writing letters, and there are but few in existence, especially relating to the later years, during which he deluged his friends with cables, preferring even on occasions a long train journey, with a satisfying discussion at the end of it, to the delays of correspondence. However, now when he was trying to mature one scheme after another, seeking to discover his true bent, he sent his friends long rambling letters, full of enthusiasm, alternately praising and blaming them, and in either case often unjustly. Once he had made up his mind, he could not bear to have the decision questioned. The only attitude that he allowed was one of unqualified support. The more he lost his temper, the longer were the letters, word tumbling over word. He was on the war-path. His own intimates were brilliant; he had met many fine talents in his travels. They must all be brought together and made to stand for a common aim. Western Europe must be made to reckon with them and with him. If they disliked organized societies, so much the worse for them. His was the will-power that was lacking in Russian cultural circles. He must convert his friends first to a full realization of their power, and then together they would attack the public. Peter the Great, looking ever to the West, was his ideal; but if part of him was Peter, part also was Oblomoff, Gontcharoff's immortal character, that explains so many Russian inconsistencies of character. He was energetic and lazy by turn, enthusiastic and apathetic, downcast and disillusioned if his plans came to maturity without a really hard struggle.

His first scheme came after his travels abroad. His artistic purchases represented an ideal and stood for more than the mere collection of a young enthusiast. Here was the basis of a museum of modern art. Benois, who had been living in Paris for some time, was the recipient of his confidences.

This first letter, in the summer of 1895, is addressed to Albert and Alexandre Benois:

"For a long time I have wanted to write you a few words to remind you of myself, but I could not collect my thoughts: firstly because I did not have much time, and then because after having visited twenty-four museums and fourteen painters' studios it is not easy to express the quintessence of all my impressions. That is why I am leaving to our meeting and long talks certain questions in the domain of art which I came across during the last months.

"I declare that this coming winter I shall give myself entirely into the hands of Shoura [Alexandre Benois], and I shall make him officially into the curator of the Serge Diaghileff museum. Something may come of it, and perhaps in a few years we shall be able to create something solid, since the basis of it all is there. But I do not wish to speak of my acquisitions, nor to spoil the effect.

"I hope Shoura will answer my call and take the museum into his hands, because I am convinced, without harbouring colossal illusions, that for three or four thousand roubles a year one can do something. That is the practical side of my journey. Forgive this incoherent note."

The impetuosity shown in that letter he retained till the end of his career. Difficulties did not exist. That was the lesson his stepmother had taught him. The museum idea was soon abandoned for something more living and practicable.

§ 7

At the age of twenty-five, two years after his self-revelatory letter to his stepmother, Diaghileff made his first bow before the public, as an organizer, with an exhibition of British and German water-colours in the big hall of the Stieglitz Museum. The exhibition contained nothing startling, it was just, as Benois has said, "*une manifestation élégante*," which was in itself at that period both a novelty and a challenge. There was no social message in these water-colours by Lavery, Guthrie, Brangwyn, Liebermann, Bartels, and others; they were just so much paint on paper with the idea of producing certain æsthetic results. It required a great amount of courage, especially in an unknown, to organize this seemingly simple affair. Many critics were scandalized at the trivial uses to which art had been put, but all were agreed that the organization and the manner of presentation were novel and wholly admirable.

Benois says that this simple exhibition marked a date in the artistic annals of Russia, in so much as Diaghileff and his friends were prepared to submit to the public's judgement what they themselves considered significant in art. It was a timid, but unmistakable, manifesto, the first shot in the war against the *Ambulants*,[1] and their purpose pictures.

Elated by this success, Diaghileff proposed to the Society for the Encouragement of Fine Arts to organize for them an exhibi-

[1] See Chapter IV.

tion of Scandinavian painting, which was then entirely unknown in Russia in spite of the great popularity of Scandinavian literature.

Diaghileff's prestige being in the ascendant, the Society accepted, and gave him every facility for the necessary travel. The exhibition was held in the autumn of that year, and so the meeting with Edelfelt and Thaulow in Paris was turned to profit, and they exhibited together with Zorn, Liliefors, Prince Eugène of Sweden, Kroyer, Carl Larssen, and others.

Again the exhibition was an instant success, especially with the younger generation of artists and art lovers.

Mamontoff himself, with his group of artists, led by Korovin and Serov, arrived *en bande* at St. Petersburg for the occasion, and Diaghileff gave a big banquet in honour of Anders Zorn, who had come over with the exhibition, and was painting Princess Tenischeva's portrait.

This banquet, attended by artists of both capitals, marked the real union of the artistic youth of Moscow and St. Petersburg, the termination of their years of fierce rivalry However, two of the most important representatives of St. Petersburg, Bakst and Benois, were absent in Paris, and without them Diaghileff was turning more and more towards Moscow, encouraged by Filosofov, who was strongly nationalist in outlook, and who saw Nouvel, Benois, and Bakst as "semi-foreigners" incapable of appreciating the depths of the Russian soul.

The results of that banquet were to give Diaghileff a backer and powerful allies in the days to come, and the fact that Moscow had followed him *en masse* to St. Petersburg clearly indicated that his powers of leadership were gaining recognition.

He wrote feverish letters to Benois, full of his plans, and it is now that they begin to take shape and to centre around the idea of a magazine.

"Nothing has come out of Albert's [Albert Benois's] society

because the creators are —— ——, that is why I am forming my own progressive society. Every year, following upon the decision of the meeting of young painters that took place in my house, an exhibition will be held in my name, so that not only every painter, but every picture will be chosen personally by me. Afterwards a society will be created to carry on the work. The exhibition will be held at Stieglitz from January 15th to February 15th, 1898.

"You understand, of course, who will form the nucleus of the society—the Petersburg youth, the Moscow people, who have taken hold of my ideas with great enthusiasm, the Finns—of course they are Russians too—and afterwards some of the Russians abroad. . . . I hope you will join us and not Albert's backwater.

"This is not just a project, but something definitely fixed upon. Reply immediately what you feel about it all. One of these days you will receive from me a detailed and official letter.

"When I said about two years ago that I wanted to have nothing to do with the Russian painters, except to take revenge upon them for their ceaseless vulgarity, I was right. I have had to deal with French, German, English, Scotch, Dutch, and Scandinavian, and have never met with such difficulties as with our own countrymen.

"This time even you and Bakst have not missed a chance to be unpleasant to me. Bakst insisted, as you will see from the official letter, that a society should not be created the first year, so personally, with my own money and sweat, I am arranging an exhibition of Russian youth. Serov was also on Bakst's side, but from a different point of view. He is tired to death of red tape, and on principle loathes every kind of society. Bakst is behind it all.

"I feel that you do not understand things, but really, sitting in this backwater, I cannot write about it. In a word, everyone and everything annoys me. No one has any broadness of mind or a spark of fine feelings. Everyone mixes up financial interests with artistic principles. It is nothing but cowardice and rows.

"I want to nurse Russian painting, cleanse it, and bring it to the notice of the West—make it big and known."

"I am terribly busy, and that is why I have not found time to reply to your charming letter. You know already from Kostia [Constantine Somov] that I am all plans, one more grandiose than the other. Now I am planning this magazine in which I mean to embody all our artistic life—for instance, the illustrations will be real paintings; in the articles I shall speak freely my thoughts; in the name of the paper I shall arrange a series of yearly exhibitions; and, finally, I intend to make public, through this magazine, a new branch of artistic industry developed in Moscow and Finland. In short, I am contemplating the future through a magnifying-glass; but I want help, and to whom should I go if not you? I am sure of you as I am of myself. Is that not so? I expect from you at least five articles a year—good and interesting stuff on no matter what subject. Kostia has already helped by promising the cover and the poster. Apropos of Kostia, what an amazing talent! He gives me intense joy and interest. He says I am letting myself go when I praise him. My friends, does it matter? It is so beautiful to be really enthusiastic. You cannot imagine what progress he has made, his summer's work is enchanting. I expect the same from you.

"The Finns are extraordinary. . . . Fear their competition and try to outshine them. I am awaiting my packages with impatience.

"The Princess [Tenischeva] is in St. Petersburg, and I am very friendly with her. She is full of enthusiasm, and, I believe, money. She wants to buy in the Scandinavian exhibition, and she has asked me for guidance. Of course I will see that she gets no rubbish.

"One of these days I am expecting Zorn, Thaulow, and Edelfelt. Imagine, the first two are going to stay with me! The Princess has commissioned a portrait from Zorn. In Finland I have drummed into her about Kostia, and one of these days I will make her buy some.

". . . I don't know the name of the magazine yet."

Every undertaking had in it for Diaghileff something in the nature of a crusade. He dramatized it, he dramatized himself and his friends. He is full of reproaches in one of his unfair letters to Benois, who had not reacted strongly enough to some suggestion or other. It is couched in extravagant language—a type of imagery that he adopted in his dramatization:

"When you are building a house, the Lord knows how many masons, carpenters, painters, and builders surround you, how much worry and work there is in all the details, either bricks, beams, or wallpaper. You feel that there is one thing you need not worry about—the facade will be a success, because you believe in the friendship and the talent of the architect. But what happens is the very contrary. When you climb from under the scaffolding, covered in sweat and dust, you find that the architect tells you he cannot build the house and is it really necessary. Only then you truly realize the dust of the bricks, the stench of the wallpaper, glue, and all the difficulties. That is how your letter struck me.

". . . In a word, I cannot go on arguing with you and begging from you, and I have no time to shake you or to wring your neck. That's all.

"I hope that my sincere and brotherly scolding will make some impression on you, and that you will not behave as a stranger, but put on a dirty overall like the rest of us and help to mix the burning lime."

67

§ 8

But exhibitions were not enough. Diaghileff, and the Peters burg and Moscow artists whom he had grouped around him, felt the pressing need of some organ through which they might actively propagate their ideas, and spread a knowledge of the type of art, both ancient and modern, in which they so strongly believed.

The skill that Diaghileff had shown as an organizer of exhibitions: his extraordinary energy; his facility in gaining connections, sympathy and help; his faculty of sensing movements that were in the air, and of expressing the ideals of the new generation—all these indicated him as the man to lead the movement. And he *willed* it. Ambitious, never for a moment in doubt as to either his skill or his strength, he assumed the position of authority. The *Mir Isskustva* (*World of Art*) came into being because it had to, because of the association of such men.

The first and most pressing necessity was to find the funds, and Diaghileff set off in pursuit of them with vigour. It was a task in which he was to become a master. From that date, all through the difficult post-war days until his death, he never lacked someone who believed in him sufficiently to finance his projects, without any thoughts of possible profit. These backers invariably lost, but all of them were proud and satisfied to lose.

In this undertaking he was ably seconded by his cousin, who, after his stay in Heidelberg, had given up all ideas of an academic career. During the last years Filosofov had struck up a close friendship with Merejkovsky and his wife, Zénaïde Hippius, and had become a fervent of the literary, philosophical, and religious movement then sweeping through Russia, with which they were so closely identified. His interest in the *Mir Isskustva* was therefore different in direction from that of his friends. He had been promised the literary editorship, and saw therein a splendid platform for Merejkovsky and his ideals.

Now, more than ever, Diaghileff and Filosofov formed a striking contrast. Staunch friends and allies though they were, they had scarcely a single point in common. Filosofov, intelligent and erudite, was treated by his family and connections as a future celebrity. He inspired them with admiration and respect. It was only through pure chance that he had come in any way into close contact with art, through his friendship with Alexandre Benois. Actually he was never an artist, either by taste or inclination, lacking entirely any true understanding of the nature of art, which to him was but a branch of man's general culture, and an unimportant one at that, compared with the complexity of the social and philosophical ideas that occupied his mind. He was a doctrinaire always in search of a principle; but at the same time he was much more than a mere theoretician, dabbling in ideas for their own sake. He wished his ideas to be living and productive, applicable to the reality of things. His ambition was overpowering. Art for him was too limited a field. He aimed at higher things: to reform the world to create a new Christianity; to surpass Tolstoi, Dostoievski, and Nietzsche. Such was to be the literary editor of the new venture.

Diaghileff, on the other hand, was above all things sensual. He held ideology in abhorrence. Not that his mind was closed to ideas. On the contrary he played with them with extraordinary dialectic skill, when it was a question of some definite aim, when someone or other had to be convinced. With him, however, ideas never had a solid philosophical basis. He disposed of them like a pair of old gloves. When an idea seemed useful or opportune, he would impose it upon others, not only through force, but with amazing powers of reason, only to abandon it or to advance one diametrically opposite, which he would defend with equal power and conviction.

"No one was more convincing in argument than Diaghileff. He thought so quickly that it was almost impossible to argue with him. He was always in the right, always able to prove his point so persuasively that one was obliged to submit, in spite of a strong previous satisfaction, even certitude, that one had all along been in the right. Argument with him was, moreover, excessively tiring. With his extraordinary powers of resistance he never gave in, so that even when he did not prevail by argument you surrendered to him through sheer exhaustion."

He loved perpetual motion. Nothing tired him more than rest and inactivity. He had to be fighting—always. The more difficult the task, the more he loved it. So much so that he would, if necessary, create obstacles for the very joy of pushing them out of his way. First combat, then realization, was his idea of life; and that was the life he lived. He was a great realist, incapable of appreciating unproductive speculation.

It was perhaps these tremendous differences in temperament that made the cousins such ideal allies. The one bond was their ambition to command, and here there could be no clash. Diaghileff would lead the young generation in the arts, Filosofov in a spiritual and cultural direction. Between them they could divide the world.

During the winter of 1897–8, the friends, with the exception of Benois, who was then in Paris, frequently met in Princess Tenischeva's studio, to discuss serious problems and trivialities, to gossip and to wash it down with champagne, that was always consumed in great quantities. Diaghileff and Filosofov did not allow the pleasant nature of these parties to make them forget the work on hand, and used all their powers of persuasion to convince the Princess that such a review was necessary and should be financed by her. Diaghileff worked directly on her, since the rôle of Mæcenas was flattering, while Filosofov talked to her inseparable companion, Princess Tchetvertinsky, who influenced her friend in all serious matters. She was easily convinced. Mamontoff, who was then in Petersburg with his opera, was also lavishly entertained by the Princess, and drawn into the scheme, willingly enough, for he greatly admired the young Diaghileff.

It was decided to found the review, and to call it *Mir Iss-kustva* (*World of Art*), Diaghileff to be editor-in-chief, and Tenischeva and Mamontoff the publishers. The decision was duly celebrated at a wonderful feast given by the Princess, and characterized by champagne and excited speeches, outlining the aims of the new publication.

§ 9

However much energy its promoters possessed, however much money they had at their command, the new magazine to be influential must stand for something concrete as a contrast to something else equally concrete. It must be polemical, violent— in order to attract attention—and its whole *raison d'être* must be a desire to reform, to liberate art—from what?

This story of the vast artistic struggle in Russia at the end of last century, although it is indispensable in the pattern of Diaghileff's life, and first reveals the essential Diaghileff, may in its actual detail seem remote and of small account to us to-day, though only recently Soviet writers have been making a close study of the subject, and have somewhat surprisingly served it up as a novelty, disguised in the current Marxian and Leninist phraseology, as symptomatic of the class struggle that was to come.

"The difficulty of the *Mir Isskustva* problem," says one writer, at the beginning of a recent monograph, "from the Marxist point of view, lies not in a lack of concrete fact that can reveal it materialistically, but in the contradictory nature and the complexity of the group, created when capitalism was approaching its doom."

Even such an angle of approach, phrased in the slogans of to-day, cannot give actuality to the typical slogan of the nineties: "Art for Art's sake." It was the period of our own Yellow Book, and it is significant that Beardsley was a favourite of the Russians, and that Conder and Wilde, both of whom Diaghileff met in his journeys abroad, were familiar names. There is, indeed, a close parallel between the two movements, and the first numbers of the *Mir Isskustva* were also hailed as decadent.

Indeed, Aubrey Beardsley's influence on the graphic art of Russia through the *Mir Isskustva* was to be immense. From the very beginning of the journal Diaghileff sought a link with his art, and wrote to D. S. McColl:

> "45, Liteinaia,
> > "St. Pétersbourg.

"21 September, 1898.

"DEAR SIR,

"Mister Charles Conder writes to tell me that you would perhaps honour us in giving our review something like an account upon the late painter Aubrey Beardsley. Being myself one of his greatest admirers and wishing to reproduce some of his works I should like them to be accompanied by an article acquainting our public with that refined and exquisite artist's meaning, with the causes of the apparition of his art and with a general aspect of his personality. I should like the article not to be of a biographical or monographical character but rather to point out the influence that this, as yet not fully appreciated, painter has had upon culture. Mr. Conder tells me that Beardsley was a friend of yours and that you were leading an active correspondence with him.

"This certainly is a priceless material for many interesting articles. I knew Beardsley at Dieppe and can well understand what a loss it is as an artist and as a man. The dimensions of our magazine do not allow the article to be too long, not above the quantity of 35,000 letters. The price of an article of that size is of 12 pounds at our redaction. The article is requested to be here not later than for the 1st of December.

"Kindly let me know if our conditions are apt to suit you and if you agree to my demand.

"Believe me to be truly yours,

"SERGE DE DIAGHILEW."

The very drawing on the letter heading, signed L. Bakst, is a tribute to Beardsley.

The parallel with our own nineties is a close one, and the Soviet writer, for many reasons, is completely on a false scent. The particular situation in Russia was undoubtedly coloured by politico-humanitarian considerations. In the years immediately preceding the critical 1905 nothing could be altogether free from politics, although the group, as we shall see, took their stand from a purely æsthetic point of view. Where the recent Soviet historian has found a problem in "the contradictory nature and complexity of the group," he hits upon its great essential—the individualism that it is so hard for the Russian to-day to comprehend or appreciate.

The cause and the ideology that started Diaghileff and the group, and that gave them their desire for self-expression, and in particular the vehemence of their language, may seem to us out-moded, but the problems involved, their approach to them, the fight and the speedy victory, out of which the ballet of 1909 was truly born, reveal our man.

The whole history of Russian art is a subject that is almost unknown in Western Europe before the Diaghileff period, save for the ikon, some gigantic and sanguinary battle canvases by

Verestchagin, much *à la mode* last century, and Répine's "Volga Boatmen."

We have seen Diaghileff develop through contact with his friends, but the story is incomprehensible unless we trace in some detail exactly what it was that turned Leon Bakst in disgust from L'Académie des Beaux Arts, and that made a magazine, of small circulation, but presuming to invoke the Russian past and to plan the European future, into so powerful and practical an instrument of reform in the present. This forgotten artificial didactic art of Russia, unimportant in itself, becomes an integral part of our European art history from the very moment that Diaghileff and his friends made up their minds to revolt against it, and, without some knowledge of it, we cannot understand the true significance of the ballet that followed so logically in its trail.

§ 10

The history of modern Russian art [1] is an easy one to trace, as it starts, from our Western point of view, with Peter the Great, and, though there are many side issues, follows three definite periods: the learning of Western methods, declining into academism; the didactic subject painting of the Romantic-Realists, declining into academism; and Diaghileff's *Mir Isskustva*, the creation of original work that is national in a sense, but that is parallel with Western European thought, and finds its highest form of expression in the theatre.

Before the reign of the great reformer the ikon had degenerated into a precise, almost mathematical, habit, according to strict formulæ laid down by the Church. Peter said, "Let us have artists," just as he had said, "Let us have a navy," and, "Let us

[1] Some of the subjects dealt with here and in a portion of the following chapter may seem remote and without great interest for the general reader. They are dealt with at length, however, since they occupy so important a place in Diaghileff's life.—A. L. H.

have schools," and made it a feature of his general scheme of education. It is not possible, therefore, to talk for some time of a spontaneous Russian school. The people were well enough content with the emporium ikons that the ecclesiastical authorities allowed them; their religious significance, their efficacy as holy charms, was the important thing, not their value as pictures.

At first Peter encouraged the leading Europeans to visit Russia, but for many practical reasons such a plan did not fulfil his wishes for long. An excellent economist, it hurt him to see good Russian gold finding its way abroad, so he sent native artists abroad to study the best methods, and then bring their discoveries back with them for the benefit of the home market. So deliberate was the plan, so carefully calculated and artificial the start of modern Russian painting, that it is in no way out of place to use commercial jargon in speaking of it.

It is obvious that at first the Russian artists were copyists, delighted with the knowledge of new technical tricks—devices that took them further and further away from the standard ikon. Then came the brilliant reign of Elizabeth his daughter, and the first harvest of Peter's remarkable foresight.

Some of the finest rococo palaces date from that period, for the aristocracy followed the Imperial lead and built themselves worthy houses. St. Petersburg took on its present-day aspect—in every sense the city of Peter.

With the building of palaces comes the desire to fill them with worthy objects, and the natural result is the popularity and development of the family portrait. It is in portraiture that the Russian artist first succeeds. While in the beginning he does not always create a work of art, time adds dignity and interest, and these portraits assume historic importance. Some of them are magnificent works of art, and such artists as Levitsky and Borovikovsky deserve renown in any country. It is in the study of this portaiture of the eighteenth century that Diaghileff specialized for a time, and until his researches were terminated they were scattered, uncatalogued and almost unknown. We shall see later the important part that this work played in his career, both practically and in his own spiritual development. Russia is as much indebted to him as a scholar and museum man as is the whole world for the visions that followed.

Gradually the centre of gravity shifted from the court and the aristocracy to the inevitable academy, which soon had art in a stranglehold, as firm as that in which the ecclesiastical authorities had held it so short a time before. A cold and meaningless classicism was the inevitable result.

From the middle of the nineteenth century onwards the history of Russian art is the history of a series of school struggles. The *Academy* against the *Ambulants*—the movement that reacted from it—and the joint efforts of the two to fight the *Mir Isskustva*, which was certainly on paper, if not on canvas, far closer in its ideals to the academy.

The first signs of revolt came from a celebrated manifesto of Tchernichevsky's, *The Relationship between Art and Reality* (1855), in which the author lays down for art a definite programme: to follow nature slavishly, to interpret life, and to help the masses in their struggle for liberty. The artist must be a soldier in the ranks of those who are fighting for the ideals of social progress. There must not and cannot be any art for art's sake. Subject takes precedence over treatment—Russian subjects for Russian people.

Such an outlook—that of the present-day producer of propagandist films—was naturally especially easy to apply in a country containing so many illiterates. The ikon had spoken and said, "Remember God and the Church"; the new picture was to speak and say, "Remember the toiling and suffering masses"—no mention of art anywhere.

A decade later this manifesto was put into practice by a group of thirteen students of the academy, who refused to paint the subject set for the gold medal examination, "Odin in Valhalla," as being too remote from actuality. This secession, known as "The Revolt of the Thirteen," caused a major scandal, and all mention of it was carefully kept out of the papers.

One of the thirteen, Kramskoi, was the veritable founder of the school that followed. "It is time," he said, "that the Russian artist stood solidly on his own feet and rejected foreign influence. Thank God we have already beards on our chins. Why do we always walk holding the skirts of our Italian nursemaids? It's time to think of creating a Russian school."

As an artist he was mediocre, but he possessed the ability to lead and to command. He was the "trades union official" of an artistic group.

The revolt was complete, but the material question at once became paramount. How to live? The cinema parallel may hold good up to a point, only there was no box-office. The state was by far the greatest purchaser of works of art; private collectors were few and far between, and then they chiefly specialized in foreign works—French and German.

The seceding artists first formed themselves into a close communist association, *Artel des Artistes*,[1] but even then life would have been impossible without the enthusiastic support of the wealthy Moscow merchant, Tretiakov—a Mæcenas was never lacking in Russia—and thanks to his support the famous society of the *Ambulants*[2] was started.

For twenty years till the advent of Diaghileff their domination of Russian art was complete.

The very name itself, the *Ambulants*, was a programme, implying the decentralization of art from St. Petersburg, a travelling of exhibitions from town to town to gain close contact

[1] Workmen's association.

[2] Its leading members were Répine, Verestchagin, Sourikov, Makovski, Vasnetzoff, Nesterov, Kramskoi, Gay, and Polenov.

with the Russian people as a whole. Russian art must concern itself with Russian domestic problems, cut off from the rest of Europe. This is the very reversal of Peter the Great's aims, a retrograde move.

The attitude towards French art—then at one of its most brilliant periods—of the most prominent of the *Ambulants* shows the fight that Diaghileff and his followers had to turn the tide towards Europe again, and also the full extent of the victory, without which no ballet of 1909 would have been possible.

Répine, in a letter to the *Mir Isskustva*, complains bitterly of the prices fetched by French paintings—Degas and Millet in particular. He finds them mediocre.

"Degas's jockeys, which have been sold for 40,000 francs, are worth at the most 400 roubles. On the other hand one can buy paintings by Meissonnier and Fortuny at well below their true value. If unknown to you a nymph by Neff were introduced into a picture by Puvis de Chavannes you would go crazy with enthusiasm; if Polenov's 'Ivan the Terrible' were signed by Delacroix you would carry it aloft in triumph. It may be thought that I am the sworn enemy of all new tendencies in art. Not at all. I have an infinite admiration for all original talent, and there are even pearls in the actual decadence, such as Böcklin, Stuck, or Klimt."

Thus spoke Répine, the most inspired follower of Kramskoi, an artist of crude strength and unlimited personality; from Delacroix to Monet, French art is one gigantic bluff.

From time immemorial civilization had penetrated Russia either from Germany or through Germany. At this particular period Munich represented the last word in painting. Young artists who would in the past have gone to Rome to complete their education now went there.

Although there was a permanent French theatre in St. Petersburg (Théâtre Michel), with a first-class company, from which

Lucien Guitry sprang, and cultured circles conversed in French and were interested in French literature, there was no close contact between France and Russia. This was especially the case in painting. Répine himself had been to Paris, but had clearly gone there in a hostile and non-receptive spirit. Even Benois and his friends, the most advanced group in Russia, at first knew little of what was actually going on in Paris, and only knew the works through reproductions in magazines and catalogues. In St. Petersburg there were no collectors of "advanced" painting. Only in Moscow were there some fine collections of French paintings, but even these were not entirely up to date.

Benois, the best informed of all, was far more enthusiastic over a Menzel or a Böcklin than about anything from France, and it was more through Munich publications than direct that they learned of French activities.

It is only with the beginning of Franco-Russian friendship that a more direct relationship was reached.

The story of the reaction from the *Ambulants* is also the story of the substitution of Paris for Munich, brought about by the travels and friendships of the Diaghileff group, of which I have already written.

The *Ambulants* were remarkable for their rigid discipline and their common ideal. Whatever their contribution to art, they spread a universal interest in painting that only the "every picture tells a story approach" could have achieved. The *Mir Isskustva* would not have been possible without them, and they were only ripe to be attacked when they themselves had become thoroughly bourgeois, and had lost their original fervour. Later on, Benois himself was frightened and well aware of this. In a letter to Lanceray, he says:

"Take care our bourgeois family life does not swallow you. There is a lot of good in it, because it represents public order, the basis of government, but there is nothing lofty or beautiful in it, and for a painter there is more harm in it than for a mason or a postman. I am very much attached to that life, but I must drive it out of me. The free soul must lose everything that restrains it and drags it down."

The name of the magazine, and the movement that followed, *Mir Isskustva (World of Art)*, is not as banal as it might at first seem. It implies not a closed all-Russian association of people with a common purpose, an *artel*, but something appealing to the world at large—a loose group of individuals with an individualistic outlook, their only aim in common being the sufficiently comprehensive purpose of liberating art from the crushing hold of their predecessors, museum academism, and the telling of anecdotes.

Those individuals we know, and also something of their background. The *Ambulants* had mostly been of a lower social status, many of them but lately freed from serfdom, or whose ancestors were serfs, while these men had leisure, and were acquainted with several languages. They had made their grand tours, and they were not class-conscious.[1]

It is here that the Soviet historian makes his false interpretations. If the *Ambulants* had avowed politico-sociological aims, it does not follow that their opponents had, or that they were fighting on the other side in a social war. On the contrary, it was never a case between these two of Right-wing politics *versus* Left, but of politics in art *versus* no politics in art. To misunderstand that is to be wrong about the whole struggle.

It is true that one can talk glibly of the unconscious in the class struggle, but in the name of the unconscious many a false thesis can be written. We are only concerned here with the conscious acts of our characters, so far as we can ascertain them. The *Mir Isskustva* was strictly without politics.

[1] The *Ambulants* extolled liberty where the *Mir Isskustva* took it rather for granted.

CHAPTER IV

"THE WORLD OF ART"
1899–1905

Initial difficulties—The Vasnetzoff controversy—Diaghileff's editorial—The policy of the paper—Enemies and partisans—Success of the international exhibition—Financial difficulties —Diaghileff's brutality—Help from the Tsar—Serov offends the Empress—Offshoots from The World of Art—*Bakst's "mania"—End of the journal.*

"Diaghileff avait en lui tout ce qu'il fallait pour être un meneur d'hommes, pour être un 'duce' . . ."

ALEXANDRE BENOIS

As soon as the necessary backing had been found, Diaghileff left for Western Europe to select the artists for the international exhibition he was planning for the following winter, and also to study the technical aspects of his new work.

In Russia at that time the necessary equipment for running an artistic review scarcely existed. Printing was entirely commercial, and primitive at that; no one thought of the artistic production of books, and, when a printer set out deliberately to do such a thing, the result was lamentable.

Diaghileff's difficulties at the start were almost insurmountable. He had to create the whole mechanism of the thing before there could be any thought of publication. In his monograph on the genesis of the *Mir Isskustva* Benois says that at that time, while still in Paris, he himself had no idea through what difficulties his friends had had to pass to produce what they did. It was necessary to have an almost religious fanaticism in order to succeed. Benois quotes an extract from an article by Filosofov

81

(1916)[1]: "Twenty years ago, from a technical point of view, we lived in a desert."

There was no suitable type. Diaghileff and Filosofov dug out of the Académie des Sciences some old characters dating from the time of Elizabeth (1742–1761), and used them as a model for the new. It was impossible to find good paper for the reproduction of blocks, and it was only two years later that it was improved. Laid paper was unknown, and was only made during the third year of the publication. All blocks had to be manufactured abroad, and when they arrived the workmen did not know how to print from them, so that it was often necessary to spend whole nights supervising the work.

"It was not until 1901," writes Filosofov, "that the make-up was more or less satisfactory to the editors. Till then each new number proved a deception and sometimes brought us to despair."

Filosofov speaks with conviction, for it was he who took on the ungrateful task of supervising the production, where his great gifts of hard work and his scrupulous sense of duty were essential. He was always ready to sacrifice himself for a cause.

Apart even from this, his was the major influence during the early period. He had brought in with him on the literary side his friends the Merejkovskys, Minsky, Rosanov, and others. Unfortunately he wished also to have his say on artistic questions, which immediately produced vast divergences of opinion which came to a point when Diaghileff returned to St. Petersburg, and began to preside at daily conferences in his flat. The principal members of the staff were then Diaghileff, Filosofov, Bakst, Nurok, Serov, Korovin, when he was in St. Petersburg, and Nouvel. Benois, in Paris, was kept informed of the happenings by letter, and these letters are to-day our best sources of information.

[1] Never published.

Nouvel wrote, "The composition of our editorial board is as follows: Dima on the right, Bakst and myself the left, while the President, Serioja, listens to the declarations of the left and upholds the right. Korovin and Serov are of the left, but they are not often there, and Nurok represents a fraction of the left, with which we are not always in agreement. While the left holds the majority, the right is often victorious, because it has behind it the public, and more especially the publishers. This only makes our discussions more vigorous and heated . . . who will win, I cannot tell. I doubt if we shall, at any rate in the near future."

At first all these arguments centred round a certain painter, Victor Vasnetzoff, to whose work Diaghileff, and especially Filosofov, had decided to dedicate the first number, together with the works of Levitan, the great landscape painter. While the "left" admired the latter, they could not abide Vasnetzoff, whom they found mediocre and in bad taste. Matters were further complicated by the fact that he was the idol of Moscow and a great protégé of Mamontoff's. Filosofov saw in him the renovator of Russian religious art after the degeneration and decay of the ikon, and had even succeeded in convincing Diaghileff. From particular the arguments became general, touching the very principles of art.

Nouvel writes to Benois: "The discussions are very interesting. Recently in the matter of Victor Vasnetzoff and the French draughtsmen Forain, Steinlen, Helleu, and others we discussed the principles of superior and inferior art. For some time, ever since their last trip to Moscow, Serioja and especially Dima have a veritable veneration for Vasnetzoff. They consider him as the torchbearer of the new Russian art, proclaim him as a genius— a phenomenon, an idol before whom one must kneel and worship. Our protests—protests of people who refuse to confound cultural and historical considerations with those purely artistic

—are met with accusations of ignorance, of not understanding Russia; they even call us 'foreigners.' Naturally, in view of their attitude as regards Vasnetzoff, Dima and Serioja had to show themselves hostile to the French draughtsmen, and yesterday Dima went as far as to call their art 'brothel art.' All this delights me, because it gives rise to serious struggles, and it is only in this way that anything good can happen."

"Looking back," says Nouvel, "this makes one smile. With what childish passion, with what sincerity and belief did we fight to make our cause triumph! Also, time has proved us right. Such essentially Russian natures as Korovin's could not understand this cult for Vasnetzoff, any more than could Serov, but since his mother was a Jewess, his evidence might seem suspect, and so he took no part in the discussion. At the same time we had a profound admiration for another artist essentially Russian, who also painted religious subjects, but with true depth—Nesterov."

There was another cause of disagreement in the efforts to encourage applied art in the Russian style that was so dear to the hearts of the publishers. This struck the Left as being forced and artificial, but again Diaghileff and Filosofov carried their point.

The first number, in spite of all opposition, was devoted to Victor Vasnetzoff, and Benois nearly withdrew in disgust, which at once brought a violent letter from Diaghileff, accusing him of desertion, and calling on his conscience, his friendship, and his love of the common cause. Benois remained in the fold.

That was the usual way with Diaghileff—"the common cause" meant above all things the cause in which he himself was interested at that particular moment. He would tolerate no disagreement.

These artistic disputes on topics long since forgotten are interesting, since they reveal the young Diaghileff as a man who could be swayed by purely sentimental reactions, applauding many of those things that it afterwards became his mission in life to destroy; a man who could be narrowly patriotic—even parochial—in outlook in a way that would never give one reason to suspect that he could ever gain the slightest recognition outside Russia. His motives are not clear. There was the strong influence of his cousin, the fierceness of the opposition, and the necessary fight which he enjoyed for its own sake, also the diplomatic aspect of keeping well in with his backers. Later, in his cult of Levitsky, and in his work connected with Russian music and ballet, he showed himself a patriot, but a highly discriminating one, identifying himself closely with "the Left," and going very considerably beyond them.

"I was then attached to the ministry of the Imperial court," says Nouvel, "and lived entirely on my salary as a civil servant. In August, when the Emperor left for the Crimea, I was forced to follow my minister, much as I should have liked to have remained in St. Petersburg while the first number was under discussion. I remember a bitter letter from Filosofov, accusing me of betraying the cause for purely interested reasons, sacrificing my friends in my own interest, and so on.

"It was always like that, the 'cause' was so closely identified with their own individual interest that they could see no other point of view. This unfair pressure, exerted on all their friends by the cousins, pushed one to revolt, and accounted for the innumerable violent quarrels that always ensued. It was also perhaps due to these demands, and to this domination, that Diaghileff and Filosofov, and, later, Diaghileff by himself, were able to squeeze the very maximum out of their collaborators.

"I found my stay in the Crimea more and more insupportable. I wanted once again to plunge into the stimulating atmosphere of our editorial, with its constant movement, its easily stirred passions, its violent enthusiasms, and its hates. I found an excuse to leave for St. Petersburg in October, just in time for the great event, the appearance of the first number on November 15th.

"I had scarcely taken any part in it save in the general discussion that June. Benois, Bakst, and myself were bitterly disappointed. Artistically nothing of the kind had ever been seen in Russia, but still it was a long way away from our ideal. There were many errors of taste, starting with Korovin's cover, and then there were those pictures by Vasnetzoff, and the specimens of peasant art that so greatly shocked us. It seemed to betray the high purpose outlined in the prospectus: 'Above all, our efforts will be turned in the direction of improving taste in all branches of our national art.' "

§ 2

The text of the first number, as well as containing articles by Merejkovsky and others, had a long and grandiloquent manifesto by Diaghileff, in close collaboration with his cousin, outlining their profession of faith. Filosofov's share was the learned historical preamble, full of innumerable quotations on the nature of art, from Tolstoi, Dostoievski, Tchernichevsky, Nietzsche, Ruskin, Zola, Baudelaire, etc., while Diaghileff assumed the aggressive attitude of running down the established artists of the day, the Press, and the public for their bad taste.

Reading this to-day, much of it, in spite of its vigour and youthful arrogance, seems a trifle childish, and even insipid; but at the time of its publication it burst like a bomb, loosing the bottled-up enthusiasm of the young and the indignation of the old. It could not be ignored. It was essential that everyone should be on one side or on the other.

Diaghileff dealt especially with the label "decadent," with which the old taunted them, saying that to be decadent, it was necessary to fall from a certain height, but that such a height had never been reached by the preceding generation, so that the *Mir Isskustva* must inevitably be an advance and not a falling off.

Individualism was made the common rallying ground of this scattered group of artists and thinkers who interpreted history as "the development of individuals." "Man does not depend on exterior circumstances, but on himself alone." Diaghileff stressed this in his very first editorials:

"If the beauty of the world is the expression of God's will, man is the highest creation of that will."

"One of the greatest merits of our times is to recognize individuality under every guise and at every epoch."

Diaghileff started the attack by defining art as a free and disinterested act taking place in the soul of the artist. "The artist is confined in a mysterious way."

Loudly he proclaimed the freedom of the artist, and this whole charter of freedom was a direct blow at the *Ambulants*.

"The creator must love only beauty. He must only commune with beauty, when his divine nature is manifest."

"The reactions of art to earthly difficulties are not worthy of the soul of the Divinity."

And again and again the paper hammers at the fact that art cannot recognize the struggle for life:

"The sole function of art is pleasure, its only instrument beauty. . . . It is blasphemous to force ideas."

This invocation of a rather nebulous ideal of beauty, and all the talk about inspiration, is very typical of its period, in Russia just as in France and England, and in the *Mir Isskustva* Diaghileff claims to speak for his generation. He hails a new school of criticism—critics who are subjective and self-revelatory.

"The desire to make a science out of criticism will never solve the importance of the relative merits of talent. One must sing art, hail every new manifestation triumphantly."

This is youth speaking, but to the end of his days Diaghileff truly "hailed every new manifestation triumphantly."

Even before the founding of the *Mir Isskustva* he had written:

"The criteria of objective criticism will in time become dried and faded formulæ, they will lose the undying charm of the personal approach, in which, as well as in the work of the creator, you will see the soul of the critic."

In later years he was to be very bitter about the soul of the critic when one of his favourite works was in question. "Most people learn from experience, critics never," I have heard him say on more than one occasion.

Benois himself, most scholarly of critics, sang the praises of subjective criticism, and the *Mir Isskustva* became the confessional and the platform of a group of men who agreed only definitely on one point—that it should become so.

Criticism is given a still higher function. Not only must the critic guide the public, and so reveal himself; "the modern critic must guide the groping and bewildered painter and show him the true links with his national past."

It was in that practical guidance, in speaking to the painter as well as to his public, that Diaghileff was unique, and it is there that one can truly claim for him a creative gift. Criticism at that point ceases to be academic. Diaghileff was not just the spokesman of·a group, but a distinct leader, whether or not they knew it or were prepared to admit it.

Such a magnificent association could exist only as long as it was run by young enthusiasts in face of a common enemy. It could be vital, self-assertive, and infinitely destructive. The wonder is that it could build. By the very nature of the association this should not have been the case—a dozen individuals, rejoicing in their individualism, whose aims and interests pointed in a variety of directions. It is clearly Diaghileff, the will-power, who can knit them together and translate their talk into deeds.

That is the first revelation of his greatness, the essential quality from which all the rest springs. He does not shirk the issue. What is beauty? The question might legitimately be put to them by their opponents. He is ready when the time comes, when he has destroyed sufficiently, to show what is his conception of beauty.

It is the *Ambulants* who are the main enemy, since the Academy after all was also aiming at "art for art's sake" in its own particular manner.

Diaghileff had already started the attack before the foundation of his own paper. In the *Novosti* of 1897, he wrote:

"It is about time we stopped admiring these inartistic canvases, with policemen, rural guards, students in red shirts, and young women with cropped hair."

In his own paper he became more and more violent:

"Tchernichevsky wishes to make logarithm tables out of pictures, touching art with unwashed hands, and out of poems he would concoct prescriptions for all the nasty ills of civilization."

Benois, in a neat phrase, described the movement as, *"Une gifle à Apollon."*

The paper was run on a nationalist and a European basis— nationalist first, and then "away to conquer wider fields."

"We must play our parts not by chance participation in exhibitions, but permanently in the march of art. This solidarity is essential. It must exist in two ways—in active participation in European life, and also in drawing European life to us. We cannot do without it; it is the only possibility of progress, the only way to fight the routine that has shackled our painting."

Peter the Great might well have said something of the kind.

Peasant art was greatly idealized, and movements to encourage it vigorously applauded, in spite of internal disagreements. Princess Tenischeva was an enthusiastic supporter of such things as Lenin has since described as "masked capitalism."

The artist in the first number who represented the national element was Victor Vasnetzoff, whose work in the ikon manner showed little freedom or originality. To-day the reason for his choice is difficult to understand, unless, as Benois suggests, it was as a cautious beginning, to inte: est and gradually educate a larger public.

The choice of artists in general, too, was magnificently eclectic: Diaghileff constantly acclaimed Puvis de Chavannes, Böcklin, Beardsley, Polenova, Rops, Levitsky, and Degas. Puvis and Burne-Jones were soul seers, far removed from reality, singing eternal harmonies; and Böcklin, fortunate in the approval of both Répine and Diaghileff, was "The Titan" and "The Modern Michelangelo."

In 1899 they were still very far from the Impressionists, whose message was even spoken of somewhat slightingly. "At that time," Benois has told me, "Diaghileff knew probably less of Impressionism than we did, although later he went much further in his admiration of modern and advanced movements than any of us."

In the second year of the paper, the nationalist tendency took the form of the discovery of Russian architectural beauties; Benois edited *The Artistic Treasures of Russia,* Lanceray painted the architecture. Diaghileff was busy with researches for his monograph on Levitsky. Societies were formed to preserve the amenities of old St. Petersburg. While Benois was sighing for the architectural past, Diaghileff mischievously praised the modern in architecture, particularly ornate just then. He shocked his friends by saying that what the public wanted was important, and must always be considered, which involved him in a controversy with Merejkovsky, and, worse still, he praised the American millionaire as a collector of works of art. He might be studying the eighteenth century assiduously, but both his feet were planted firmly on nineteenth-century soil.

A study of the paper shows us that Diaghileff, Benois, and Nouvel had great hopes for the future, while Merejkovsky and Filosofov were more austere—full of philosophical doubts.

§ 3

All this created a host of powerful enemies, among them Répine, who had been sympathetic at the first, and who had promised his collaboration. He immediately broke off diplomatic relations, and started a violent controversy with Diaghileff in the Press. This did not prevent the paper from devoting a number to his art according to the original plan.

"In the beginning of December," says Nouvel, "I left again for the Crimea, taking with me two copies of the paper, which were presented to the Emperor and Empress through my minister. They seemed pleased with it."

Later, when funds grew low, the Princess having retreated before the storm of abuse and ridicule, the Emperor himself gave some funds for the paper, at the request of Serov, who was then painting his celebrated portrait.

With each number the Review improved in quality, both in text and in appearance. Benois, coming to St. Petersburg for a few weeks, gave Diaghileff his critical advice and somewhat counterbalanced the influence of Filosofov. The second number contained Levitsky's famous series of portraits of the pupils of the Smolny Institute, and a further number was devoted to the centenary of Pouchkine. Both Levitsky and Pouchkine were later subjects of very special study by Diaghileff.

The work was divided as follows: Diaghileff had the general management, and consequently possessed dictatorial powers, which he chose to exercise on the artistic conduct of the Review, the policy, the reproductions, and the actual physical make-up. He consulted the other members of the editorial, listened to their advice, and, once having made up his mind, would take no notice of any objection. He was not fond of writing himself, but contributed for the first year a series of critical articles. The literary side was run by Filosofov, but under the supervision of Diaghileff, while the comments on current events were done in collaboration round the table where the old *nynya* presided over the samovar. These editorial meetings were held daily from four to seven, when every event was passed under review and enemies were pilloried as bitterly as possible. Nurok was a specialist at this, pointing out the weaknesses in people and denouncing them with glee. At the back of all this was the desire that Diaghileff held all his life—to *"épater le bourgeois."* When this went too far, the austere Filosofov would call the meeting to order, and remind them that they were conducting a serious review.

One of the rooms was gaily decorated with caricatures of the various artists and friends, a task at which Bakst and Serov excelled. They were often brutal, and spared no one.

In January 1899 Diaghileff's large international exhibition was opened with all the pomp and ceremony that he always loved. Everything worth doing must be done on a large scale. For the first time contemporary Russian art hung side by side with the very best in Europe, and made a surprisingly good showing. Among the foreigners were Renoir, Degas, Besnard, Whistler, Boldini, Raffaelli, Liebermann, Lenbach, Carrière, and Conder. Now that time has acted as the supreme critic, the list seems curiously mixed, but at the time it was truly representative and in the vanguard of artistic development. The Emperor, Empress, Grand Dukes, and Duchesses visited the Exhibition. The Grand Duke Vladimir, Diaghileff's future patron, as President of the Academy of Fine Arts, paid several visits, and took a genuine interest in the movement.

It met with a great success from sympathizers, and increased the influence of the magazine, but it also aroused the opposition to fury, and the hostile Press stopped at nothing in their rage, accusing the *Mir Isskustva* of "corrupting youth, breeding ugliness, morbidity, and depraved tastes."

There was more than one incident, but none had any lasting result. An old critic of the influential and reactionary *Novoie Vremia*, famous as a malicious and witty pamphleteer, had written an especially venomous attack against Diaghileff and his friends. Diaghileff and Filosofov, aroused to indignation, decided to chastise him. When they rang, he opened the front door himself, and, seeing his visitors, promptly slammed the door in their faces, only giving Diaghileff time to touch his cheek with his inevitable top hat.

These exhibitions continued with success till 1903, when the exhibitors, revolting against the domination of Diaghileff, seceded and formed their own society, after which the artistic level dropped and he abandoned them to their own devices.

The third exhibition was perhaps the most notable in organization. It was held in the vast halls of the Académie des Beaux Arts, an invasion of the sacred home of the academy itself; a favour that had been especially hard to obtain. Many of the academicians were horrified at the very idea, but Répine, although at war with the *Mir Isskustva*, generously spoke for Diaghileff and, thanks to the goodwill of the Grand Duke Vladimir, the victory was won.

Diaghileff was not content with having gained the hall. He wished to arrange it in his owner manner. The walls were decorated with villainous copies of the masters, a deplorable background for an exhibition. Aided by carpenters from the Imperial Theatres he erected wooden partitions, split the vast halls into small well-lit rooms, and hid the offending paintings. Every effort was made to stop him, and at the last moment rumours were spread that the structure was unsafe. The exhibition was a success from every point of view, and the publicity of the struggle greatly added to his prestige.

In the spring of 1900 Diaghileff went to the Universal Exhibition in Paris and saw the complete triumph of his cause: Serov winning the medal of honour, Maliutine and Korovin gold medals for painting, and Vroubel and Golovin for applied art. Each one belonged to the group.

§ 4

At the end of 1899 Diaghileff and the *Mir Isskustva* went through a difficult period that was totally unexpected. Mamontoff, whose affairs were in a parlous state, found it quite impossible to continue his subsidy, and almost at the same time Princess Tenischeva withdrew. Benois thinks that her reasons may have been the following: The affair had cost considerably more than she ever anticipated, and the dictatorship of Diaghileff and Filosofov had robbed her of the important rôle she certainly intended to play. Further, she became frightened of the increasing number of enemies that the movement was making, and the Press held her up to ridicule, one paper coming out with a caricature of her as a cow being milked for the benefit of Diaghileff and his friends. In a sense this was too near the truth for her to take it as a joke, and nothing could persuade her to remain. At the beginning of 1900 the paper was entirely without funds. Then a group of friends and admirers came to the rescue, and guaranteed its existence for a further year; among them were Ilya Ostroukhoff, a rich Moscow merchant and a collector and painter himself, and Dr. Serge Botkine, professor at the medical academy. Diaghileff's whole career was marked by these last-minute rescues of his expensive enterprises.

After this reprieve the artistic appearance of the paper improved with each number. Benois was permanently back in St.

Petersburg, and more than counterbalanced the influence of Filosofov, bringing back the paper to its original artistic policy. Diaghileff had interested Bakst, Lanceray, Somov, and Doboujinsky in graphic art, and in their decorations for the magazine was inaugurated a school of book illustration second only in importance, because it was local, to the theatrical movement. Korovin and Serov came more and more frequently from Moscow. Of all the group, Serov was the most respected. His position was one apart. He was seven years older than the rest, and already a celebrity. He now rightly ranks as the greatest easel artist Russia has produced. He was a pupil of Répine, and at first a member of the *Ambulants*, but threw himself whole-heartedly into the new movement as soon as it was started. He had an immense admiration for Diaghileff, while readily admitting his faults, and he guided him, advised him, and even reproved him at times. Diaghileff regarded him as an elder brother, and he was perhaps in his whole career the only person for whom he had an entire respect, and before whose judgement he would readily incline himself. Serov merited that respect and became the final arbiter in all the disputes that arose—and there were many.

"I remember one dreadful scene that took place," says Nouvel, "though I have completely forgotten its cause. It degenerated into a contest of abuse between Diaghileff and Filosofov on the one hand, and Bakst on the other. There was constant conflict between Diaghileff and Bakst, provoked by their utter differences of nature. Bakst was a delightful person, full of imagination, often highly comical, sometimes without meaning it. His greatest fault was his excessive vanity and his love of publicity, which he exploited in a manner not always pleasing to us. He was touchy and unbalanced too, so that it was not always possible to trust him completely. Diaghileff disliked this, and Bakst resented his domination. That particular evening I had sided with Bakst and gone out, slamming the door. The next day I learned that Bakst had stayed on, continued the quarrel, and had been literally thrown out of the room by Diaghileff. That recourse to physical brutality infuriated me and I quarrelled with Diaghileff, but it was the gentle Somov who was the most disgusted. Any violence or injustice revolted him, and he wrote a letter to Diaghileff, speaking out his mind Diaghileff took affront, and was almost ready to challenge him to a duel. I was chosen as intermediary, and with great difficulty, and after interminable negotiations, managed to smooth things over. But from that day things were never the same again between Diaghileff and Somov. They stopped calling one another by the familiar second person, and only met on a strictly business footing. In spite of all Diaghileff's warm admiration, Somov had never had any sympathy with his brutality. Bakst himself soon made the peace."

In this way Diaghileff forfeited the collaboration of an artist who might have excelled in the decoration of the early romantic ballets.

But in spite of such scenes of violence there was always much laughter and good humour. Diaghileff could never sustain a quarrel for long. He had no false pride, and usually rather than that the work should suffer he would be the first to make friendly overtures whether he had been the aggressor or not.

Later, when low in funds once again, there took place an event of capital importance to the group. Serov received the commission to paint a portrait of Alexander III in Danish uniform, which Nicholas II wished to present to the Danish regiment of which his father had been colonel. This portrait naturally had to be done after photographs, but Serov had kept such a vivid impression of the late Emperor that he succeeded admirably in producing both a vivid likeness and a great work of art. Shortly afterwards he painted a magnificent portrait of the Grand Duke Paul in his Guards' uniform—which won him the

Prince Serge Wolkonsky

Isadora Duncan by Bakst, 1905

Original poster of the Russian Ballet 1909,
Pavlova by Serov

medal of honour at the Universal Exhibition in Paris—and also the portrait of the old Grand Duke Michel Nicolaievitch, the Tsar's great-uncle.

These successes gained him the commission to paint the Emperor's own portrait. He told his friends of the sittings, and of the simplicity and charm of the Emperor. They saw that he had the royal sympathy, and Diaghileff, greatly daring, suggested that he should invite the Emperor to subsidize the *Mir Isskustva*. This was done, and the sum of 10,000 roubles a year (£1,000) was guaranteed for a period of five years, assuring the continuance of the magazine. The portrait was an immense success, the finest in fact ever painted of the Emperor, and it was given to the Empress and hung in her private apartment until the taking of the Winter Palace by the Bolsheviks, when it was wantonly destroyed.

A little later Serov painted two further portraits of the Emperor, one in the uniform of the Scots Greys, for presentation to that regiment, and another for a Caucasian regiment. During the painting of this latter portrait an incident occurred that completely spoiled the good relationship between Emperor and painter. Serov had already quarrelled with the chief of the court chancery about the price of the portraits, fixed at the modest sum of 4,000 roubles (£400), and had written him a very violent letter, his pride hurt by the insinuation that he was taking undue advantage of the fact that the price had not been agreed upon in advance. This, however, had no ill results, as opinion was firmly in Serov's favour. The incident that finally caused a rupture was with the Emperor himself. During one of the sittings, the Empress came in and began criticizing the painting to the Emperor, in English. Serov could not understand the language, and was deeply offended. Turning to the Empress, he offered his palette and brushes, saying, "If your Majesty wishes to paint it herself—*voilà!*" She at once left the room, and the sitting was continued in silence. It was the last.

Later, in 1911, when Serov died, an application was made to the Tsar for funds for the widow, left without resources. He readily consented, saying, "Although he offended me grievously in the person of the Empress, I bear him no trace of ill will."

§ 5

Thanks to the stimulating influence of the *Mir Isskustva* activities were started in every branch of the Russian world of art.

The Imperial Society for the Encouragement of Fine Arts founded a review, *The Treasures of Art in Russia*, and offered the editorship to Benois, who accepted. Diaghileff, always jealous when his friends undertook any activity apart from himself, was alarmed. He saw not only a potential rival, but the end of Benois's invaluable co-operation. Finally they came to an agreement by which Benois was to continue his work for Diaghileff and confine the new magazine purely to matters of ancient art. The first number of the new magazine was published in 1901. In the autumn of the same year, Nurok, Nouvel, and some friends founded Les Soirées de Musique Contemporaine. Their resources were slender, only permitting them to hold concerts of chamber music, but their record is a remarkable one. For the first time in Russia works by French composers from Franck and D'Indy to Debussy and Ravel, by such Germans as Reger and Schönberg, and, among the young Russians, Stravinsky and Prokofiev received auditions.

Once again Diaghileff was angry at not being invited to participate, and Nouvel's reasons for this omission are revealing.

"There were two reasons why we did not invite Diaghileff: we were afraid of his dominating character, and we were quite certain that the modest scale on which we were operating would not interest him. He only cared for big enterprises.

"He readily accepted this explanation, and there was no further misunderstanding between us."

Also arising out of the *Mir Isskustva*, Filosofov, Merejkovsky, and their followers founded Les Assemblées Religieuses et Philosophiques, which met periodically under the presidency of a highly placed ecclesiastic. They were aiming at a restatement and rejuvenation of Christianity. Benois, Nouvel, and even Bakst were present from time to time, chiefly out of curiosity. Diaghileff stayed resolutely away. He had a loathing for such things, though he greatly appreciated the intelligence of Merejkovsky. It was in the *Mir Isskustva* that his celebrated essay on Tolstoi and Dostoievski first appeared.

The far-reaching effect of Diaghileff's effort will be seen from these three examples. In these and their many offshoots the influence lasted right up to the time of the Revolution. Long before 1909 and his conquest of the West, Diaghileff had performed a task that he might have been justified in regarding as a life's work.

§ 6

These activities paved the way for still further changes. Benois had a sharp quarrel with the Society for the Encouragement of the Fine Arts, resigned his editorship of *The Treasures of Art in Russia*, and went for a few months to Rome. At the same time the Merejkovskys and their group formed a journal of their own, *The New Path*, for the propagation of their religious and mystical ideas. Now that they had their own organ, Filosofov lost all interest in the *Mir Isskustva*. This rid the paper of an element that had never had the sympathy of the artists, but at the same time it threw an immense burden of practical work on Diaghileff, so that, as soon as Benois returned, Diaghileff proposed that he should become joint editor, and continue the work he had been doing in *The Treasures of Art in Russia*. From January 1st, 1904, the Review appeared under their joint signatures, the ancient art controlled by Benois, the contemporary by Diaghileff, in alternate numbers. It proved an ideal partnership, the two men complementing each other; but this was to be the last year of the paper, and Diaghileff was already faced with the practical problem of its further existence. The Emperor's five years' subsidy had now come to an end, and the enormous expenses incurred by the crown during the Russo-Japanese War made its continuance out of the question. Both Diaghileff and Benois were feeling the weight of their task. During the last six years they had said all that they had to say, the fight was well won, and without a fight there could be no zest in working. They had destroyed, but they had also built up and sustained a whole new generation of artists, according to their ideal. Nevertheless they made one final attempt when they approached Princess Tenischeva again, but she proved to be so cautious after her previous experience that she laid down certain conditions which they judged quite impossible of fulfilment.

The kernel of the little group, the soul of the paper, was rapidly scattering.

Bakst had fallen ill with pneumonia, and, at all times highly strung, his illness had brought him to the very verge of madness, due in a large part to his marriage with a daughter of Paul Tretiakov, for whose sake he had had a year previously to be converted to the Orthodox faith. He was essentially a Jew, and in his weakened state he imagined himself irrevocably condemned to death for his betrayal of Jehovah. Recovered from his pneumonia, he still believed this, fell into a profound melancholy, locking himself in his room and refusing to see anyone, literally motionless, awaiting his punishment. He quarrelled with his wife, in whom he saw the cause of his misfortune. Doctor after doctor reassured him, but he would not believe. "They do not like to tell me the true state of things." This breakdown lasted through the winter. Fortunately, just at that time, a law was promulgated permitting Jews, who had been forced for some reason to become converted, to abjure Christianity and to return to their former faith. Immediately Bakst profited by this, and rapidly became his old self once again—a gay, care-free man about town.

There was nearly always something just a little comical about Bakst, even in his most tragic moments. It was a part of his charm, and at times he even took a certain pleasure in provoking laughter at his expense. On this occasion, too, comedy had entered largely into the story. As soon as he had decided to marry, and consequently to become converted to Christianity, he looked about him for the quickest and least troublesome way. He was told that it was easiest to be received into the Anglican Church by a certain clergyman in Warsaw. This he did, intending to be confirmed on his return to St. Petersburg, since this was the essential before marriage. He went to the English Church, and was told that the bishop alone could perform the ceremony.

"Where is the bishop?"

"In England, he has just left, and he won't be back in Russia for another two years."

Vainly Bakst went to the Lutheran and the Protestant Churches, but they would not confirm him, and finally he had to be received into the Orthodox Church. The simplest way had turned out to be the most complex and the most farcical, but it was a tragedy to Bakst.

Filosofov had followed his own bent, perhaps happy no longer to play the unexpected rôle of second fiddle to his young cousin. Soon after they had a violent quarrel that broke up the intimate friendship and alliance of fifteen years. Filosofov had had a large share in the forming of Diaghileff, but now there was nothing left, and the rupture was complete. They saw one another from time to time, always by chance, the last occasion being in a Warsaw restaurant in 1928, after a lapse of twenty years. They exchanged politenesses, but met as strangers.

The end of the *Mir Isskustva* marks the end of Diaghileff's critical life, and the next period is one of action. Seldom has any periodical with a circulation of under four thousand exerted so powerful an influence on the whole culture of a period, and in the process of educating the public it moreover educated its founder.

DIAGHILEFF AND PRINCE WOLKONSKY
1899–1900

*Prince Wolkonsky—Diaghileff as a subordinate—The story
of a historic quarrel—Diaghileff and Wolkonsky's successor.*

"If I was an *enfant terrible* in my management of the theatre and the desire to
reform, Diaghileff was a raging lion."

PRINCE WOLKONSKY

On July 22nd, 1899, in excellent time to prepare for the important winter season, Prince Serge Wolkonsky was appointed
director of the Imperial Theatres, a day full of promise for the
group. Here at last was a vigorous young man in charge, instead
of the usual courtier or antiquated bureaucrat; a friend and a
sympathizer of theirs, who would most certainly give them an
early opportunity to put their many theories into practice. Much
as they were interested in every branch of art, the theatre was
their great and special love. They realized, too, its importance
as propaganda. With such opportunities Russia would soon be
convinced. A friend of theirs now held the keys to the finest
stages in the world.

Wolkonsky succeeded his uncle, Vsevolojsky, a man of erudi-
tion and culture, even something of a reformer in his time, but
now definitely of the old school and no longer receptive to new
ideas, especially with regards to *décor*—naturally enough, since
he was himself an enthusiastic and indefatigable designer of
costume. Now when, after seventeen years' reign, he made way
for his nephew, and was given the post of director of the Imperial Hermitage by way of compensation, it did not seem to him

103

—as it seemed to the authorities—that the calm of the museum would be a welcome rest after the noise and bustle of the theatre, and he is credited with the pathetic remark:

"I am surrounded by goddesses and cannot even clothe them."

In theory, Wolkonsky should have been the ideal man for the position, and, in addition to his personal qualities, he had an ancestry not merely of blue blood but of noble achievement.

His love of the theatre was in no sense that of a wealthy, aristocratic *dilettante*, but an all-consuming passion that had dic-- tated the whole course of his life. It began when, as a schoolboy, he went with his brother to see the Italian actor, Rossi, in *Othello*. The impression was overpowering. It started not only his love and knowledge of the Shakespearian drama, but it set in motion that element of hero-worship that is shared by the gallery girl, the fashionable first-nighter, and even the most cynical of *impresarios*, and that, when it is accompanied by a fine critical faculty, becomes an irresistible creative force. Diaghileff, too, as we have seen, began his artistic pilgrimage as a fervent seeker after autographed photographs, and worshipped the great even while he was learning to understand them.

The young Wolkonsky purchased a photograph of his hero and, accompanied by his brother, went backstage to get it autographed. They were in no wise disillusioned to find their hero, the jealous Moor, puffing at a huge black cigar. They stood in the wings, thrilled at this first intimate contact with the theatre, to watch the Moor's *entrée*, but Baron Küster, the then director, soon turned his successor of twenty-two years later off the stage, and with a scolding.

"From that time," says Wolkonsky, "it was surprising how my attention was drawn to the methods by which certain effects were attained. In moments of the greatest excitement I did not lose interest in the technicalities of the art; my feelings were completely overcome by *what* he did, but all the time I was watching *how* he produced his effects."

This is the attitude of the complete theatre man, who can share the pleasures both of the stage and of the auditorium from his privileged position in the wings.

His early balletic education is of greater importance to us, and shows us vividly with what, first Wolkonsky himself, and afterwards Diaghileff and his fellow workers, had to contend in their struggles against popular opinion and prejudice. It is interesting, while reading such an account, to realize that the fight was lost from the start, and that to this very day in Soviet Russia the abuses that Wolkonsky mentions exist and elicit applause: the *Red Poppy*, for all its revolutionary scenario, is nearer to the *Fisherman and the Naiad* than to anything in the Diaghileff repertoire.

"I do not want you to think of me as a confirmed *balletomane* from the start," Wolkonsky tells me. "In fact, I doubt whether I really ever became one at all in Russia in the strict sense of the word. The first time I went to the ballet it was to see the *Fisherman and the Naiad*. I was a child. I liked the fairy side of the performance, I liked the *corps de ballet*, but, frankly, I disliked the soloists. Even in those early days I felt shocked at their affectation, and the technique, which was stressed to an almost acrobatic extent, left me quite cold. I could neither grasp the difficulty nor the charm of it, so tremendously did the 'untruth' of it offend me. It was true to no convention, illogical, absurd, unnecessary. You will understand something of it when you compare early theatrical photos with those of to-day.

"Then Zucchi came to me as a great exception and a great revelation. I saw that ballet dancing could have a 'meaning.' She was one of the greatest mimes I have ever seen. Everything about her seemed to speak—eyes, shoulders, hands, and fingers. I shall never forget her lovely expressive back, when she turned it

105

to the public. There was an indifferent ballet called *Brahma*, to music by Pugni, Minkus, or even worse. In it there was a scene where she never failed to make people cry, as she implored the priests to spare her. Just think of it—she had to conquer music, story, and *décor*, and the mood of an audience who had come to see—not art, but physical prowess and tricks! What was important was the fact that her movements, in their preparation and in their climax, fell in time with the music. That may seem obvious to you now, but in those days music and movement were very far apart. This, then, became to me the main exigency to which mime in dancing must respond, and it was the main exigency just because at that time it was the most neglected one. Little by little through my interest in the mime I was won over to see what vast possibilities lay in ballet, and began to interest myself in the purely dancing side."

Zucchi's share in converting the reformer, and making him visualize ballet as it ought to be, cannot be too greatly stressed. To-day her name means little to us, but, by directly inspiring Kchesinska, and by moving Wolkonsky, Benois, Nouvel, and others, it may have been she, more than any other single artist, who saved ballet, and gave to it its new importance; and thus it is that the great dancer survives, if not always in memory, yet in actual concrete service to her art, long after she has ceased to dance and to live.

Through his early but reasoned infatuation Wolkonsky became a fine connoisseur and a very excellent amateur actor, travelling extensively abroad, learning at every opportunity from the foreign theatre. He followed a definite line, and knew what concrete forms he would accomplish—given opportunity.

His was an education parallel to that of the group, and pointing in very much the same direction.

Then he was confronted with the machine, and visions of art and idealism remained but visions, as he struggled hard to keep it in motion. Had he been more of the *tchinovnik*, mentally black-coated, and less of the artist, he might have held down his post and have become an honoured nonentity; had he shelved reform and played the social game for all it was worth, as did his successor Teliakovsky, evidently a master at playing for safety, he would also have survived, and marked time in comfort.

All St. Petersburg envied him his position at the early age of thirty-nine, and, indeed, it was socially of first-class importance. As a court rank it gave the director the right of *entrée* to the Emperor whenever he was present in his box at any of the Imperial Theatres, and, as Nicholas II was an ardent theatre-goer, this meant a frequent and close contact with all the advantages that a schemer or self-seeker could have wished.

Wolkonsky was none of these things, and from the very first was even diffident about accepting, fearful of the social and administrative duties involved; and when finally he accepted, it was only to give pleasure to his father.

"In fact, the only people who could really take the fullest advantage of the position are the relatives of the director. All that they have to do is to select their performance with care, and then to watch it and to be seen watching it from the prominence of the director's box. When I resigned, my brother went about telling everybody that he had 'resigned the position of the brother of the director of the Imperial Theatres.' "

However, he started full of zeal, only to meet opposition from the very first day. Actors, dancers, society, and especially the Press, were in close alliance against the director, everyone playing some little game of his own. He found that each insignificant incident, however private and personal it might have seemed to him at the moment, was magnified, published, and discussed. When, on one occasion, he turned up the ends of his trousers to avoid the dust and cobwebs of a scenery storeroom, this lack of dignity on the part of a high official went the rounds for over two years. A triviality—but highly irritating, nevertheless, to one who was dreaming of new scenic effects, of perfect diction, and of a more intense realism. The Press caricaturist, too, being forbidden anything of a political nature, was ever on the look-out for a theatrical titbit, and there was no risk involved even in being really malicious.

One of Wolkonsky's first "interferences" in the sacred realm of ballet was an attempt to modify the very short skirt, so ill-becoming and uncharitable to any but the most perfect legs. "How dare he interfere with what has always been," cried the *balletomanes*, and a caricature appeared straightway of Wolkonsky conducting a rehearsal of *coryphées* clad in sacks right up to their chins. Curiously enough, this was the only theatrical question that interested the Empress, or about which she ever expressed an opinion—a most decided one, and altogether in the director's favour.

The ballet was sacrosanct, and it is almost impossible for us to realize at the present day the position then held by the dancer. Gradually, under the Diaghileff régime, the dancer sank into comparative anonymity, giving way to the ballet as a whole. Any parallel that we might try to make with a favourite film star or with a world-famous athlete would be quite inadequate. It was not just a question of swaying a vast public, of receptions, ovations, and photographs everywhere. The great dancer swayed her public, but that public was not merely the vast popular one that paid for its seats, applauded, and then thought little more about it. That is popularity—not power. The devoted public of the great Russian dancers consisted of publicists, ministers of state, the Grand Dukes, and, on the very summit of the pyramid, the Emperor himself, who was ready to intervene on occasion if he felt that ample justice had not been done to some favourite artist. As the director never had the last word, his task was impossible from the start. Wolkonsky started, too, with the unmerited reputation of being hostile to ballet—because he did not accept it blindly in all its forms—and his early attempts at reform were received either unwillingly or without understanding. Some historians of the period have accused him of wishing to change the ballet technique for Dalcroze eurhythmics. Wolkonsky was certainly impressed by the Dalcroze methods when he saw them—but that was not until ten years later, and at the time of which we are speaking he signalled his revolt by a logical appeal to artistry and common sense, that had its birth in no system, but in his own development. Its direction, which others pursued after him, was to save the ballet form and not to jeopardize it.

"I remember at the very beginning of my directorship a new production of *Tannhäuser*. The dances in the first act, the bacchanal in the Venus grotto, had been staged by the great Petipa himself. At the dress rehearsal I was horrified. It was just 'tiptoe-tiptoe' the whole time. The nymphs were *ballerinas*, never forgot it themselves and never let the audience forget it. Think of it; during that wonderful accord which an invisible chorus sings behind the scenes, we saw three *ballerinas* cross the plateau on their points, grinning sweetly and triumphantly to the enraptured audience.

"I gave orders for the scene to be changed but, even if there had been time, nobody would have understood in the slightest what it was I wanted. The dances had elicited applause—how could there possibly be anything wrong?

"In the whole Imperial dancing school there was not even a class of mime. There was a choral singing class, but none in musical appreciation. I instituted a mime class under old Gert, but he was too fixed in the stereotyped fashions of his time to give anything to his pupils.

"It was only with Fokine in the Diaghileff days, in *Shehera-*

zade in particular, that I saw the practical realization of my dreams and became a true ballet lover."

Tannhäuser bacchanal *sur les pointes*, hand on heart, lovers' sighs—that is the setting of the scene for the advent of Diaghileff and the struggle that had to follow.

Had Wolkonsky himself been weaker and less honest—or stronger and less honest, he would have succeeded, and the collaboration with Diaghileff would have reformed the Russian stage in Russia itself instead of abroad. As things happened Wolkonsky must go down in history as an important would-be reformer, and one of the first to visualize the path that Diaghileff himself was to follow so resolutely. His relations with Diaghileff are of the utmost importance, and proved a turning-point in Diaghileff's career. They strengthened the belief of the whole group that their mission was world-wide, and not something local—on however large a scale. If Russia was unwilling to accept them, then so much the worse for Russia! They gave Diaghileff his first practical contact with the theatre, and disproved conclusively the comfortable proverb, so often quoted by parents, headmasters, and the military, that "he who wishes to command must first know how to obey." His Maryinsky experience made him, if anything, more ruthless and direct in his aims.

Wolkonsky and Diaghileff first met at the house of Madame Panaïeva Kartseva, Diaghileff's step-aunt and a highly talented singer, while Diaghileff was still an unknown student.

"You should meet my nephew, Diaghileff," she had said, and the young man made an immediate impression. He was in congenial company, and had no need of arrogance to make his effect. Since that meeting he had begun to make a name, and now Wolkonsky saw in him the very man he required to help him put new life in the theatres through a close alliance with the *Mir Isskustva* group of artists.

While Wolkonsky had an instinctive sympathy for Diaghileff, from the very first he did not quite trust him or feel happy with him.

"Not so much," he says, "because of anything that I felt myself, but because of what others felt. He had the gift of putting people's backs up from the very start. He was arrogant, and people never quite knew how to take him. You must remember —and it may be difficult for you who only knew him in the later years—that he was not yet by any means acknowledged as a great or an important man, but he had all the *allure* of one, and people resented it. I felt that the theatre needed him, so against all advice—and it poured in from every direction—I engaged him and attached him to the service for 'special missions.' There was a storm, of course—there always was a storm when Diaghileff was anywhere near. My action was considered so mad in certain quarters that a critic, Bourenin, writing in the reactionary *Novoie Vremia*, referred to the engagement of 'this Diaghileff whose only title to fame is a predilection for multicoloured waistcoats of rare design.' That, incidentally, was one of the politest things said about him, and many of the innuendoes were of a disgusting character."

The first task given to Diaghileff was the production of the *Imperial Theatres Year Book*, an official annual publication. His handling of it was a triumph,[1] and began a new era in Russian book production. Artistically, nothing better could be hoped for, but from the bureaucratic, official point of view he had made a very bad mess of things. Firstly, the allowance assigned him was exceeded—bad enough—but even that could be overlooked, only that—horror of horrors—he altered the format and increased the bulk that had been customary from time immemorial, an unpardonable sin in an unpopular man on the threshold of success. The book had to go through the post, and regulations would be infringed. High officials had to be interviewed, and they took

[1] See note, p. 120.

keen pleasure in keeping the dandified young man waiting in anterooms, and snubbing him in all the unimaginative ways that come natural to the petty official. He took umbrage, went to his chief in a rage, and the unfortunate Wolkonsky, none too secure himself, had to spend hours on the telephone before he could set matters right.

The book was a success, but total failure would have been easier to forgive. Diaghileff provoked more and more scenes, and the solemn touchy officials could understand neither his arrogance nor his particular humour, perhaps because he did not condescend to be charming with them. They saw affronts everywhere.

"You mustn't sneeze on the stage," he told the chorus at rehearsal; "it is an offence against Imperial orders and subversive of discipline."

What exactly did the fellow mean? Was he making fun of them or of the sacred institution?

These brushes with officialdom made Diaghileff himself more and more irritable. One day, while eager to discuss some question with Wolkonsky, he was kept waiting while the director listened to a singer. The next day there was an aggrieved note:

"I am sorry to notice that apparently you have no more sympathy with me or my ideas. I had something really important to discuss with you, and it seemed scarcely necessary to postpone it to listen to a singer whose work you knew already."

Wolkonsky calmed him, but a succession of such notes proved irritating.

The work went on well, however. The first new artist brought in through the association was Apollinaire Vasnetzoff, and the production of *Sadko* that resulted was a triumph, and a triumph that was especially gratifying, as it delighted Rimsky-Korsakov, whose works had had very rough treatment at the Maryinsky,

Anna Pavlova, 1908

Chaliapine as Ivan the Terrible, 1909

Fokine and Fokina in *Daphnis and Chloe*

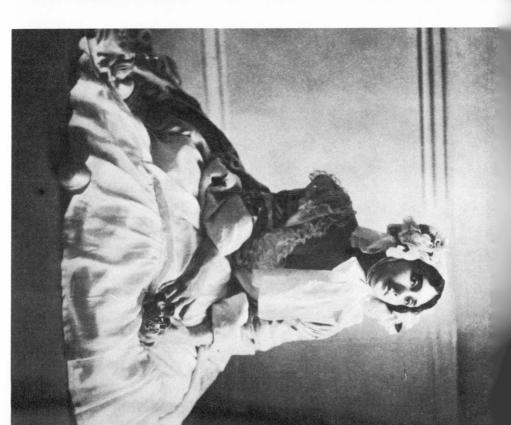

Tamara Karsavina in *Le Spectre de la Rose*

being invariably vetoed by Alexander II before they even reached production.

Diaghileff's unpopularity grew steadily, and malevolent people now began to pay close attention to his morals and to talk scandal. The director received visits and letters of complaints; Diaghileff himself received a powder-puff as an anonymous gift, and a deluge of similar insults followed, until the situation became so intolerable that one night after the performance the director sent for Diaghileff.

"I like you, Sergei Pavlovitch, for your ideas and for your energy, and especially for the fact that you do things on your own initiative without ever having to be urged by me; and so what I am going to say is very difficult for me. We are speaking man to man—*en ami*—I hope.

"First you offend people by your whole manner, which negatives all your constructive work and may destroy you. I know and can sympathize with all your difficulties, because so many of them are my own.

"There is a further matter, however, which is exceedingly awkward for me to mention, and it is this. I have not the slightest desire to act as a censor of morals. Your private life is no concern of mine, unless it obtrudes itself in such a way that the prestige of the theatre is involved and the work suffers, and then as an official I *must* intervene.

"People are talking about you, and, whether what they say has any foundation in fact or not, you must be more discreet in your whole conduct."

It was a difficult speech to make. Diaghileff indignantly denied the truth of any of the rumours, and even warned the director against certain persons of such habits themselves, who might have started the stories.

"I can remember the interview to this day," says Wolkonsky, "and it hurt me deeply. I greatly believed in the man, he was my choice for the post, and I wanted so much to help him. I was helpless, but I had to speak, and my official position gave me a sort of assumed superiority, as of someone sitting in judgement, that was very far from what I really felt.

"It was a bitterly cold night; after I had taken leave of Diaghileff, I put the lights out and went to the window; and then I saw him leave the house, and stagger wildly down the street like a drunken man."

However, Diaghileff's unpopularity continued, and he seemed unwilling or unable to conquer it. He could be charming on occasion to certain people whom he respected on account of their brains or because of the positions they occupied; but it was clearly impossible for him ever to fill a subordinate position, and this year must have been the hardest in his life—a break was inevitable.

After the success of *Sadko*, Wolkonsky gave the order that the production of the ballet *Sylvia* should be entrusted to Diaghileff. The music had long been a favourite with the various members of the little group, especially with Benois, and this type of retrospective romanticism fitted in with their programme at the moment. The *décor* and costumes were to be entrusted to Benois, Bakst, Lanceray, Korovin, and Serov, a combination of all that was finest in St. Petersburg and Moscow.

The order was to be published in the official gazette the next morning, but that very day something like a general strike occurred. All those whom Diaghileff had in any way offended—and there were many—now saw their opportunity, and a deputation waited on Wolkonsky to tell him that such was the feeling that they doubted whether the work could ever be carried out.

After due consideration, the order was rescinded and Diaghileff informed of the fact. He felt—and rightly so—that, whatever the circumstances, he had been very badly treated. He promptly countered by a written announcement that he refused to continue the editorship of the journal. Then the inevitable happened. Many of those who had protested so vigorously against Diaghileff now took his side and threatened to strike, and so the director found himself in a dilemma. He has been accused of weakness in that he failed to fulfil his promise; undoubtedly he was weak, but the conditions must not be forgotten. He held an official administrative post; all scandal must be avoided, all personal considerations laid aside. He was the official representative of the Emperor, and the theatre must be kept running smoothly. Diaghileff himself by his whole previous conduct had raised the opposition, and, however brilliant, however right in principle, the director felt that he must be sacrificed. Levinson has hinted that the whole trouble was on account of Wolkonsky's jealousy, but this suggested explanation does not fit the facts. The only other course open to him was his own resignation, but, although he was by this time heartily sick of the post, he had obligations, and the main consideration was to avoid, if possible, a first-class scandal.

Wolkonsky called on Diaghileff to resign his post of *attaché* for special missions, which was an honorary one. He refused, saying, "If you want a scandal, then I'll give you one." The next step was to send in his name for enforced resignation or dismissal, a humiliation that carried with it the impossibility of further work under the state. Then the real trouble began. Diaghileff used all his influence; the many who were hostile to the new director rallied to his side, and, as usual, through devious channels, the matter reached the Emperor, who ordered a postponement of the order till after a conversation with him. At first he supported Diaghileff, saying, "Were I in his position I would not leave," but after a review of the correspondence the Emperor, being urged by the minister, a stern disciplinarian, upheld Wolkonsky, though only when the order was actually published two days later could he be sure that it would not be rescinded.

The Emperor was so easily persuaded, and there was much pressure brought to bear. The minister acting in the absence of Baron Fredericks wisely decided to be *not at home* on the day intervening.

The order went through, and it was publicly announced that Diaghileff had been dismissed from his post.[1]

This meant a breach of diplomatic relations between the Theatre and the whole *Mir Isskustva* group, whose valuable co-operation was lost. It also meant an entirely new orientation, and from that date they may be said to have set their eyes towards the West.

Wolkonsky's reign was brief. A few months later he came into collision with the great Kchesinska, fined her for a breach of the regulations, and lost in the gigantic scandal that followed.

"If I was an *enfant terrible* in my management of the theatre and my desire for reform, Diaghileff was a raging lion. I sympathized with him and had to dismiss him. As people saw me leave my box to go to the beautiful palace assigned me, they may well have envied me; they could not guess my difficulty, but I was going through hell. Later, when I read of Diaghileff's first triumphs, of his applause by the banks of the Seine, when the short-sighted people of the Neva were still laughing at him, I rejoiced to see their noses put out of joint, and I enjoyed those triumphs as if they were my own."

The disgrace of enforced dismissal was shortly remedied. It was obvious that Diaghileff had been harshly treated. Six months later a special *prikaz* was issued in which Diaghileff was considered to have resigned of his own free will, and he was reinstated in another branch of the service. This was purely nominal, and was intended as an act of rehabilitation.

[1] In later years Diaghileff dramatized these events almost beyond recognition. In a letter to W. A. Propert he attributes Wolkonsky's subsequent fall to these happenings, and states that the late Emperor disliked and distrusted him.—A. L. H.

For ten years neither of the protagonists spoke to the other. Bakst, the good-natured, was the first of the friends to capitulate. At the Châtelet, Wolkonsky was struggling with a group of officials at the pass door—always exceptionally difficult to negotiate in France—when Bakst came up and said, "*Monsieur le Prince passera*," and they made friends. One by one through chance meetings the little group capitulated. Then one day in Rome, at the Umberto restaurant, Wolkonsky met Diaghileff, went up to him and expressed his admiration. They shook hands, and the incident was closed, but Diaghileff had not completely forgotten or forgiven. Years later in London, when he asked Wolkonsky to collaborate with him, he used the words: "I would like to have you with me. You are the sort of person who would do things on your own initiative without having to consult me."

The phrase was slipped into a long conversation. It may have been accidental, but Wolkonsky was the last person to grudge Diaghileff a belated revenge, and his criticisms in the Press were whole-heartedly generous.

I know Wolkonsky well to-day, and have discussed these things at length with him. To know him is to relive this whole drama of men with similar ideals and dissimilar characters who were accidentally thrown into opposition. With Diaghileff it was but an episode in his education, an episode among the many that he was to encounter in his long journey from Perm, with its many contacts. Wolkonsky can discuss it with regret, but with no trace of bitterness—objectively, as an episode in bygone history. This idealist of yesterday is an idealist to-day. He still sees the curtain rise with all of a schoolboy's thrill of anticipation, and the cinema has become for him a serious study. He does not decry to-day in the name of yesterday, and to-day the brilliant child Baronova finds his favour as did Zucchi then. "Diaghileff should have seen these young people, and how he would have rejoiced over such rich material."

There is something of the old actor about his whole manner. Tall, slim, pointed beard, eyes that are still full of fire, he gesticulates and mimes to illustrate a point, his voice takes on the inflections of mimicry as he recreates some scene from the past.

A very noble gentleman.

But Diaghileff was waiting. His struggle and temporary defeat had given him a new energy.

§ 2

Diaghileff continued to keep a hopeful eye on the Imperial Theatres. He was too much of a fighter to consider the incident completely closed, and he had plans that were demanding fulfilment. He had already attracted attention, made many powerful friends, and a change of régime might easily see him called upon again. Shortly afterwards the change came. Prince Wolkonsky fell, and Teliakovsky was named director of the Imperial Theatres.

Teliakovsky, in everything the opposite of Wolkonsky, was an ancient guards officer with no special artistic culture, narrow-minded and stubborn, but well able to hold his own in the political intrigue so essential for the position. He was completely dominated by his wife, who painted and designed costumes herself, and had pretensions to understand advanced art. Through her he was able to play at reform by employing many of the finest artists, yet without the ability to guide them or to strike out on a definite line of his own. His wife admired Korovin and Golovin, and with their advice he imagined that it would be easy to replace Diaghileff and to carry out his ideas himself. He did not for a moment realize that Diaghileff's schemes needed not only the finest artists, but a master brain to control them. Frequently since that time managers have made the mistake of engaging the best available talent, all the names made famous

118

by Diaghileff himself, and then of imagining that in this way they had discovered his secret, only to be amazed and disappointed by the results.

Between Teliakovsky and Diaghileff there was from the first a strong mutual antipathy. The director was jealous of Diaghileff's fame, and saw the one man who could replace him, while Diaghileff despised him, even hated him for having taken his ideas and ruined them in the execution. There was latent warfare between them, only thinly veiled by an assumed admiration of the director for Diaghileff. It was no easy task to upset Teliakovsky. He understood the political game, and the minister Baron Fredericks, who had appointed him, was also an ancient guards officer. He had filled the most important posts at court with former regimental comrades, and between them all there was a solidarity that it would be difficult or impossible to break.

Teliakovsky was highly sensitive to criticism, and especially frightened of the *Mir Isskustva*. Diaghileff did not spare him. In the second number (1902) Benois attacked the new production of *Don Quixote*, finding fault in the first place with the revival of anything so musically feeble as a work by Minkus, with Gorsky's new choreography and even with the *décors* by Korovin and Golovin. Publicly he dissociated the whole group from this production, though he admired the young choreographer's desire to escape from a worn academism. "We are not going to deny the talent of Petipa. We know some groups and figures which are finely conceived and highly effective; but one must admit that he is far from true art. His ballets are well-made academic drawings, but devoid of all soul and of all artistic temperament." The new choreography goes to the other extreme. He calls it a continuous Spanish bacchanal, and the direction is blamed for its sad misuse of true talent. In the same article he also condemns them for a revival of his beloved *Sylvia* in an old and unworthy setting. The same sentiments, naturally expressed with still

greater violence, are to be found in an article by Diaghileff himself, "Delibes' Ballets," published a few months later. Each one
of these criticisms was justified, and the passive watching of this
flirtation with his ideas must have been torture.

So far Teliakovsky had only used those artists who had
worked for him previously in Moscow, but now he turned to the
members of the St. Petersburg group, and on October 14th,
1902, Bakst made his début as a decorative artist with Merejkovsky's version of Euripides' *Hippolytus* at the Alexandrovsky
Theatre. The performance was poor, but Bakst at once proved
himself to be in the very front rank. This success was followed
by the *décors* for a ballet *La Fée des Poupées* and for *Œdipus*.
No one was more stunned than Bakst by a success which all his
intimates had foreseen. Till then he had looked upon himself as
a graphic artist and portraitist, with the decorative work as a
side-line. At the same time Benois too made his début with the
Twilight of the Gods, also a sensational success.

Teliakovsky had raided Diaghileff's preserves, but there was
no room for the man who had paved the way and prepared the
public mind. However, he had scratched the surface, leaving the
essential Diaghileff ideas untouched, and the fine ballet production as an entity of music, *décor*, and dancing was still to be
attempted, though never in Russia.

NOTE ON
THE YEAR BOOK OF THE IMPERIAL
THEATRES, 1899–1900
Edited by Serge Diaghileff. 244 pages

The actual cost of the production was 30,000 roubles,
(£3,000), over £1,000 in excess of the sum allotted.

Baron Driesen, who edited the volume five years later, states
that he still remembers the scandal, and the resulting upset in
the budget.

The writer possesses a copy of this remarkable volume. It is truly a triumph of editing and production, as unlike an official publication as one can imagine. It shows both hard, conscientious work and real imagination. It is far in advance of its times. The other volumes in the series are but a prosaic record of past events.

The editor assigned to his friends a good proportion of the work. The cover and the various tailpieces are by Leon Bakst, and there are delicately coloured reproductions of the programme covers of the Hermitage Theatre by Bakst and Somov. Benois contributes a learned and profusely illustrated article on the architecture of the Alexandrovsky Theatre.

A special feature, introduced by Diaghileff as a commentary on various period pieces given in the dramatic and operatic theatre that year, is the reproduction of historical portraits parallel with the photographs of the actors and actresses who undertook the various rôles.

The year book also emphasizes the fine state of the Russian stage at that date. No other state has ever subsidized its theatres in so lavish a manner, or attracted so many distinguished foreign visitors.

The second part of the book is a catalogue of the plays presented during the year, and of the actors and actresses employed, with the year of their graduation.

That year in the Maryinsky ballet there were fifty-five performances and twenty-six different ballets, with four new works, the most noteworthy being Glazounov's *Seasons*. Pierrina Legnani receives a benefit performance; Petipa is in the list for his forty-third year, and nearly the whole repertoire is by him. Kchesinska reigns supreme, and her famous ballet, *Esmeralda*, is revived, complete with its pet goat in the cast. Pavlova II— Anna Pavlovna—is beginning to make a great name; Trefilova, Egorova, and Preobrajenska are applauded, and in Moscow

Gheltzer is the star, and has remained so almost till to-day. There are other names that count to-day, and that have remained true to the theatre through each régime—Vaganova, brilliant technician and, as a teacher, guardian of the tradition at the present day. Fokine is emerging; there is a photograph of him with Pavlova II, and there are many names that will figure in the programmes of the editor himself: Astafieva, Will, Kyasht. Sometimes there are whole dynasties with regal numbers I, II, III, IV.

In the list of those who graduate from the ballet school that year is the name of one Serge Grigorieff, never absent from a Diaghileff programme, 1909–1929.

———CHAPTER VI———————————

THE GREAT SUMMING-UP
1905

The Revolution of 1905—Diaghileff and the Soviet—The historic Portrait Exhibition—Diaghileff as author—Diaghileff's prophetic speech.

"We are doomed to die to pave the way for the resurrection of a new culture, which will take from us what remains of our weary wisdom."

SERGE DIAGHILEFF

Diaghileff's last and greatest Russian enterprise took place in the midst of revolution, and the great upheaval of February completed for a time the disorganization of the group.

Benois, who had a horror of all noise or violence, speedily left Russia for the calm of Versailles, his spiritual home, where he remained for two years. Serov, always an independent spirit and a fierce lover of social justice, had witnessed by chance the doings of that Black Sunday, from a friend's window, and, horrified, immediately sent in his resignation from the Academy, whose president was the Grand Duke Vladimir Alexandrovitch, commander of the troops that fired into the crowd. Yet he could appreciate the strong man, the autocrat—these were the very things he admired so greatly in Diaghileff. With him, too, there was the same apparent contradiction: always simple himself, he nevertheless liked pomp and luxury, and enjoyed painting the court and society beauties. While Bakst, who more than anyone appreciated court trimmings, and whose only revolutionary fervour born of his race was an intense unreasoning hatred of the Orthodox faith, drew for a satirical paper. ". . . If the editor is

123

put in prison, I will edit it myself, and lead it from the swamps of political caricature into the beautiful paths of artistic research. I will combine art and sociology, *mais forcément à outrance moderne.*"

Theirs was essentially a romantic revolution, a revolution purely of the imagination, seen in the rich colouring of Delacroix's "Sur les Barricades," and far removed from political reality. In their own social conduct they were of the Left, class distinction and anti-Semitism were unknown to them; artistically they were of the extreme Left, while in their hearts they liked the idea of a court with its attendant luxury, seeing it doubtless in terms of the seventeenth and eighteenth centuries. They were not blind to the extreme weakness of the present monarchy and its many shortcomings, yet monarchy was their ideal—monarchy supported by the strength and genius of a Peter. Their liberalism stopped well to the right of the "cadets," [1] favoured party of the *intelligentzia*. They welcomed the constitution of 1905, because they saw the necessity for a change, but they wished that the means might be less violent. Stability was an essential for the realization of their ideals. That was their general outlook, though there were, of course, many shades of difference in their reactions as individuals.

To Diaghileff, who hated calm—"there is all eternity to rest in"—and was at his best in an atmosphere of feverish agitation, all upheaval was welcome, especially since it might easily be turned to the advantage of his artistic ideals. Not only had he no settled political convictions, but he did not wish to have any. He was always amazingly well-informed as to politics, but reserved to himself the right to change his opinion at frequent intervals.

A vague liberalism of ideas, or, more accurately, of conduct, was a family tradition with him—his grandfather had freed his

[1] The party later led by Miliukov, who favoured a constitutional monarchy of the English pattern.—A. L. H.

serfs before 1861—but that liberalism did not include or understand republicanism. It existed together with a profound respect
for strong monarchy, and the two could be reconciled, because
they were emotional and were never examined at all closely. In
Diaghileff's own life of action they were combined; he was an
absolute autocrat but, apart from sudden fits of blind rage, generous and humane in all his dealings, especially with subordi-
nates.

When the October revolution came, he addressed a memoran-
dum to the Secretary of State, offering to found a Ministry of
Fine Arts, that would remove art from court control, and he
even took part in a project for a politico-satirical theatre in
which Gorki and Meyerheld were concerned, but all the same
the idea of revolution was abhorrent to him, and for a time he
thought seriously of leaving Russia "until the dawn came." In
a letter to Benois he admitted the inevitability of the conflict,
praised its æsthetic effect in the detached manner of one watching a sunset, and cried out loudly for his lost comforts, torn
between a desire for action and for the settled order of things.

To-day such an attitude is reprehensible to the Bolsheviks, as
it may well be to the Whites, because it is completely incomprehensible. Yet in every type of state and society the perfect non-
political artist with æsthetic loyalties must have his place, and in
spite of their sneers at the *Mir Isskustva*, and the attempts to
unite the artists in a "common front," the Soviet Union in practice is forced to allow the artist a wider latitude of opinion than
any other class of society.

For a time Diaghileff hoped and believed that sooner or later
Teliakovsky would lose his position and be replaced by Count
Jean Tolstoi, a friend of Witte's, who was favourable to Diaghileff and his ideas. Autonomy was in the air, the cherished aim of
each institution, the very schoolchildren passed solemn resolu-
tions, and this spirit spread to the theatres, and to the ballet in

particular. Diaghileff was not content to watch passively. A romantic in politics proper, he was a realist in the politics of art. A movement for autonomy within the ballet was started, led by Pavlova, Karsavina, and Fokine, and the latter often came to him for advice. Diaghileff encouraged and egged them on, not through conviction, for he was the last man to believe in artistic autonomy,[1] but in the hope that this would embarrass Teliakovsky and lead to his downfall. However, the movement was speedily squashed, and the company, not knowing exactly what it was they wanted, capitulated and were pardoned, disheartened and horror-stricken by the tragic suicide of Sergei Legat that had become linked to the whole story.

Teliakovsky emerged from the conflict stronger than ever, and Diaghileff's last chance of showing his theatrical ideas in Russia had gone.

§ 2

Diaghileff's subsequent attitude to the Soviet is particularly interesting in this connnection. Being entirely without strong political convictions, when people at times suggested that he might become theatrical dictator of Russia he was thoughtful.

Such a dictatorship in itself meant nothing—he was already an artistic dictator in Europe, and he knew it. His hesitation came from a totally different reason—the constant haunting fear of being considered *vieux jeu*. Here there seemed possibilities for an entirely new artistic experiment on a gigantic scale, and with full official support. No longer would there be the fear

[1] The last contemporary exhibition that he organized in St. Petersburg was in direct defiance of artistic autonomy. The artists who had revolted from his autocratic control and formed their own association invited him to preside over their committee. He refused, and organized his own exhibition, with his usual success. It was the last that he held in Russia. Among the artists included was a future collaborator, M. Larionov.

of anyone supplanting him with the very latest fashion, the label *revolutionary* would serve as a kind of guarantee. It was an exciting label that he coveted. When Taïrov arrived in Paris with his Kamerory Theatre, Diaghileff did not miss a single performance, watching every detail eagerly and jealously, but, when asked, he refused to speak at the banquet given in Taïrov's honour, or to commit himself in any way.

He was especially upset when the Soviet poet Maïakovsky accused him of being both bourgeois and behind the times. "You know nothing of our new Russian art."

"You think so," replied Diaghileff, white with anger, and immediately recited two poems by Maïakovsky himself—a retort that was final. Whether it had been carefully prepared or not it was a typical Diaghileff gesture. No one ever saw him reading, but he was always well-informed as to the very latest in literature. This desire that haunted him to be always in touch with the newest activities (and that was strong enough to render his last years unhappy) was closely bound up with his almost panicky fear of old age and death. It took him many days to recover from the effects of a funeral, and his deeply superstitious nature led him into a hundred and one comical tricks to ward off death and ill fortune.

His torment as to whether he should return to Russia or not was soon decided in dramatic fashion. It was at Covent Garden, during the *première* of the *Triumph of Neptune*, before an especially elegant public, who had come to applaud the first nationally inspired ballet. He was told that two young men, his cousins [1] from Russia, wished to see him. There they stood before him, lean, hungry-looking, and unkempt, visitors from another world. He asked them how they were impressed by the elegant

[1] I have failed to trace these young cousins, and, though the story was related by Svetloff and others, it may be a journalistic invention.—A. L. H.

public and the happenings on the stage. They shrugged their shoulders.

"Poor boys. You are struck dumb from amazement. I can just imagine your youth, far removed from all the blessings of culture."

"We can assure you," one of them replied, "that even the minimum we have is far too much. You have quite a false set of values, while we have long discarded all such prejudices."

They spoke another language. He was deeply moved, but now his mind was fully made up. It was not possible for him any more to make so drastic a change, to learn an entirely new set of values. It was no longer a question of being behind the times, but of something much more basic. To go to Russia would be easy, to come back impossible. Also he doubted the freedom of creation under such circumstances—did not believe that it was possible to reconcile art with privation and political stress. He would have made any personal sacrifice to lead some vigorous new movement, but it had to be a world movement. In Russia he would be completely cut off from the rest of Europe. Already once before in entirely different circumstances, he had chosen Western Europe rather than his own much loved country, and it was too late to return now. Although he demanded little for himself, the elegances of life appealed irresistibly to him, providing as they did the atmosphere in which he could create. The austerity of these ghost cousins terrified him, and proved to him conclusively that he was right in remaining where he was. A great tragedy was averted.

In Prokofiev's *Le Pas d'Acier* he produced a work more revolutionary in spirit than anything yet shown by the ballet in Russia. If he was afraid of not being progressive, it was not the *Red Poppy* that would prove him a placid bourgeois. The *Red Poppy* stood for the old order of things that he himself had long ago destroyed—for *Tannhäuser* with the grinning *ballerinas* on their points. As far as ballet was concerned, Diaghileff was very much on the Left wing to the extreme Right of the Soviet.[1]

It is extremely doubtful, had he returned and been left in sole control, whether things would have been very different. Each work of his from *Les Sylphides* to *Le Pas d'Acier* was the result of a careful and deliberate system of education of the public. He maintained a constant balance between classicism and novelty. The juxtaposition between *Aurora's Wedding* and *Le Sacre du Printemps* in a typical programme did more than please two different types of public, it explained the new work in relation to the old. However much he hankered after the revolutionary label, and was given it at times, he followed an evolution with caution instead of inspiring a revolution. He did not upset the constitution, he added amendments to it. Not one of the later ballets would have been tolerated out of its sequence. *Les Sylphides* paved the way for *Les Biches*. It required fifteen years of careful propaganda to arrive at the point where he now was. Russia had remained pre-*Sylphides* and he could never have followed the whole difficult path again.

§ 3

The friends, as we have seen, never had a Slavophil cult, they were no believers in the current cant of the mystic mission of Russia. From the first they had looked to the West, partly because they felt themselves not sufficiently appreciated at home, and partly also to display abroad the artistic resources of Russia. Diaghileff was undoubtedly the most nationalistic of them all, and therefore in his outlook already suited to be the greatest propagandist.

Diaghileff had thrown himself into the study of the portrait-

[1] He was highly flattered when Madame Lunacharsky told him that in hearing him talk to Lunacharsky one would have thought Diaghileff the revolutionary.

ure of the eighteenth century with a passion and an enthusiasm that amazed his friends. It seemed for a time as if he had discarded the present in his discovery of the past. His turning back before going boldly into his explorations of contemporary European art has been misunderstood by many astute critics, who were writing too near the event to obtain a clear perspective.

The late André Levinson wrote:

"Is it surprising, then, that the retrospective attitude got the upper hand more and more, and that the offshoots of this movement were *sacrificed* to a propaganda of the past?" In a further passage, he is more definite still:

"For a time Diaghileff allowed himself to drift. As usual he treated this craze for the past on a grand scale."

Craze it undoubtedly was; every interest was a craze, every craze was on a grand scale; Diaghileff saw things that way, but drift he did not. Though the process may then still have been unconscious, each successive *craze* added something definite to his equipment, and he invariably knew when to stop in time. It wearied him before it did his public, and the next step, however irrational it appeared, was the perfectly logical outcome.

Many papers that followed the *Mir Isskustva*, and were inspired by its success, also under the art editorship of Benois, were admirable and scholarly productions, but they remained on the same lines when Diaghileff had left the past far behind and was busy preparing the future.

His craze in this case served an admirable purpose, both for his own inner development and for his ultimate success.

The work of research showed him how to employ his energy in a practical, disciplined manner. It gave him an immense root in things Russian that could maintain him in his long exile, and keep the original nature of his enterprise, when it was threatened with a violent change of atmosphere through prolonged contact with Paris. The Swedish Ballet rapidly became the plaything of French poets and painters, the Russian Ballet used them and was never submerged, because so deep were its roots that it preserved its nationality intact.

Finally, for him, it was of value as a farewell to the old, to Russia and tradition, before plunging boldly into the new— 1905 St. Petersburg, the Russian Historical Portrait; 1906 Paris and the Salon d'Automne; 1907 Paris, the Concerts; 1908 Paris, *Boris Godounov*; 1909 Paris, the Ballet—and then all the world save Russia.

By 1905 Diaghileff was already an acknowledged expert with a successful book to his credit.

§ 4

Diaghileff's only published work, a monograph on the great Russian portraitist Levitsky, is curiously unlike what one might have expected from his character. There is no trace of impulse, and the painter is not made a peg upon which to hang an artistic controversy, or to air his own æsthetic theories.

The work is scholarly almost to the point of dryness, concerned at considerable length with the question of attributions. The case for each work is examined with the thoroughness of a legal expert and carefully catalogued, and the history of every sitter is briefly outlined. This work, the beginning of Diaghileff's summing-up of the Russian past, clearly shows the word *craze* in the sense used to have been unjust. It was the result of nearly a year's patient and difficult research. The field was previously unexplored. In 1901 an appeal was inserted in the *Mir Isskustva* for any information that might be of use to the author, and the following year the book appeared. Half of the hundred portraits reproduced were discoveries, each one of which required the most careful study. The make-up of the book, under Diaghileff's own direction, is extraordinary even at the present

131

day. At that time in Russia, and for many years after, nothing of the kind had ever been seen. If in its text it summed up the past, in its presentation it was a pioneer work. It was originally intended as a trilogy, and Diaghileff had already gathered much material for the next two volumes—Vol. II on various eighteenth-century painters, Vol. III on Borovikovsky—but lack of funds prevented their completion. It met with an immediate success. The Académie des Beaux Arts had guaranteed the purchase of 100 copies by way of subsidy, and the remaining 400 [1] copies were speedily acquired by collectors. It was a rarity shortly after publication, and there are very few known copies in existence to-day. In 1904 the Académie des Sciences awarded to Diaghileff the Ouvaroff prize, and this official recognition certainly helped in the success of the following year's exhibition. This Levitsky monograph, unknown in Western Europe, and in its subject matter of no great interest save to the specialist, is nevertheless an imposing monument to Diaghileff. It reveals in him the scholar; it shows a solid basis in reason for the *flair* that is primarily associated with his name. No one more than he used the knowledge and gifts of others to advantage, but he had proved himself capable of hard, patient, and unspectacular work —the monograph throughout uses the impersonal "we"—in acquiring knowledge; work that must have required immense self-discipline, since he loathed the physical labour of writing. To-day the book remains as a learned piece of research, as a thing of great beauty, but most of all as a proof of character.

§ 5

Diaghileff had soaked himself in the atmosphere of Russia. But careful study culminating in a book was not enough. These

---

[1] I cannot ascertain whether the edition consisted of 300 or 500 copies, but the last figure is certainly the maximum.—A. L. H.

portraits must be seen by the public, and take their proper place in art history. He undertook a hundred journeys to country houses in remote provinces where rumour or his own researches told him that he might unearth treasures.

The choice of the Palais Tauride itself was an inspiration and a magnificent piece of showmanship. The palace that Catharine had built for her favourite Potemkin was lying neglected, like so many of the pictures that Diaghileff had unearthed. Once or twice a year, at most, it had been used for some charitable function. It was a certain distance away from the centre of the town, but its architecture and associations made it ideal for the purpose. Once again Diaghileff did not merely hang the pictures in chronological order upon the walls. He prepared the whole setting with care, in order to create a living effect, borrowing furniture and porcelain of the period. In this exhibition he combined his gifts of artist and scholar. The detailed catalogue of over three thousand exhibits was drawn up by him, and many of the exhibits that figured in it were saved from destruction in the revolution of that year, when the peasants began their pillaging of the country estates.

The success of the exhibition, and its distinguished patronage, gave Diaghileff a new public and, after the failure at the Imperial Theatres, a patent of respectability. It also gave the educated Russian, who had looked abroad for his art, a pride in the products of his own country, and the very natural attitude, "If they have done these things in the past, these things that are so definitely a part of me, my family and my country, then I will believe in them in the future."

Had Diaghileff arrived abruptly as a revolutionary, with the latest products from Paris and nothing else, he would have pleased the few alone. He could never have hoped for extensive support for his schemes. The exhibition also gave him, in his frenzied search throughout the Russian country houses, many valuable introductions.

One Russian has told me of Diaghileff's visit to his house. "We knew about him; his tastes and extravagances were a by-word at the time. We were annoyed. Why had this pushing fellow come to worry us? Out of sheer good nature we gave him the run of the house. In the attic he unearthed some dusty pictures that we had placed there when my father returned from the grand tour, bringing with him the latest works from Germany. He seemed excited at his discoveries, and because we were gratified we gave him the loan of them for his exhibition. Later, when everyone was talking of them, when they had a definite value and looked different to us hanging on the fine walls of the Tauride Palace, our views of him altered completely. 'Fine fellow, Sergei Pavlovitch, and a great connoisseur, you can trust his judgement.' From that moment I watched his every move with active interest, and once when he needed some assistance I was able to give it to him without hesitation."

§ 6

While the rattle and boom of the guns of the 1905 Revolution were still echoing, Diaghileff made a prophetic speech in the very building where the Duma, symbol of a mighty change, was soon to hold its sessions.

The occasion was a banquet given in Diaghileff's honour to celebrate the success of his immense effort. His reply was far from the conventional thanks that are expressed on these occasions. It was a prophecy—a solemn warning that must have had a startling effect on all those present in that big hall, surrounded by the serene, untroubled faces of their ancestors. It was the first and only time that he explained himself fully and made clear his own exact position as to the past, the present, and the future. He

was no rebel, but a man caught up in the midst of a vast upheaval, fully conscious of it and seeking to assist at the birth of
a new culture that should arise from the old. *This speech makes
every subsequent artistic action of his abundantly clear, it points
a consistent direction to what may seem at times a zigzag path.*
In the hall where he spoke, symbol of his country itself, the
change from old to new was not easy, the passing did not preserve the amenities of life, and we are still witnessing the period
of transition.

Instead of a graceful speech of thanks, Diaghileff poured out
his heart to this gathering, and when he sat down his investigation of Russia and the past was complete. He had lived through
one of the richest experiences of his life, and now he was ready
to look to the West and to assist in building the future.

§ 7

"The honour that you have shown me in to-day's gathering
is as pleasant as it was unexpected. Having heard only yesterday
of the projected meeting, I was deeply moved, and I felt that I
was not ready to receive such a touching expression of attention
for everything that we have done, suffered, and achieved.

"Every festival is a symbol, because when we honour a person
we at the same time do honour to his ideas. I do not feel like discussing the justice of our beliefs or the realities after which we
have been striving. We are used to thinking ourselves in the
right, and only our conviction—that it must be either ourselves
or no one—upheld us in this unequal struggle for a truth that is
only too obvious.

"I want to consider the sense of to-night's gathering from a
different point of view. There is no doubt that every tribute is a
summing-up, and every summing-up is an ending. Far from me
the thought that to-night's banquet is in any sense the end of the

aims for which we have lived up to now. I think you will agree with me that thoughts of summing-up and ending come to one's mind more and more in these days. That is the question that struck me the whole time I was working. Don't you feel that this long gallery of portraits of big and small people that I brought to live in the beautiful halls of the Palais Tauride is only a grandiose summing-up of a brilliant, but, alas! dead period of our history? Impregnated as I am with the æsthetic point of view, I am moved by the theatrical brilliance of the eighteenth century as before the legendary brilliance of the sultans of the eighteenth century, but these fairy-tales I remember only from old wives' tales. The fertile Dan, with a note of imperceptible sarcasm, makes us realize that we cannot any more believe the romantic heroism of terrifying helmets and heroic gestures.

"I have earned the right to proclaim this loudly, because with the last breath of the summer breezes I ended my long travels across the immensity of Russia. It was just after those acquisitive expeditions that I became convinced that the time to sum up was before us. I saw that not only in the brilliant portraits of those ancestors, so far removed from us, but more vividly from their descendants, who were ending their lives. The end of a period is revealed here, in those gloomy dark palaces, frightening in their dead splendour, and inhabited to-day by charming mediocre people who could no longer stand the strain of bygone parades. Here are ending their lives not only people, but pages of history.

"That is what completely convinced me that we live in a terrible period of transition. We are doomed to die to pave the way for the resurrection of a new culture, which will take from us what remains of our weary wisdom. This is shown us by history and by æsthetics. Now, since I have gone through the history of artistic portraiture, and cannot be reproached as an artistic radical, I can say boldly, and with conviction, that what I am about to say is right.

"We are witnesses of the greatest moment of summing-up in history, in the name of a new and unknown culture, which will be created by us, and which will also sweep us away. That is why, with fear or misgiving, I raise my glass to the ruined walls of the beautiful palaces, as well as to the new commandments of a new æsthetic. The only wish that I, an incorrigible sensualist, can express, is that the forthcoming struggle should not damage the amenities of life, and that the death should be as beautiful and as illuminating as the resurrection."

It was the Diaghileff that Paris and London knew for over twenty years that left the hall that night, and, as if he felt the upheaval soon to come, he took with him the best of Russian art, to plant it firmly in Western Europe.

PART II

———

IN WESTERN EUROPE
1905–1929

CHAPTER VII

DIAGHILEFF LOOKS TO THE WEST
1906–1908

*Diaghileff rejects an honour—Salon d'Automne, 1906—
Scope of the exhibition—French attitude to Russian music—
Historic concerts, 1907—Quarrel with Scriabine—Preparations for* Boris Godounov, *1908—Hostility of French Theatre
staff—The gallant wigmaker.*

"Ce qu'il voulait? Trois choses précises: révéler la Russie à la Russie, révéler la
Russie au monde, révéler le monde—nouveau—à lui-meme."

R. BRUSSEL

"He was the kind of man who never goes under."

M. CALVOCORESSI, *Music and Ballet*

After the resounding success of the Historic Portrait Exhibition,
which would have been still greater under more normal conditions, the Grand Duke Nicolas Michaïlovitch proposed to obtain
for Diaghileff the office of *gentilhomme de la chambre* as a reward for his work. Nothing could have given him greater pleasure than a position at court, not only on account of the real joy
that he took in the picturesqueness of such surroundings, but as
a very complete answer to his enemies, who were numerous in
court and society circles. He felt, however, that this office—the
first step in the court hierarchy, and one to which so many were
appointed—was beneath his dignity, and he therefore insisted
on being nominated as master of ceremonies, to obtain which
would have been a rare and exceptional favour. The Grand Duke
nominated him, but the opposition was fierce, and he failed.
This was a very severe blow to Diaghileff's pride.

More and more he turned his thoughts to the West. There

141

was no longer anything to retain him in Russia; the *World of Art* had achieved its purpose, and was finished; the artists had realized their strength and formed an association of their own without him; the Imperial Theatres, having adopted his ideas in part and then distorted them, were closed to him, and there seemed no hope of Teliakovsky's removal in the near future. Russia represented his past, and he had summed up the past in his eloquent address at the Palais Tauride. This summing-up was more than a symbol, it outlined a definite course of action; but in going abroad Diaghileff had as yet no conscious aim. He wished simply to amuse himself—to leave behind him for a certain time the threatening repressive atmosphere of Russia, and to forget his own personal disappointments, especially his rupture with Filosofov, which he had greatly felt. He wished to know Greece, to see the latest discoveries in archaic art, to visit his beloved Italy once more, and to go back to Paris, which he visited yearly. He was already very much of a Parisian, and the intense artistic life, where all the latest tendencies were centralized and world movements grew, appealed to him irresistibly.

In Paris he saw Benois, who had been living in Versailles for a year, and from him and the many French painters whom he knew he learned of the growing interest in advanced circles in all things Russian, after the Universal Exhibition, where there had been a Russian pavilion, decorated by Korovin. He saw here an immediate opportunity for another of those difficult and gigantic tasks that he so greatly loved, and he immediately put himself in touch with the organizers of the newly formed Salon d'Automne—a concentration of all those young minds best able to understand him—and its members accepted his proposal with enthusiasm. It was decided to reserve a large section at the Grand Palais for an *Exposition de l'Art Russe à Paris*. Naturally Diaghileff had seen to it that the absolute control, both artistic and organizing, should lie in his own hands.

Back in St. Petersburg, and assisted by Bakst, he set out in search of exhibits with all his accustomed energy, and also took every means in his power to ensure its social success. His great patron, the Grand Duke Vladimir, was president of the exhibition, while the presidents of honour were M. Nelidov, Russian Ambassador in Paris, la Comtesse de Greffulhe, and M. Dujardin-Beaumetz, Under Secretary of State to the Ministry of Fine Arts. A patrons' committee under Count Jean Tolstoi was also formed, composed of artists, writers, and, of course, the indispensable men of wealth, both French and Russian. Diaghileff's official position was that of Commissaire général de l'Exposition.

Diaghileff returned to Paris with Soudeikine, Paul Kouznetzoff, and Walter Nouvel, whom he had lured unwillingly away from the fascinating calm of a *milieu* of poets and philosophers. Bakst was in charge of the general *décor*, and, as with the Palais Tauride Exhibition, had arranged with trellis-work a formal garden in which the sculpture was exhibited. A special room, hung with old golden brocade, out of which priests' chasubles were made, was set aside for the ikons. The exhibition occupied twelve rooms, and contained seven hundred and fifty items, many of which had been lent to Diaghileff from the Imperial palaces, museums, and great private collections. The confidence in him now was such that he could command full official support for all his ideas. He had begun his service as Russia's artistic ambassador to the West. This opportunity of presenting an exhibition of Russian painting in the very centre of the world's artistic life was an admirable occasion to take the first steps in the directions outlined in his Palais Tauride address. Paris was the field from which he could best direct his researches for the new æsthetic.

He outlined the scope of the exhibition, and the ideas that lay behind it, in a simple foreword to the catalogue:

"The aim of this exhibition does not consist of presenting in a complete and scrupulously methodical fashion the whole of

Russian art throughout the different periods of its evolution. To accomplish such a task would present insurmountable difficulties, and would be of doubtful utility. Many names once famous have to-day lost their glory, certain of them temporarily and some for ever. Many artists, to whom their contemporaries attached an exaggerated importance, seem now devoid of all value, having produced no influence on the art of to-day. That is the reason for the deliberate omission of the work of many painters who have been too long considered in the West as the representatives of artistic Russia, and who have too long disfigured in the eyes of the public the true character and importance of Russian national art.[1] The present exhibition is an *aperçu* of the development of our art as seen by the modern eye. All the elements that have exerted some immediate action on the contemporary thought of our public are represented. It is a faithful image of the artistic Russia of our days with its respectful admiration for the past, and its ardent belief in the future."

In this brief foreword once again Diaghileff reveals his point of view, his belief in a living art. He has done far more than actually select the exhibits; it is he, with his six years' campaign in the *Mir Isskustva*, who has made "many of the names once famous" "lose their glory." No single manifestation of his must be taken out of its place. In the present case it would be easy to see him just as the highly efficient organizer of an exhibition instead of as the man who had deliberately moulded public and artistic opinion, and had made them see things through his eyes. All those who have sought to detract from his work, either through malice or through a lack of knowledge, have done so merely because they considered each manifestation as something apart, and have ignored the systematic preparation of what went before. To organize an exhibition required nothing more than

[1] The defeated opponents, the *Ambulants*, were kept out of the exhibition.

hard work and a certain judgement, but to make Paris take that exhibition seriously, and to make that exhibition itself the result of a very personal point of view, belongs to a definitely creative order of things. That creation was in the past—out of it; it is the Diaghileff touch to create something for the future, both through an education of the public, and the more concrete aspect, the making of new contacts.

It is also characteristic of the respective rôles of the two men that Benois contributed a scholarly historic survey of Russian art to the same catalogues. In it there is an interesting passage, especially significant to-day, revelatory of the whole *Mir Iss-kustva* attitude to current events.

"In this exhibition," he writes, "there is nothing to remind one of the terrible crisis that threatens our country, and which is one of the great causes of the dark outlook of the present day. Yet Russian art is well—almost completely—represented. This state of things, is it not the result of the great gulf which exists between the Russian artists and Russian life, or rather does not the actual crisis show that purely political movements do not reach the sphere of pure ideals? Whether by chance or by intention, it is certain that, in the twelve rooms containing this manifestation of Russian art, there is a unity, and that that unity is very different from the general ideas current about Russian art.

"Without trying to resolve these questions completely, let us hope that this unexpected aspect may correct a little the preconceived notions that have been formed of Russia, great and mysterious."

This hope of Benois was immediately fulfilled. The exhibition was an unqualified success, showing, as it did, to the French public the force of the contemporary Russian artist. Also it revealed Diaghileff as an organizer of immense ability. That was the first aspect to strike the Western public.

145

The exhibition led logically to the historic concerts, just as the concerts were to lead to the opera and the opera to the ballet. Diaghileff never contrived any segregation of the arts in water-tight compartments. The exhibition was enhanced, and the bridge between that year and the next made more solid, by the playing of Russian music in the exhibition hall, and by the singing of Felia Litvinne.

For his share in the organization Diaghileff was offered the Legion of Honour, but the idea did not appeal to him—it was not uncommon or picturesque enough, and at his suggestion it was awarded to Leon Bakst and Alexandre Benois.

§ 2

Diaghileff had shown Russian painting to Paris, and the following year, 1907, the idea of a series of historic concerts came as a matter of course. The musical ground had been prepared much more fully than in the case of the painting, which was totally unknown before 1906, but it is through these concerts that Russian music became truly known to the West, and it is important, in assessing Diaghileff's achievement, to know something of the French attitude and knowledge of Russian music before 1907. Walter Nouvel writes:

"In the summer of 1904 I was living in Pavlovsk, near St. Petersburg, and Vincent d'Indy had come to direct some symphonic concerts that were given yearly in the Vauxhall. I immediately made his acquaintance, went to all the rehearsals, and we dined together nightly. It is then that the *Prelude de l'Après-midi d'un faune* of Debussy and *l'Apprenti Sorcier* by Paul Dukas were given for the first time in Russia. In spite of certain divergencies of taste, I was soon entirely under D'Indy's charm, lost in admiration for the nobility of his character, his distinguished mind and his ardent and disinterested love of art, so that when he went away we maintained a constant correspondence. The next time I was in Paris we met again regularly, and at one of our meetings he invited Paul Dukas, whom I wished particularly to meet. Dukas was a Jew, and of the Left politically, while D'Indy was of the old nobility, Catholic and a royalist—but they were the best of friends, and D'Indy appreciated his colleague both as a musician and as a man of vast intelligence. Wisely we refrained from discussing politics. The principal theme of our conversation was Tchaikovsky. At this period French musicians were enthusiastic about Russian music, but only for that of the famous "Five," the so-called "Koutchka" [1] and its adepts. Tchaikovsky was loathed. They found him trivial and vulgar, and refused to see in him any Russian characteristics. It was in vain that I told them that we considered him to be the most national of our composers, that he alone knew how to render the soul of the Russian nineteenth century and find a spontaneous and sincere echo in the people, while the music of the "Five" was a somewhat artificial reconstruction of popular melodies, strongly Germanized by the influence of Liszt and Wagner. All my eloquence was in vain, and what amazed me still more was the fact that they were unwilling to admit even his purely musical gifts, his technique, his sense of rhythm, and the mastery of his orchestration."

This interest in Russian music, which was then manifest in French musical circles—in Debussy [2] amongst others—had been roused principally by the works of Moussorgsky and Rimsky-Korsakov, and it was the knowledge of this that decided Diaghileff to follow up his art exhibition by a series of historic concerts. The project was received with enthusiasm by the French, and Diaghileff obtained the necessary patronage, notably that of the invaluable Comtesse de Greffulhe, President of the Grandes

[1] Handful.
[2] Debussy as a young man had been tutor in the Von Meck family in Moscow.

Auditions de France, without much difficulty. It was decided to hold these concerts at the Opéra, in the spring of 1907.

Immediately Diaghileff had concluded the winding up of the exhibition, he set about the organization of the concerts. As usual, he took the shortest cut to success by interesting the necessary people—one in particular, Alexandre Tanéieff, head of the Emperor's private chancery. Tanéieff was an ardent *amateur* of music, a composer in his spare time, and a sound musician who had studied composition under Rimsky-Korsakov. He had composed some works of importance—a symphony, an opera, and some chamber music—but apart from a certain taste and technique they were devoid of any originality; they were *pastiches* in the manner of the "Five," and Russian musical circles and Diaghileff himself did not take them at all seriously. But he was a person of great influence, his help was invaluable, and Diaghileff for once made a concession to expediency by promising to perform his symphony in Paris. This assured him all the help of an influential man, and smoothed his path, but all the same he felt uneasy.

Curiously enough Diaghileff was greatly encouraged in this by the French critic of the *Figaro*, Robert Brussel, whom he had invited to Russia to take charge of the publicity. Brussel was a great admirer of the "Five," and a bitter opponent of Tchaikovsky. He was enthusiastic about Tanéieff's symphony, so that Diaghileff, while retaining his opinion, was reassured and convinced that it would not damage his prestige in Paris. Apart from this necessary concession, he selected his programme with meticulous care, realizing, however, that it was essential to reckon with French public opinion, even at the sacrifice of his own tastes, and so his beloved Tchaikovsky was omitted. The "Koutchkistes," with the exception of Cui, who had no longer anything in common with them, were richly represented, and among the young there were Scriabine and Rachmaninov. Nouvel, the musical representative in the *Mir Isskustva* cabinet, took an active part in all the preparations. As usual Diaghileff was ready to welcome advice, though when once his mind was made up the final decision rested with him.

The programme was an ambitious one, containing whole acts of operas with soloists and chorus, and Diaghileff had engaged the most famous singers of the St. Petersburg and Moscow operas, led by Chaliapine, whose Paris début this was to be. Among the pianists he had selected Hofmann and Rachmaninov, who was to play his second concerto. Hofmann was essentially an interpreter of classical music, but Diaghileff was able to persuade him to play two Russian concertos by Scriabine and Liapounoff, which responded but little to his musical tastes. Diaghileff had chosen the Liapounoff concerto for the sake of conciliating the French, who saw in him a typical representative of Russian music, although he was in essence a shadow of Balakireff, his master, both of them being strongly influenced by Liszt and Chopin.

In the question of conductors, once more Diaghileff envisaged things on a gigantic scale. There were five. It was a mania with him to have works conducted by their composers, by no means always an advantage [1]; but he thought, and with reason, that this would enhance the importance and the prestige of the manifestation. Diaghileff's artistic outlook was fundamentally theatrical, and, both here and in the exhibitions, with their careful settings, he was as much the producer as the organizer.

It was decided that Glazounov, Rachmaninov, and Rimsky-Korsakov should conduct their works in person. The first two readily accepted, but Rimsky-Korsakov, who was already ill and fearful of the fatigues of the journey, and who in general hated all such exhibitions, would not hear of the proposal. It took all

---

[1] "Tchaikovsky, Glazounov, and Rimsky-Korsakov had amongst us the reputation of being mediocre conductors."—W. N.

Diaghileff's charm and tenacity to persuade him.[1] For the *ensembles* and the works of other composers Diaghileff had engaged Felix Blumenfelt, the excellent *chef d'orchestre* of the Imperial Opera of St. Petersburg. But still that was not enough. He wished for a big "star," and his choice fell upon Arthur Nikisch, then at the summit of his fame. He had specialized in the music of Tchaikovsky, and had no great sympathy for other Russian composers, but his was a great name, and this fact it was that attracted the theatrical Diaghileff. Afterwards he regretted it, for the first number that Nikisch conducted at the opening of the series, the overture of Glinka's *Rousslan and Ludmila*, was taken so slowly that the entire effect was lost.

As soon as he had found the necessary funds for this exceedingly costly enterprise,[2] which, as usual, was planned before a penny piece was in the bank, Diaghileff left, with Nouvel, for Paris, where the usual feverish struggle began. Not only were there the daily rehearsals of orchestra, choir, and soloists, but there were the Press and public opinion to be prepared, by the system of whispering propaganda that Diaghileff never neglected. He was everywhere, working at top pressure, making others work for him, and, unlike many dictators, he did not surround himself with nonentities, but with the best qualified of specialists. One of the most important tasks was the preparation in French of an explanatory programme by Nouvel, and there was the new collaborator, Calvocoressi, who was to be associated

---

[1] "I don't lose hope that you will take part in Paris. With all the infinite difficulties which this enterprise presents it is impossible to work without the thought of help from the dear and beloved master. Think how sad we shall be if you refuse, and what is more what harm you will do to the work you have approved. For God's sake agree to what we ask you. The journey won't be tiring. We shall take the greatest care of you, shall be entirely at your disposal. You will be doing us an immense favour and will be helping as no one else could have done." Diaghileff in a letter to Rimsky-Korsakov. Korsakov replied, "If we must go, we must, as the parrot said when the cat pulled him out of his cage!"

[2] Ten thousand roubles were contributed by a rich St. Petersburg music lover, Gilse van der Pals, through the intermediary of Nouvel.—A. L. H.

with him during the next four years. "I shall always look back with pleasure," says Nouvel, "on our collaboration, and on the precious help that Calvocoressi brought to us."

Calvocoressi himself gives the following first impressions of Diaghileff: "From the first, I found him to be endowed with a good deal of taste, but a taste so catholic and mutable as to be most disconcerting until we remembered that he was the type *par excellence* of the cosmopolitan Russian. . . . Looking back after all these years, I still doubt whether, left to himself, he would ever have determined upon and followed a steady and original artistic policy." This, as we can see, is the truth, but not the whole truth. There is an amazing consistency in the pattern of his artistic life, taken as a whole. He was not "left to himself" —that was a part of his policy—but he used his collaborators to follow "a steady and original artistic policy" of his own—a very exact balance of classicism and modernism, tradition and experiment.

At last the day of the first concert arrived: "the vast opera-house was crowded with all fashionable and artistic Paris," [1] and Chaliapine secured an immense personal triumph with Galitzky's song from *Prince Igor*. It was the start of his world success.

The result of these concerts was to popularize Russian music as a whole in Paris for a considerable time. It was Moussorgsky, in particular, who had made the deepest impression, and from this time dates his world fame. Borodin also was an immense success, while Scriabine, the Moscow "genius" of the moment, made little impression. The new Russian music of Prokofiev and Stravinsky was not yet born.

Everywhere the large party of Russians was dined, wined, and fêted, everywhere the French showed to Rimsky-Korsakov

[1] This phrase might serve for all Diaghileff *premières* from 1906 to 1929. One year he said, "If the theatre were to burn down to-night, the best artistic brains and the most elegant women in Europe would perish." It was literally true.—A. L. H.

and Glazounov the warmth of their admiration, but there could be no frank interchange of compliments. These one-time innovators had closed their ears to all modern music; they would admit neither Debussy, Dukas nor Ravel, even César Franck and D'Indy were anathema to them. This hardening of artistic arteries was Diaghileff's main fear. He was never to suffer from it, always ready to welcome the new, sometimes only because it was new. The little free time that was left they passed at the Café de la Paix in heated discussion. Scriabine explained to them the constituents of his *Poème de l'Extase* and revealed his plans for *The Mystery*, which on his untimely death remained unfinished. Also they discussed his theories on the relationship between sound and colour.

There was but one small incident to mar the general atmosphere of success and rejoicing. Scriabine, whose piano concerto was to be played by Josef Hofmann at the second concert, had just had a rough passage in the United States, where the attitude of the public to his fellow traveller, subsequently his second wife, had been threatening. There had been a considerable amount of small talk, which soon assumed the dimensions of a real scandal that threatened to become a second *affaire* Gorky. Once the Press lighted upon the trail, things came to a climax somewhat suddenly, and Scriabine had deemed it wise to make a sudden departure for Europe, and, having spent the night in packing, he embarked at 8 A.M., arriving in Paris with some thirty francs in his pocket to find the whole city devoting itself to the worship of Russian music. It may have been the combination of the residue of his nervous condition with a return of confidence in himself as an artist which inspired his attitude towards Diaghileff, but this attitude in any case requires a measure of explanation.

On the evening of the second concert, at which his symphony was to be played, he discovered at a late hour that his complimentary tickets had not arrived, and they actually reached him only as he was leaving his quarters. During the *entr'acte* he approached Diaghileff, and roundly upbraided him for having left the despatch of the tickets until so late a moment. "Think, but for a miracle they might have arrived after I had left the house!" Diaghileff was never a man to stand such aggression, especially in the midst of a triumph. He replied, in his usual strong language, that he was not obliged to worry about Scriabine's (a string of unpleasant adjectives) tickets, he had better things to do, and for the future he had better take charge of this evidently important department himself. The scene that followed defies description. . . .

"Is it possible," said the infuriated composer, "that you dare address me in such fashion. . . . Let me remind you that I am actually a chosen representative of Art itself . . . whilst you, you are privileged to gallivant about its fringe. . . . But for the likes of me such people as you would find it difficult to supply a reason for your existence! . . ."

Diaghileff was so completely overcome by the force and virulence of this unjust and unexpected attack that for once he was reduced to a condition literally verging upon speechlessness. . . . "To think that you, Alexander Nicolaievitch, that you——"

§ 3

The success of Moussorgsky and the triumph of Chaliapine in the fragments of *Boris Godounov* at once suggested to the untiring Diaghileff the nature of his next enterprise. At last his dream of mounting a large theatrical presentation was to be realized. Not only could he show the Parisians a work of genius, but also all the best resources of the Russian theatre, with *décor* and production undreamed of in the West, and Chaliapine would be revealed not only as a singer, but as a dramatic actor of genius. The prospect was grandiose. A Diaghileff alone could have carried it off, and as usual it was decided upon before any investigation of the material difficulties.

Since this was Diaghileff's first actual contact with production and scenery, it is interesting to study his methods, and his outlook in some detail.

As in the later productions, this was essentially a piece of team work with Diaghileff in control, listening, discussing, rejecting, or accepting—with Benois, ever fertile in suggestions, and now a practical man of the theatre, at his elbow. Teliakovsky's marked hostility to Diaghileff was not without its effect, even outside his own domain. Golovin had been commissioned for some of the costumes. He was a Teliakovsky man, and could not assist "the enemy" openly or with too good a grace. He delayed and temporized—and finally did not deliver them. The designs were then entrusted to Bilibine and Yuon, while Benois himself undertook the whole Polish scene.

The scenery was painted on the stage of the Hermitage Theatre, and the costumes begun in St. Petersburg. Immediately Diaghileff threw himself into the new work with enthusiasm, spending hours selecting and matching silk with his meticulous and untiring eye. His rooms in the Hôtel d'Europe were like a warehouse, bright-coloured silks, piled high on the floor, spilling their colour over bed, tables, and chairs. He visited the rag market with Benois, and together they bought from the Tartar and Jewish dealers all the gold-embroidered eighteenth-century neckerchiefs that they could find—some hundreds of them. These were cut up and made into the boyars' collars—one of the most effective scenes in the production. That was Diaghileff, at the very beginning of his career, setting a standard for himself from which he never departed; unique gold embroidery cut up to be used for one short scene. Always everything must be perfect—time and expense need not be taken into account.

It is at this time that he began the habit of making his many business visits in a closed *coupé*. There had been a few cases of glanders in St. Petersburg, and he had a morbid fear of all infection. On entering or leaving the carriage he muffled up his face to protect it from possible germs, and inside he pulled up the windows. Venice was his greatest joy. There he could truly relax these tiring precautions, since there were no horses. The invention of the motor-car finally delivered him from a nightmare.

For the musical part of the opera Diaghileff consulted Walter Nouvel, and also his new adviser, Calvocoressi. Nouvel writes: "We were not always of the same opinion. Diaghileff was ever drastic in cuts and revisions. He had entirely suppressed the tavern scene as being too *ambulant* in tendency, also he had changed the order of many scenes. In his version, the coronation came after Pimen's cell, and the camp of Kromy before the tableau of the death of Boris, which from a chronological point of view was an absurdity, but which by its graduation of effects was a great gain dramatically. Diaghileff always laid stress on dramatic effect, was terrified of boring his audiences, and on that account never hesitated to make cuts that musicians and critics might consider sheer vandalism. It is true that the majority of Russian operas are too long and badly constructed, and would greatly benefit by such methods."

He was dissatisfied with Rimsky-Korsakov's version and with his orchestration, and had replaced the carillon music that had been cut, and by this means he gained an important dramatic effect. There were no words to this music, and it was necessary to devise some action. At the last moment Benois hit upon the device of making Chaliapine recite Pouchkine's great dialogue from the dramatic poem *Boris Godounov*. There was no time for him to learn it, so the book was propped up on the table, lit by a concealed lamp. The stage was in darkness save for a moonbeam

155

that crept nearer and nearer to the clock as it chimed, finally lighting up the procession of figures that moved around the face —penny toys, gilded by Benois. "At the dress rehearsal," says Benois, "wearing no beard or make-up, Chaliapine in this scene gave a piece of dramatic acting I have never seen equalled. It was one of those theatrical miracles."

But it was the coronation scene, for which he asked Rimsky-Korsakov to amplify the orchestration, that was Diaghileff's chief joy. He had made a profound study of coronation ritual, and, although it may be doubtful how much realism remained when he and Benois had finished their embroidering, the effect was dazzling.

A great problem that confronted him was how to bring in the false Dmitri. He was never fond of horses in general, and a horse on the stage revolted him.[1] At Bayreuth, Brunhilda's horse invariably misbehaved in the middle of the stage and completely spoiled his enjoyment. He got out of his difficulty in an ingenious manner. Dmitri was brought on in a sleigh. So great was his popularity that it was drawn by the enthusiastic peasants themselves! From his very first practical contact with the stage, Diaghileff proved himself a great theatre-man, and that is the essence of his work. However much the academic may have blamed him on occasions for his use of music, he was justified, since his aim was "good theatre." He understood their objections—even anticipated them. His decisions were the result neither of ignorance nor of neglect. In the case of *Boris Godounov* he spent many hours with Moussorgsky's original score, and that of Rimsky-Korsakov, in an attempt to find a combination that would satisfy him. In this he was aided by numerous musicians.

Diaghileff laid special stress on the scene that represented riot

---

1 "To start with, once on the stage it never looks like a horse at all," he said. during the production of *Contes Russes*. In this case he substituted a wooden, painted horse.—A. L. H.

and revolt on the stage, and drew attention to it in interviews. Sanine produced and took part in it with a rare fervour, and the unfortunate actors felt the weight of his knout on more than one occasion. This operatic realism was entirely new to the French, and that, together with the beauty of the choral singing and Chaliapine's double triumph, subsequently occupied the chief attention of the Press.

§ 4

Before leaving Russia everything had been carefully planned, but the Russian contingent did not take possession of the Paris Opéra without considerable difficulty. There was then no theatre in the world more bureaucratic and conservative, and the chauvinistic officials and employees looked askance at this "horde of Asiatics" who had come to invade their sacred precincts. Also the French and Russian conceptions of working hours were entirely different. Nothing on earth would induce the Frenchman to remain for even a minute after hours—*déjeuner à midi* was sacrosanct, and he must, moreover, be continually running out for *un coup de blanc*. Time was short, and it was essential to press the work. Benois was in charge of the stage preparations, running from the *atelier de couture*, where the costumes were being completed, to the paint-room on the fifth floor, retouching standards and ikons. Still another difficulty lay in the choice of "walkers on." In Russia a permanent group had always been attached to the theatre, so that the designer knew the actual man who was to wear his costume. Here it was different. The very sweepings of the street were employed, given beards, dressed in cloth of gold, and transformed into Russian boyars. "The smell of these great unwashed in the dressing-rooms," says Benois, "was indescribable."

A fierce cabal—headed by the chief mechanic—soon started

against the Russians, and on one occasion, when the work had continued beyond midnight, there was a small revolution that was only quelled after an impassioned speech by Sanine, who, standing on a table, reminded the astonished workmen that they were fellow artists, and must behave as such. That, together with some bribes, quelled the rising, and the chief mechanic now resorted to a policy of discreet sabotage, determined at all costs to delay the production. He had already delivered the ultimatum that if the scenery did not arrive by a certain date it could not be hung in time. It was a day or two late, and the mechanic-*saboteur* rejoiced. Diaghileff cajoled him, and finally forced him to hang it, but once in place there was a gap of several feet between the floor and the ends, and the Frenchman joyfully blamed the Russian manufacturers.

The *répétition générale* was imminent.

"Shall we be ready in time?" asked Diaghileff.

"Quite impossible. There can be no performance; we can't have the scenery ready so soon."

"All right, then. No matter—but we *shall* give the performance, just the same. All Paris will be there, and we'll carry on without scenery."

The threat worked, and the victory was with Diaghileff, but the mechanic had come to within an ace of succeeding.

The night before the performance the weary and disgusted Russians had gone *en masse*, artists and workmen, for a hasty supper at Larue's. Chaliapine was insisting on a postponement, terrified of a sensational failure, and he managed to talk the others round without much difficulty. They were all thoroughly disheartened by then. The matter was put to the vote. The decision for postponement was unanimous, and an announcement to the Press was being worded, when a thick, peasant voice cried out: "Impossible. We must go on—we can't allow ourselves to be beaten. What sort of people are we if we give in? I won't have it."

The indignant man was Chaliapine's wigmaker, a simple worker, but a veritable artist in his work. His words supplied courage to everyone, and it was decided to give the performance at all costs.

On the night itself everything was ready—but only just. While the great public was assembling, Benois, in dress clothes and top hat, stood on a lofty ladder, touching up damp spots in pastel, amid cries of "For God's sake get down, the curtain's going up any minute now," and his descent actually coincided with the closing bars of the overture.

Boris was a success, but by no means the immediate and striking triumph that the Russians had expected. The first performance was crowded with an elegant public, but for the next two or three there were many gaps, and it was only at the last two of the eight performances that the work was fully appreciated.

This was Diaghileff's third success in the space of three years. He had made new and powerful friends, he commanded confidence, and the public awaited further manifestations for the following years. They were not to be disappointed. From 1906 to 1929, with the exception of the war years, all Paris came to the Diaghileff *premières*—always with a thrill of expectation— and the result never disappointed the most critical and fickle public in the world.

———CHAPTER VIII————————————

THE BALLET AND DIAGHILEFF

THE STORY OF AN EVOLUTION: PART I, FROM PETIPA TO FOKINE

Duncan's first appearance in Russia—The decay of ballet—
Vsevolojsky and the Italian school—The Russian Renaissance
—Fokine—Diaghileff's raison d'être *in ballet.*

"The subjects that are treated in dancing are usually senseless, and only show a confused tangle of scenes sewn together as badly as they are interpreted; however, it is usually indispensable to subject oneself to certain rules."

NOVERRE: *Letters*

"De grâce, si vous le pouvez, rendez-nous les beaux ballets d'autrefois, donnez une grande importance à la pantomime et à la symphonie, soyez savoureux, soyez sublimes, mais ne proscrivez pas la danse, cet art délicieux, en qui la femme a trouvé des grâces nouvelles que la nature ne lui connaissait pas."

THÉOPHILE GAUTIER

"I am the enemy of ballet, which I look upon as false, absurd, and outside the domain of art . . . I thank God that a cruel destiny did not inflict upon me the career of a ballet dancer."

ISADORA DUNCAN

"This is how in the past a ballet was created; all the collaborators and the principal interpreters worked each one for himself. . . ."

VALERIAN SVETLOFF

"There is more poetry in Zucchi's back than in all the modern poets of Italy."

SKALKOVSKY

In 1905 a girl from the Middle West, devoid of all dance tradition, came to Russia, and at St. Petersburg, the very centre of the rigid art of ballet, was acclaimed for dancing in a manner that ignored the five positions, cast aside the sacred shoe, very symbol of grace, and substituted a loose Greek tunic for the inevitable stiff tarlatan, framework of the human top. The

160

Tamara Karsavina in *Le Pavilion d'Armande*, 1911

Les Sylphides First London performance, 1911

Fokine conducting a rehearsal Karsavina in foreground, Paris, 1910

dancers wondered, and then applauded her; the younger generation applauded her; the *balletomane* cried blasphemy, and thought that the world was coming to an end.

At Pavlova's house, at supper one night, Isadora Duncan told Diaghileff of her aims. She said to him defiantly, "I am an avowed enemy of ballet. It is false, absurd, and outside the domain of art." She used a hundred arguments to prove to him her point, but she excepted certain individual dancers from her scathing condemnation. Pavlova, their hostess, was "beautiful, æthereal, tragic," and of the veritable high priestess of traditional ballet, Kchesinska, she said, "I could not help applauding her fairy-like apparition, more like a bird or some charming butterfly than a human." That was praise indeed. She admitted that ballet had reached a peak from which she intended to topple it.

As she talked, Bakst sketched her, showing her proud, defiant, triumphant, like those statues in Greece which both he and she had so greatly admired. When she paused in her onslaught, he read her fortune in her palm. "You will attain, but you will lose the two beings dearest to you." Fortunately she could not then understand. A few more happy years still remained.

This woman, hostile to their art, according to all their standards a complete amateur, became to many, to Fokine and Diaghileff himself, a living symbol of the freedom of the dance. She pointed the way. And all the while the *balletomanes* fumed, one of them fighting a duel, not for the honour of a woman, but for his whole faith—the Classic Ballet. Saturated in dogma, he said, "Things have always been thus and thus, and so they must always continue. This is the place for a *pas d'action;* here must come the *coda,* and here the *adagio;* else there is nothing to hold on to any more. All else is atheism." He would have said Bolshevism had the word possessed its particular significance then.

But there were many, who had long had their doubts about

the dance, for whom the dancing of a few great *ballerinas* was not sufficient compensation. Noverre had warned dancers in his letters, but his warnings had not been heeded. Outside of Russia, in the very cradles of the art, Paris and Milan, it appealed to but a few, and then merely as a matter of habit—a quaint survival that would give fragrant sentimental memories of Taglioni, Elssler, and the *pas de quatre*. Outside of Russia it was a dying art, and even in Russia by the end of the reign of Alexander II it was in decay, maintained by habit rather than by anything else.

§ 2

When Vsevolojsky became director of the Imperial Theatres (1882) he did everything in his power to raise the standard, and so to attract a new public, for on ballet evenings the theatre was often sadly deserted. The leading rôles were always divided between the same two *ballerinas*—Eugenia Sokolova, a charming dancer in the French style, with no great technique, and Vasem, reliable, strong technically, but without much charm. Among the men only the character dancers and mimes were at all appreciated. Russian ballet was at its lowest ebb, and doomed, apparently to extinction, as was ballet throughout the rest of Europe.

It was then that various Italian troupes visited the capital, dancing in the wooden theatres on the islands in settings quite unsuited to serious artists. The troupes themselves were poor enough, but they always included one or two first-class stars who created an enormous impression by use of the famous Italian technique—hitherto completely unknown in Russia.

The artist whose success caused the entire revaluation of dancing was Virginia Zucchi. I have already quoted Prince Wolkonsky on the effect that she produced, but since without her perhaps the Russian Ballet, as we know it, might never have come into existence, I will also quote Walter Nouvel, who must surely have communicated his enthusiasm to Diaghileff himself, making him look upon ballet with a more kindly eye:

"Some of our critics and the public were inclined to make Petipa responsible for the bad state of the ballet, saying that he was growing old and merely repeating himself. Vsevolojsky wished at all costs to do something positive. He had already given Petipa an admirable opportunity in *Coppélia*, with a charming dancer, Nikitina, who later was to be a remarkable Blue Bird in *The Sleeping Princess*. Now, at the grave risk of shocking all the nationalists, he engaged Virginia Zucchi (1885). It was a masterstroke that awoke our dancers from their long sleep. Zucchi was a genius, so vital and stimulating that no one could remain indifferent to her influence.

"She remained for two consecutive seasons at the Maryinsky. Of all our editorial group only Benois, Somov, and myself had seen her. We were only schoolboys, but she was our idol. I remember, when she came back to dance in a small theatre, how we waited for her at the stage door, and when she appeared took off our coats and spread them on the ground in front of her carriage. She gave us a charming smile, and we were proud and happy that night.

" 'There is more poetry in Zucchi's back than in all the modern poets of Italy,' said Skalkovsky, a well-known critic of this time. Her example proved that the dancer could be the equal of a Sarah Bernhardt or a Duse as an artist."

After her departure Vsevolojsky continued his policy of engaging foreign dancers, and Cornalba, Brianza, creator of Aurora, Dell'Era, the fairy of *Casse-Noisette*, and the dazzling Legnani of the thirty-two *fouettés* appeared five or six seasons running. Then Vsevolojsky achieved yet another masterstroke by the engagement of Maestro Enrico Cecchetti, and so little by little Italian technique penetrated into Russia and, imposing itself on the French tradition of Petipa and Johannsen, formed the perfect Russian school. For a long time there were sharply hostile camps, but the fact that the director's policy was a wise one became more and more evident as such native dancers as Kchesinska and Preobrajenska began to be formed—firstfruits of the new-found perfection. Cecchetti's influence was also felt among the male dancers, and soon a promising group began to appear, so brilliant that they forced the public to welcome them.

Vsevolojsky played a large part in the decorative side of the theatre, especially from the point of view of luxury. Technically the scenery was on a high level, but the order of the day was for a lavish and tasteless convention. That was largely the *point de départ* for the reforms, and his action was as decisive in music as it had been in dancing. Hitherto it had been entrusted to such artisans as Pugni and Minkus, and as an improvement to Drigo, composer of the still famous *Millions d'Arlequin*. Then Vsevolojsky had the happy notion of commissioning a ballet from a real composer—the biggest of the day, Tchaikovsky. This was daring in the extreme, and even shocking to the faithful old guard, the *balletomanes*, who had supplied the scanty audiences throughout the bad times. *The Sleeping Princess* had an immediate success, and in 1892 the director boldly followed it up with *Casse-Noisette*. Then he produced a revival of *Swan Lake*, newly devised by Petipa and Ivanov. When first produced in Moscow during the lifetime of the composer it had been a dismal failure, but now the public was prepared and it was a triumph. These examples turned the attention of serious composers to ballet, and Rimsky-Korsakov introduced a choreographic tableau into his opera *Mlada*. Vsevolojsky's boldest stroke, however, was to commission *Raymonda* from Glazounov, then known as a revolutionary and an ultra-modern. It was a success, and was followed by *Les Ruses d'Amour* and *Les Quatre Saisons*.

§ 3

This was the state of things when Diaghileff began to take an interest in ballet. Of this *entourage*, Benois and Nouvel—ever since La Zucchi—were confirmed *balletomanes*, and Bakst, Serov, and Korovin were mildly interested. Filosofov despised it not a little, and considered it a low form of art. It was therefore Benois and Nouvel who first opened his eyes, and at that moment there were wonders to be seen—a whole constellation of young Russian dancers, many of whom were later to gain a world-wide reputation under Diaghileff's banner.

It was perhaps the young Serge Legat, a charming Russian classical male dancer, who moved him the most.

Legat finished school, at the age of eighteen, in 1896, and with a complete disregard for convention Vsevolojsky entrusted him straight away with the leading male rôle opposite Legnani in the ballet *Barbe Bleu*, and the following year in *Raymonda*. Alas, his brilliant career was a short one. In 1905, in an access of madness, he cut his throat. Some attributed it to the effect of the revolution, others to an unfortunate love story. As a young man he had fallen in love with the beautiful and temperamental Marie Petipa, twenty years his senior, and it was said that he was not sure of her fidelity and suffered from fits of jealousy. In the ten short years of his career he delighted every *balletomane* in St. Petersburg. With Legat, Pavlova and Fokine all showing promise, by the turn of the century Diaghileff was a confirmed *balletomane* with definite ideas of his own for the further reform of the art, which unfortunately he was not able to put into practice during his tempestuous year in the Imperial Service.

§ 4

Russia had taken to itself all that was still vital choreographically in the person of the little ballet master from Marseilles, Marius Petipa, who had danced with Fanny Elssler herself, and all the dancers of Italy and France followed him, secured their triumphs under his banner, and left an example for their Russian successors. He was a great innovator, a genius who laid down for all time certain immovable principles, and, with Vsevolojsky to prepare the ground for him and Tchaikovsky as a partner, left behind him certain ballets that will never grow old. But now his reign had extended over forty years, and no man could go on finding always fresh inspiration for sixty full-length ballets and more. While he still worked actively, such was his prestige that no one could dispute his position, but now that he was getting old one of his own pupils, Michael Fokine, had certain ideals and theories of his own. He had been carefully trained as a dancer in the rigid discipline of the master, had worked in the dramatic school, and painted for his own pleasure. He was well fitted to express the feelings of the new generation. His first attempt, *Acis and Galatea*, arranged for the students of the school, aroused a storm from those who would defy the laws of nature and keep an old man for ever young, but the old man understood, recognized his true successor, and generously hailed him—"You will be a great *maître de ballet* some day."

La Duncan then appeared on the scene. She danced to the music of great masters, and, instead of shocking, it pleased a vast public, and artists flocked around her. Already Fokine had his own very definite ideas, but here was both an inspiration and an encouragement.

Diaghileff in later years, when writing of the beginnings of Fokine, and consequently of his own ballet, assigns to Duncan too positive a part.[1] He was, of course, in a position to know, but his own statements, often dictated by the moods and necessities of the moment, are always extremely unreliable.

Duncanism was not at the back of all Fokine's creations, for there was no Duncanism, only Duncan, an individual, and he had mapped out his course before she came on the scene. *The Dying Swan*, one of the earliest examples of his neo-classicism, was set a few months before her visit.

Fokine's own task was different and far more difficult, and that not merely because of the fact that he had to fight a powerful organization supported by fanatical followers. Duncan was concerned with her own body, and her own individual needs. She started with a clean slate. First she learned to walk, and then she danced as the fancy suited her. She created a revolution, while Fokine followed an evolution.[2] He had no wish to discard the valuable system that had given him his own training. He did not wish to destroy, but to build. To follow Duncan completely would have meant chaos. She was in no sense, and her later efforts prove it, a *chef d'école* but an isolated individual expressing simply herself; and it was only natural that in Russia, last stronghold of the dance, her message should be taken seriously. It was a source of strength, an inspiration, that could be converted for use in the already existing machinery, but never something to be followed closely in every detail.

During the end of Petipa's reign there was a veritable galaxy of great talent that Duncan herself had admired. Petipa, a foreigner, Johannsen, a foreigner, Cecchetti, a foreigner, Legat of

---

[1] *J'ai beaucoup connu Isadora à Petersbourg, et j'ai assisté avec Fokine à ses premiers débuts. Fokine en était fou et l'influence de Duncan sur lui était la base initiale de toute sa création.*"—Diaghileff, in a letter to W. A. Propert. See W. A. Propert, *The Russian Ballet*, 1921–1929, p. 88.

[2] Her direct influence can only be traced in his actual Greek ballets, such as *Eunice, Narcisse*, and *Daphnis and Chloe*, but not at all in his Russian, romantic, or oriental works—the major part of his production.—See *Balletomania*, by Arnold L. Haskell, pp. 135–7.

foreign descent, had finally [1] overcome a firmly rooted superstition that the Russian was never able to dance as well as did the visiting artist. The first harvest of really great native dancers, superior in artistry to their Italian competitors, and rapidly gaining an equality of technique, was now at hand. With Kchesinska, Trefilova, Preobrajenska, Egorova, and Pavlova all appearing at one time, Russian Ballet was truly born—the perfect style that had taken to itself the strength of Italy and the grace of France. All that now remained to complete the national triumph was a Russian choreographer. Petipa had fulfilled his task admirably, but it was now time for him to quit the scene. His work could not perish. Everything that came would be a monument to his memory, and later his ballets would be revived with new understanding and live as the classical basis of a flourishing art.

From the point of view of the actual dancing there was to be a shifting, too, in the transition from Petipa to Fokine, and later to Fokine-Diaghileff. The old ballet, however ridiculous at times in its rigid conventions, had produced its quota of great dancers, greater as individuals, perhaps, than any that the new convention was to produce, because they triumphed in spite of its difficulties—against it, in fact, and with no emotional support from the music. The new conception of music, in which Duncan had led the way, meant that the dancer would have to revise all her standards. Previously she had required a good ear to follow in rhythm the accompaniment of the ballet music—she now required, in addition, a true feeling for music. She would have to interpret as well as to follow. The word *soul*, always vague and unsatisfactory, took on a newer, more definite meaning.

In the past, and in a work so tawdry and artificial that it would have produced tears of laughter if danced by anyone less

[1] There were previously great Russian dancers such as Grantzeva and Mouravieva who had even appeared in Paris.—A. L. H.

than a genius, Virginia Zucchi could evoke genuine tears from even the most sophisticated audiences. The new conception could help both dancer and audience; it could make every dancer appear in a much better light, so that its final result would be to substitute for one great figure, and for a mechanical background, a number of interesting personalities. It meant the death of the *ballerina assoluta*, and in her place twenty *premières danseuses* of merit; a whole evening of intelligent entertainment that could be analysed and justified afterwards, rather than some rare and breathless moments of indefinable excitement in the midst of boredom and tinsel.

As technique became more and more a means to an end, fashion, too, would become less shifting. Gone from the scene is the dancer, who "dates," who pleases the audience of one generation by a series of well-executed tricks, and afterwards goes on making their children laugh by the repetition of those selfsame tricks.

All this was brought about by Fokine, thinking first in terms of the dance, and subsequently in terms of ballet, accelerated by Duncan's example and success.

This thinking in terms of the dance led to certain inevitable conclusions: acting or mime could no longer exist as a thing apart, since music was now the inspiration, and action and music are bound up together; the whole body must be expressive—dancing means arms, legs, trunk, the head and the very smile on the dancer's face; and the logical conclusion of all this, as Duncan had discovered in practice, was that no music was in theory out of reach of the dancer. The toe was no longer the sole focal point. Those nymphs tripping on tiptoe to the music of *Tannhäuser* were for ever banished. Dancing must be in a style appropriate to both music and poem. Henceforth music and costume are decreed equal partners with the dance.

169

§ 5

These new ideals bring a number of new people into the ballet scene: composers who understand atmosphere, and who are working on original lines instead of measuring out so much rhythm with a yardstick; rhythm that could be slashed unmercifully, if too long or too short, and that could have inserted in its midst, as was the custom, the inevitable Russian dance, by some other composer; painters who understand what the music and the action is about, and who dress the idea as well as the dancers.

Finally someone entirely new is needed, someone who now makes his appearance for the very first time in ballet, the man who will bring all these elements together, reconcile them, dovetail them, and weld the pieces into a harmonious whole with a unity of its own. That such a person, made logically indispensable by new conditions, has to this day no name is the greatest tribute to the man who created the function If to-day such a person exists at all, we call him "a second Diaghileff" and leave it at that.

Fokine's great evolution was possible just because the artists and composers he needed were coming round to the same way of thinking, and because the *Mir Isskustva* group, in its crusade of art for art's sake, had seen in the theatre an admirable medium. As individuals, they were equally interested in music, painting, and the drama; and for them the arts were never tidily arranged in watertight compartments. They may have been specialists— but each of them understood the other man's specialty. Benois, Bakst, and Nouvel in their line, Fokine in his, had completely prepared the ground. It is in marshalling their resources to the full that Sergei Pavlovitch showed himself to be a true creator. He had created a function previously unknown—a function for which there is still no name but his own.

For a previous book I consulted a number of Diaghileff's collaborators, and asked of each the same question—Was he creative?

For the most part their reactions were identical. They looked surprised, as if the idea had never occurred to them before, and said, almost as if it had been a formula, "He was a wonderful organizer, a very great man. He let me create, he showed my creations—I can remember no concrete idea of his," and the like. I do not for a moment believe that they would grudge him such an admission, especially as so many readily admitted that he had discovered and launched them. It was simply that they could not know. They were each a part of his creation. Every time they sat around a table with him, and talked till the small hours of the morning, he was creating. Each individual, full of his own ideas, could not have noticed the change of direction that Diaghileff gave to the conversation, how the trivial remark would be seized upon and expanded into something practical that would set the telegraph wires humming between St. Petersburg and Paris. Each time he introduced some painter from Paris to a composer from Italy, he was taking his share in creating the idea that these two men under his guidance would produce. The very notion in his mind that, when these two men met, certain significant results might be achieved was his undisputed creation. Nothing could be further from the truth than to talk of hypnotic influence, a totally false deduction from the facts that Diaghileff himself was neither painter, dancer, nor composer. We have seen how he added to his *flair* such knowledge in every branch of art as was needed to bring about these results. Even were it not possible to adduce a single idea that came from him direct, it is still logical to call him a creative artist, a claim that I do not base on the obvious one—the one that he himself was proudest of—that he was a discoverer of talent Diaghileff himself, for all his arrogance, was never intent on laying claim to original ideas. On the contrary he preferred to credit them to his collaborators, for his one pride was always in the discovery of genius. When asked by reporters what he himself had contributed to the performance, he invariably said, "You can tell your readers that I have looked after the lighting." He did that too, and attended to a hundred small details, but his real work was accomplished long before the first rehearsal, in tracking down the germ of the idea and assisting in its development. Often some cherished idea would be laid aside through lack of the requisite artists.

From the moment that in 1908–9 the ballet was launched, Diaghileff became a fully creative artist.

The education that we have followed in the first part of this book, the feverish racing after new people and new impressions, was his solid material. Hitherto we have known only one period of his life, the second, and that too well to understand him properly. Like an iceberg the solid base of his being exists in this first period, the time of the *Mir Isskustva*. Everything that followed, that was to make him into a world figure, was the result of those years of searching, and only understandable through them.

Such a view of Diaghileff need not in any way lessen the value of his collaborators. Those early friends first formed him, and then they, and all who were to follow, continued to create, each within his own specialized sphere, while Diaghileff's was not specialized, but embraced them all.

He had to learn to think in terms of three media combined, and in an interview he outlines this. "The more I thought of that problem of the composition of ballet, the more plainly I understood that perfect ballet can only be created by the very closest fusion of the three elements of dancing, painting, and music. When I mount a ballet, I always keep these three elements in my mind. That is why almost daily I go into the artists' studios, watch their work and the actual execution of the costumes, examine the scores and listen to the orchestra with close attention, and then visit the practice-rooms where all the dancers practise and rehearse daily."

This method of thinking led to those productions where the three elements were in perfect harmony, each partner expressing the same idea. So much so that it is impossible subsequently to pick the work to pieces and to tell with whom the work originated. To whomsoever belonged the germ of the idea, the fusion of the three was Diaghileff's. He was fully at home with a score, he could sketch out a *maquette* sufficiently well to explain an idea to an artist, and, while he seemed to pay less attention to the choreography, that in fact was not the case. His choreographers were always with him, soaked in the atmosphere of his ideas, translating them into dancing without the need of direct or detailed suggestion.

CHAPTER IX

GENESIS OF THE RUSSIAN BALLET IN WESTERN
EUROPE

1908–1909

*Genesis of the Russian Ballet of 1909—Nijinsky—Pavlova—
Astruc—Diaghileff's explanation—The first programme:* Le
Pavillon d'Armide, Cléopâtre *and* Ida Rubinstein—Les
Sylphides—Prince Igor—Festin—*Selecting the company—A
financial "plot"—Death of the Grand Duke Vladimir.*

"Diaghileff's flat—A Chancery and a Parnassus in the limited space of two rooms."

"I had seen a Japanese performer, once, exhibiting feats of quadruple concentration.
I failed to be impressed by him; I had seen Diaghileff at work."

KARSAVINA, *Theatre Street*

Once an idea has become concrete and has then passed into history, there is always some mystery as to its actual conception,
and everyone in the vicinity at the time claims his share of the
glory. Books and articles of reminiscence have done this in
regard to the origins of the Russian Ballet,[1] but actually there
can be no mystery, and its origins will be clear to all of those
who have followed the story so far.

Romola Nijinska, in the Life of her husband, attributes the
whole thing to a chance remark of Nijinsky's; but this would
appear to be an overstatement, because actually there was no sort
of intimacy between the two men at this time, and although
Diaghileff admired Nijinsky—at a distance—such a suggestion
from him could have carried no weight, notwithstanding that

[1] I use the words "Russian Ballet" throughout where the sense is clear, though it
should be called, more accurately, "The Russian Ballet in Western Europe."—
A. L. H.

Nijinsky's astonishing artistry undoubtedly did. Dandré suggests that Diaghileff was influenced by Pavlova's [1] success abroad, which must undoubtedly have encouraged him. But the most detailed, and the most dramatic, story is that of Gabriel Astruc, whom Diaghileff had met at the Comtesse de Greffulhe's during the *Boris Godounov* season, and who afterwards became his French *impresario*.

Dining at Paillard's, after one of the performances of *Boris Godounov*, Astruc mentioned to Diaghileff how beautiful he had found the production and the dancing [2] in the Benois-designed Polish scene, and the talk passed on to ballet in general.

"You seem so fond of dancing," said Diaghileff, "you ought to come to St. Petersburg to see our Imperial Ballet. You, in France, do not honour dancing any longer, and the art is incomplete as you show it to-day. You possess fine *ballerinas*, but you have no idea of what a male dancer can be. Our male dancers are stars in Russia. . . . Nothing can give you an idea of how fine our Vaslav is—I believe that nothing like him has been seen since Vestris."

"Does he dance alone?"

"Yes—but sometimes with a partner who is almost his equal, La Pavlova. She is the greatest *ballerina* in the world, excelling both in classicism and in character. Like a Taglioni she doesn't dance, but floats; of her, also, one might say that she could walk over a cornfield without bending an ear."

"But you must have great producers and *maîtres de ballet* to use all those fine talents."

[1] In May 1908 a group of artists of the Imperial Theatre left home for the first time on a short tour under the direction of M. Edouard Fazer. The group consisted of Mmes Egorova, Will, and Messrs. Obouhof, Legat, Bolm, and Chiraev, with Anna Pavlova as *prima ballerina* They visited Helsingfors, Stockholm, Copenhagen, and Prague, and, early in 1909. Berlin. Pavlova met with instant success in the type of programme she adopted later on. Adolf Bolm was artistic director of the tour. —A. L. H.

[2] One dancer alone, Vasilieva, came for this polonaise, which was simple and easily taught to the French dancers.—A. L. H.

"We have. There is the old Cecchetti, master of us all, who carries the torch of classicism. Then there is a true genius, Michael Fokine, a descendant of the greatest *maîtres de ballet* of all time."

"Nijinsky, Fokine, and Pavlova *must* come to Paris—next year."

"But Paris will never come to see whole evenings of dancing."

Astruc then goes on to tell how he convinced Diaghileff and overcame his objections.

"Who is to provide the money?"

"If your dancers are all that you say, bring them over with the productions. I will look after the hiring of the Châtelet, the organization, and the publicity. A guarantee of 100,000 francs will be enough."

The very next day, says Astruc, the contract was signed, and he went off in search of the guarantee. His list was headed by Isaac de Camondo, André Bénac, Henri Deutsch (de la Meurthe), Henri de Rothschild, Basil Zaharoff, and Arthur Raffalovitch.

Actually, as will be seen, the launching of the Russian Ballet was not so simple an affair. The idea had long been a cherished one with Diaghileff and his circle, even without the intervention of Nijinsky, Pavlova, or Astruc, and the recent actions of Teliakovsky had brought it still more to the fore. Years after, when interrogated as to the origins of his ballet, Diaghileff himself said:

"I had already presented Russian painting, Russian music, and Russian opera in Paris, and from opera to ballet was but a step. Ballet contained in itself all these other activities."

That is the simple and obvious explanation, but where the paintings, the music, and the opera already existed and were exported from Russia, however much they were enhanced by their presentation, in the case of the ballet Diaghileff wished to

Matilde Kchesinska in *Carnaval* in 1911

Leonide Massine in *Carnaval*

Nijinsky in

L'Apres-midi d'un faune, Paris, 1912

Nijinsky in

Le Spectre de la Rose

show something that was not yet brought to perfection in Russia itself, though all the necessary talent existed.

The desire to present a Russian Ballet abroad came about because there were first-class artists and a programme all ready to be presented, without the slightest possibility of doing this at home so long as Teliakovsky was in power, and the composition of the first programme gives us the *raison d'être* of the whole enterprise.

§ 2

Its cornerstone was *Le Pavillon d'Armide*, the ballet entrusted to Alexandre Benois by Teliakovsky in 1907. This ballet was entirely Benois's creation, for not only was he in charge of the *décor*, but he wrote the scenario, chose the composer, Nicholas Tcherepnin,[1] who was considered the most gifted of the pupils of Rimsky-Korsakov, the choreographer, Fokine, and the principal dancers. The whole production was supervised by him in the closest detail and under the greatest difficulty Teliakovsky, taking a page out of the Diaghileff programme, had employed Diaghileff's closest friends and collaborators, but at the same time he was bitterly hostile to them, and did everything to throw obstacles in their path. During a rehearsal of this same ballet, at the Maryinsky, Diaghileff, who had been invited by Benois, was asked to leave the theatre under some pretext that an official request had not been made. Jealousy could go no further, moreover the director was totally unable to speak the same language as they did.

His was a vulgar and trivial mind. Diaghileff could always forget the injuries of an enemy he respected, but not of one he despised, and to him a lack of taste was unforgivable. Benois tells of how he came with Tcherepnin, full of enthusiasm, to outline

---

[1] Tcherepnin was Benois's nephew by marriage.

177

the idea to the director. It had been in his mind for three years. He began to tell the story, but was interrupted:

"Is there a waltz?"

"Yes."

"Well, I want to hear it."

Tcherepnin sat down at the piano and played. Teliakovsky approved. "But I must have another waltz as well—the waltz is the basis of the whole thing."

That sums up the whole artistic outlook of the man. The additional waltz was composed, only to be withdrawn for the Paris production, when a balance was re-established. There were difficulties, too, from the start with the rôle of Armida. Kchesinska had been selected, but withdrew at the very last moment, and Pavlova stepped into her place. This rôle was never to prove popular with any *ballerina*, and for Paris, when Pavlova declined, it was entrusted to Karalli, who did not make a success of it. However, in spite of innumerable obstacles, Benois finally triumphed, and *Le Pavillon d'Armide* was one of the most complete and artistic productions ever shown on the Imperial stage. Its choice for Paris was obvious. It was largely to show *Le Pavillon d'Armide* that the enterprise was started—a *Pavillon d'Armide* shortened, and amplified by a score or so of expensively clad walkers-on.

§ 3

The next ballet to be selected was Fokine's *Nuits d'Egypte*, first produced at the Maryinsky, and now entirely revised by a patchwork process into a new ballet, *Cléopâtre*, built around the dazzling beauty and personality of Ida Rubinstein.

Ida Rubinstein was an orphan of good Jewish family, brought up by an aunt, Madame Horwitz. Not unnaturally in the case of such a beauty, the girl became stagestruck, learned dancing as a private pupil with Fokine and declamation at the dramatic school, and, in spite of fierce family opposition, determined to go on the stage. When she came of age, she gained not only her independence, but a large inheritance that enabled her to fulfil her ambition. She wished to play Oscar Wilde's *Salomé* but, as in England, the censor intervened and she only performed the dance of the veils, arranged for her by Fokine, to music specially commissioned from Glazounov. It was in this that Diaghileff first saw her and, encouraged by Bakst and Fokine, decided that she was the right person for *Cléopâtre*—a daring decision, since as yet she was almost completely untrained as a dancer. It was necessary to compose for her movements that would reveal her beauty without making her dance. Bakst—and Ida from the first was a living picture by Bakst—hit upon the idea that caused so great a sensation in Paris—namely, her entrance in a palanquin, swathed like a mummy, and then the gradual unfolding of those veils to reveal the perfect figure. Another dramatic effect had to be devised to show the consummation of Cleopatra's passion without causing offence, and Benois conceived the now famous scene, where the *corps de ballet* dances round the lovers with veils, making a living tent, while other dancers throw roses over them.

For Paris the music was completely altered, the kernel remained Arensky, but the Egyptian music from Rimsky-Korsakov's *Mlada* was added, Glazounov's bacchanal from *The Four Seasons*, later made famous by Anna Pavlova, and the *pas de deux* from *Rousslan and Ludmila*.[1] This musical potpourri may have been unwise, but it was arranged with the greatest skill, and it was magnificent theatre.

[1] The bacchanal was danced in tiger-skins that revealed a portion of the shoulder. The Moscow artists were scandalized and demanded tights! The date, 1909.— A. L. H.

§ 4

The third ballet was *Chopiniana*, renamed *Les Sylphides*, a title suggested by a great ballet of the romantic period, Taglioni's *La Sylphide*. This had originally been designed by Fokine for a charity performance, and was subsequently taken over by the Maryinsky Theatre. In its first version there had been the trace of a plot, a poet dreaming, but this was soon discarded and the suite of dances that we know so well was retained. This was to be Pavlova's ballet, a striking contrast to her rôle as the *fiancée* in *Cléopâtre*, and it can never have been danced more perfectly than by Pavlova, Karsavina, and Nijinsky at the Châtelet.

Diaghileff, who was on delicate ground musically, had had the music completely reorchestrated, and in *Les Sylphides* began his close collaboration with Stravinsky that lasted the whole life of the Ballet and its founder.[1]

§ 5

The remaining works were more fragmentary. *Festin* was a *divertissement* on a large scale, danced in a setting by Constantine Korovin, its principal number being Petipa's famous *Blue Bird*, temporarily renamed *Firebird*. Fokine says that Diaghileff had intended to present this ballet in the first programme, and had commissioned the music from Liadov, who was notoriously slow. One day he met Liadov in the street:

"Well, where is my ballet?"

"You will have it shortly, I have just bought the ruled paper."

"*Firebird* having been announced," says Fokine, " it was necessary to show it, so that the *Blue Bird* was renamed for the occasion."

[1] Stravinsky orchestrated the first prelude that is danced, and the final waltz. —A. L. H.

Festin also gave Diaghileff the opportunity of introducing some Tchaikovsky into the programme, and the music, the finale of the second symphony, was selected with a deliberate propagandist purpose. It was written round a definitely Russian theme, and the critics had denied that Tchaikovsky was Russian at all.

The rest of the programme was made up of one act of *Prince Igor*, containing the famous Polovetsian dances, perhaps Fokine's masterpiece. Their savagery even astonished the Russians, and when the *Balletomane* Bezobrazov saw them in rehearsal, he remonstrated with Fokine. "Aren't they—well just a little strong? Don't you think you might tone them down a bit?" "Not at all. They will be stronger still by the time I have finished with them." They were to prove the success of the season.

Since it was unwise to depend entirely on ballet, the first act of *Rousslan and Ludmila* was decided upon, as well as an abbreviated version of *La Pskovitana, Ivan the Terrible*, one of Chaliapine's most sensational roles.

§ 6

Diaghileff had decided upon this season immediately after the close of *Boris Godounov*, and there were almost nightly meetings of the group, *balletomanes*, and dancers at Diaghileff's flat, at Dandré's, or at Fokine's. It is there that Diaghileff first met his future aide-de-camp, Serge Grigorieff, then Fokine's right-hand man. At these gatherings the programme was drawn up and the artists decided upon. The choice presented no difficulties. Fokine was the foundation; Pavlova, then definitely a member of the advanced group, the central artist, the admired of the *Mir Isskustva*, and with her Karsavina and Nijinsky. Diaghileff wished to combine both St. Petersburg and Moscow, so that he engaged twenty-five women from St. Petersburg and five from Moscow;

seventeen men from St. Petersburg and eight from Moscow—a picked company of fifty-five from the best in Russia.

Again everything was planned regardless of cost. The theatre was ready awaiting them, but the ambitious productions, the salaries, and the transport had first to be paid. Diaghileff then devised a scheme that, while it may be morally indefensible, was almost excusable in the circumstances, since not a penny was to be diverted to his own uses and no one was in any way harmed by it.

In Russia there was a law that said that the heads of commercial houses established for over a hundred years could apply for patents of nobility that became hereditary. They could apply, but that did not mean that their applications would necessarily be granted without much influence and pressure from the powerful. A certain Mr. K., the head of a rubber manufactory, was devoured by such ambitions, and proposed to pay Diaghileff the sum of £10,000 if his Grand Ducal patron would endorse the application. The Grand Duke, ever sympathetic to artistic aims, was easily persuaded, and, since the application was legally in order, promised his help. The whole matter seemed on the point of accomplishment when he died, without having written the letter. Diaghileff was heartbroken at the loss of this understanding man, and not merely on account of the present predicament. He came sobbing to his friends, in his grief. The whole glorious plan seemed to have come to a standstill, there were many obligations to be met, and the Grand Duchess did not share her husband's esteem for Diaghileff, and heartily disliked the whole idea. Fortunately, at the last minute, through other influences, the scheme went through, Mr. K. became a noble, and Western Europe was able to see the Russian Ballet—on such ambitions does the fate of great enterprises sometimes rest.

Until the death of the Grand Duke the company had been accorded the right to rehearse in the Imperial Theatre of the

Hermitage, but this privilege was immediately withdrawn. This great achievement, that made Russian art known and respected throughout the world, was launched in spite of the indifference and opposition of influential Russians themselves. Almost alone had the Grand Duke Vladimir appreciated the significance of what was going on, launched Leon Bakst, and lent his powerful aid to the first four enterprises of Serge Diaghileff. All honour to his memory.

——CHAPTER X——

THE CONQUEST OF PARIS AND THE WEST
1909–1911

1. Preparations for 1909: *Valz—Astruc's* corbeille—*The* première—*Pavlova and Diaghileff—The meaning of success —Financial difficulties.*

2. Preparations for 1910: *Finding the capital—The Emperor's veto—First appearance of Dmitri Gunsbourg—The programme—*The Firebird.

"To-day, sir, dancing and the ballet are the craze; they are followed with a kind of rage, and never has an art been more encouraged by applause than is ours."

NOVERRE : *Letters*

"C'était toujours terrifiant et, à la fois, rassurant de travailler avec cet homme, tant cette force était exceptionelle. Terrifiant, parce que chaque fois qu'il y avait divergence d'opinion, la lutte avec lui était très dure et fatigante; rassurant, parce qu'avec lui on était toujours sûr d'aboutir quand ces divergences n'existaient pas."

IGOR STRAVINSKY : *Chroniques de ma vie*

"Il semblait que la création du monde ajoutât quelque chose à son septième jour."

COMTESSE DE NOAILLES

"Je dirais qu'il a créé quelque chose; quoiqu'il n'ait signé aucune des œuvres représentées par sa troupe, la part qu'il prit à leurs élaborations est celle d'un de ces collaborateurs sans qui elles n'auraient pas vu le jour. Il a créé une plastique, un gôut, un style d'époque."   JACQUES EMILE BLANCHE

"Mais il faut convenir que ces phrases sont enfantines. Les yeux qui voient sont éblouis et n'y sont point préparés."   LOUIS DELLUC

1. *PREPARATIONS FOR 1909*

After his previous experience with the executive staff of the Opéra, Diaghileff did not intend to take the slightest risk. He could well dispense with such emotions. When he arrived in Paris this time, it was with a large technical staff led by O.

Allegri, the head of the scenic department of the Maryinsky, and E. Valz, the chief mechanic. Valz was a miracle worker, as they found almost from the first day. Where the French reaction to any request was "*Impossible,*" with a shrug of the shoulders, Valz's was, "I will find a way." "You can't have the two fountains in *Pavillon d'Armide,* or even one, for that matter," said the French, "for the good reason that there's no water laid on." "*Il y aura de l'eau,*" said Valz, and on the night those two fountains played higher than they had done in St. Petersburg. This time Diaghileff was reassured that all would go well back-stage, but to say that calm reigned would be an exaggeration, for a hundred things, all of them noisy, went on at the same time. Carpenters hammered in the auditorium, Cooper rehearsed the orchestra in the pit, behind the curtain Fokine shouted at the dancers, and in the wings there was a flock of goats—walkers-on in *Le Pavillon d'Armide.* Almost day and night the whole mixed company and staff lived in the theatre, hasty meals being brought in from the *brasserie* opposite. Diaghileff himself was in a hundred places at once, busying himself with every detail, artistic and social.

The Châtelet was an old barrack of a theatre, used to blood-and-thunder melodrama and orange-eating, villain-hissing audiences, and was therefore in no way previously adapted to such a fashionable public as Diaghileff invariably attracted. The front of the house also needed *décor,* just as the art exhibitions had. Who can say that such things were superfluous or a waste of money? They all contributed to the total effect of what we must call the Diaghileff touch. He therefore proceeded to redecorate the entire house, recarpeting it throughout, converting the more popular parts into fashionable boxes, and making the *foyers* into gardens of flowers—the stage, too, was completely refloored. There was plenty of money in hand, but no exchequer could stand such a strain.

The usual elaborate machinery of propaganda was set in motion—the whispering campaign in the *salons*, the careful preparation of the Press. An illustrated brochure was ordered from a young poet, Jean Cocteau, the *enfant terrible* of all their meetings, and a faithful friend and collaborator to the end.

The very audience itself was not left wholly to chance, and the energetic Astruc turned his attention to beautifying the house in a manner surely unique in the history of the theatre.

"It was my principle to look after the auditorium on my first nights as if it had been a part of the scenery. In May 1909, the evening of the revelation of the Russian Ballet, I offered seats in the front row of the first balcony [dress circle] to the most beautiful actresses in Paris. Out of fifty-two invitations, fifty-two answered *yes*. I took the greatest care to alternate blondes and brunettes and, as everyone came on time, when the stage manager gave his three knocks, a smile of satisfaction lit up all those pretty faces, and the whole house burst into applause.

"The serious *Temps* devoted a front-page article to this innovation, which Joseph Galtier designated my *corbeille*.

"The balcony, thus renamed, kept its new title in the Théâtre des Champs Élysées and set a new fashion in nomenclature for most theatres built since then.

§ 2

The accounts of those first Paris performances have passed into history and form a part of every memoir of the period, artistic and social, and the continued repetition of the word "triumph," like the enumeration of celebrities in the house, after a little while becomes monotonous.

The ballets themselves cannot be described, since all ordinary language must be meaningless to those who have not seen them, but the enthusiasm that was aroused can at least be hinted at by a few quotations from the writings of various critics who were there:

"After long eclipse the dance will reign again over Paris." [1]

"What a joy for us to rediscover in these dances the human body in all its amazing variety, with its inexhaustible invention." [2]

"When it was said of Mlle Sallé or La Camargo that all their steps were sentiments one was already talking of La Pavlova or La Karsavina; and the mimed dance of a Nijinsky can alone give us the idea of what a Vestris must have been." [3]

"The ballet for the sake of the star is finished. . . . *To be just to the Russian troupe one should avoid all personalities.* It is even finer than the individual values that compose it. It possesses that supreme quality of being one with the work that it represents to the point of seeming born of the music and melting into the colours of the *décor.*" [4]

"Here is colour, here are real *décors.*" [5]

Each dancer was made the subject of a special eulogy, since it was impossible to avoid personalities, however perfect the ensemble.

Of Nijinsky: *"L'ange, le génie; le triomphateur du spectacle, le danseur divin, Nijinsky, s'emparant de notre cœur, nous emplissait d'amour, tandis que les sonorités suaves ou acides de la musique asiatique achevaient l'œuvre de stupéfaction et d'envahissement."* [6]

Of Karsavina: *"Si grande virtuose qu'elle soit, elle ne sacrifie rien à ces traits extérieurs, qui surprennant plus qu'ils n'émeuvent. Elle a découvert le merveilleux mystère du lyrisme chorégraphique—tout en elle est poésie. . . ."* [7] *"Vous avez compris, vous, la fille la plus exquise du classique chorégraphique que*

[1] Marcel Prévost.   [2] Abel Bonnard.   [3] Camille Mauclair.
[4] Henri Ghéon.   [5] Maurice Denis.   [6] Comtesse de Noailles.
[7] *Le Figaro.*

l'union était possible entre une tradition et une révolution artistique." [1]

Of Pavlova: *"Mademoiselle Pavlova est à la danse ce qu'un Racine est à la poésie, un Poussin à la peinture, un Gluck à la musique."* [2]

Of Ida Rubinstein: *"Elle est trop belle, comme une essence première sent trop fort."* [3]

These were not merely the words of a notoriously impressionable Press, but of the leaders of French artistic thought. A whole new literature grew around the first visits of the Russians, a whole new sense of decoration. The flaming colours of Bakst had penetrated everywhere, and *ballets russes soirèes*, and routs became frequent and fashionable. Nowhere but in Paris, where the arts are understood as a whole, where movements and tendencies are born, could a successful first night have given to an enterprise such a sure place in world history.

It is a tribute to the greatness of Diaghileff that the Press was silent about him. He rejoiced in the success of his *artistes*, of Nijinsky in particular, with whom his friendship was just beginning; but he himself kept in the background, caring nothing for popular applause. He knew that he was responsible for this triumph, and that those whose good opinion he valued also knew it—and here was reward and satisfaction enough. Diaghileff, in no sense a modest man, was always too sure of himself to relish praise. *"Les ballets russes—ce fut la triomphe de l'unité,"* said Emile Henriot—and it was Diaghileff who made that unity.

§ 3

In retrospect we are apt to lose sight of the details of this triumph and to assign the same credit indiscriminately to everyone and everything. Writers in looking back on the past have

---

[1] R. Brussel.   [2] Jean Louis Vaudoyer.   [3] Jean Cocteau.

often confounded the success of subsequent seasons with the first, and have given an impression of one continuous roar of applause.

Le Pavillon d'Armide, the main attraction, with the exception of the buffoons' dance, magnificently led by Rosai, was a comparative failure. The French may well have thought it daring of these strangers to show them the France of Louis XIV when they were looking to the Russians for something altogether exotic. For this reason too Les Sylphides was not instantly welcomed. It was a ballet blanc, and they could not yet see in it Fokine's great departure from academism. It was with the triumph of Le Spectre de la Rose, two years later, that they began to understand the new classicism, and then only did Les Sylphides come into its own. The undoubted success of the season was Prince Igor. Here at last was a thrill, the real "air of the steppes," the "wild Asiatic horde." For generations France had seen no real male dancing, and the virile Bolm and his warriors came as a revelation. A corps de ballet to them was something dull and lifeless, a necessary piece of scenery. These Russians had no corps de ballet, but a living ensemble of fine individual dancers. Cléopâtre, too, they could understand—that was truly exotic—and Rubinstein became the heroine of the day.

This distribution of success had an instant and marked effect on the whole subsequent history of ballet. Anna Pavlova was the favoured of the Mir Isskustva group, the great hope of modern ballet. The first poster of the Russian Ballet had been an inspired drawing of her by Serov, but things had turned out so that she did not secure the attention that her art deserved. In Les Sylphides she had been eclipsed by Nijinsky, in Cléopâtre by the exotic beauty of Rubinstein. The French had seen great ballerinas, even if they had never seen a Pavlova, but a male dancer and a fine ensemble were novelties, and attracted all their attention.

At the end of the season she left. Modernism had not done her justice, and she turned her genius in another direction, and succeeded against all artistic canons—because she was Pavlova.

To the end of their lives there seemed a trace of bitterness, a certain veiled hostility in both. Years later, in an interview, Diaghileff extolled Spessivtseva at the expense of Pavlova, comparing them to the two halves of an apple, "only the Spessivtseva half has been in the sun." However greatly he admired Spessivtseva, this could only have been dictated by disappointment at losing the great *ballerina*. He also said on another occasion, "Pavlova was never really interested in art as such. The only thing that mattered to her was her virtuosity, and she is a virtuoso without equal. When first I wanted her to do Stravinsky's *Oiseau de Feu*, specially designed for her, she declared that she wouldn't dance to such horrible music—Pavlova was not alone in this. In Monte Carlo, the Russian colony, with, of course, a general at its head, went to the president of the music society to ask him to ban *Petrouchka*. To-day both are classics."

The estimate of Pavlova as not being interested in art is lacking in subtlety, and, again, obviously dictated by disappointment. Pavlova's conception of art differed radically from his. She took unworthy things, and by what Benois aptly terms a "theatrical miracle" they became art once they had passed through her. It was never virtuosity that interested her, nor her material, but the quality that she could give to it. Pavlova, on her side, saw herself as the standard-bearer of classicism and beauty against his cult of eccentricity and ugliness.

When both of them died, so nearly at the same time, there died two conflicting principles of ballet: the one based upon the triumph of the individual, the other upon the triumph of co-operation. The first is dead for ever, while the second, with its foundation on reason, can live again. Pavlova has left a memory, Diaghileff a school and a system.

§ 4

"Son existence s'entourait de mystère," says his friend Jacques Emile Blanche, *"quoiqu'il fut sans secrets, toujours accompagné, public et très sociable."* From this time onwards Diaghileff lived in the limelight, and even his private affairs became the common property of a large group. He gathered to himself still more and more friends, but they did not really know him. Benois knew him, Nouvel knew him—only those of the *Mir Isskustva* period knew the real Diaghileff, and could appreciate exactly what it was that he was doing. These next twenty years were the consummation of his work in Russia. His intimates of the last twenty years can for the most part only talk of him with considerable difficulty. They can record events, but where is Diaghileff?

The success of 1909 had made him a nomad, uprooted him from Russia, the country he loved and served so well, for the desire to show to the West what his country could produce was ever present in his mind.

From now onwards Diaghileff was to have no fixed home— that was a part of the price to be paid for success. Just a series of hotel rooms, encumbered by trunks always half packed, the table cluttered up with letters, programme proofs and box files, can- vases and drawings on the chairs and against the walls.

"Come in and sit down. No—for God's sake don't put your hat on the bed, it's unlucky! It means death; no—no—not on the table, either—that means poverty."

The only thing to do was to throw the wretched thing on the floor, or to keep it on one's head.

The Grand Hotel, Paris, the Savoy, London, the Hôtel de Paris, Monte Carlo, hotels in the Lido and Venice—these were to be Diaghileff's homes for the next twenty years. The frantic applause in Paris had made that certain.

Diaghileff was sentimental, loving his country and his home, but always feeling lonely when surrounded by a crowd. Perhaps his friendship with Nijinsky would at last give him what he desired. There was something different in it from the others, something idealistic. Before, he had often been disappointed; only a few weeks ago his secretary had run off with a girl in the *corps de ballet*. It was humiliating, but actually it had been a good riddance, leaving him free for Nijinsky, who was an artist, a genius of the dance, and who could be taught, developed, and made into a great creative artist. Yet at first Diaghileff was not wholly at ease, a trifle apprehensive of the possibility of some big scene here in Paris. Prince L. had introduced them, had been desperately keen that this friendship should be made, but at the same time he had seemed a little jealous. With him Nijinsky had been bored and bad-tempered, while now he was so clearly interested and happy. Fortunately friends had seen to it that Prince L. did not subject his unbalanced nature to such a strain by coming to Paris.

§ 5

As usual Diaghileff had spent right and left without reckoning the cost. No commercial enterprise could have stood such reckless expenditure.

"The figures of the receipts," says Astruc, "were astronomical; but Diaghileff in his mania for beauty and perfection had passed all bounds."

"Once again it was necessary to make a tour of the wealthy and to ask them to realize their capital. Camondo and Bénac smiled, Henri Deutsch scolded me in a friendly fashion, Henri de Rothschild made his cheque into round figures, and Jupiter-Zaharoff frowned."

In spite of their intervention there remained a deficit of sixty thousand francs. Diaghileff left his headquarters at the Hôtel de

Hollande heavily in debt. Writs flew on all sides, and Diaghileff, according to Astruc, was finally caught at the Gare du Nord.

"Why on earth have they taken my trunks, my waistcoats, and even my pants?"

This may be a picturesque exaggeration, but it is not very far from the truth. It was a typical triumph *à la* Diaghileff, as Astruc himself was to know, to his cost, some years later, when the expenses swallowed up his management of the new Champs Élysées Theatre.

At the end of the season Nijinsky fell dangerously ill with typhoid, but soon made a complete recovery. To recuperate, Diaghileff took him to the Lido, the first of almost annual visits, where Diaghileff rested with the friends of his choice from his labours, though, even amid the calm of the lagoon, ballets were discussed and plans for the future laid. There could be no more rest once this enterprise had been started.

2. PREPARATIONS FOR 1910

Arrangements for the next year's season of ballet and opera were immediately concluded with the Opéra, Paris, once again without any definite idea as to whence the necessary money was to come. Diaghileff, by now an expert at such things, started the necessary *démarches* for an Imperial subvention. He had already done so much for the fame of Russian art abroad that he was fully entitled to one. He pulled strings, even visited Stolypine in person, but still the question was left undecided till the fatal day when it became necessary to pay the first instalment of the sum that was due to the Opéra, Paris. Nouvel then saved the situation temporarily by borrowing from a friend of his mother the sum of £1,000 for three months,[1] on a bill countersigned by Diaghileff, Gunsbourg, and Prince Argoutinsky. Whatever the outcome

[1] This sum was fully repaid, though only a year later.—A. L. H.

of the financial situation, it was necessary to economize, to drop the opera and concentrate on ballet. Nouvel and Gunsbourg were sent as ambassadors to Paris, to convince the directors of the Opéra, Paris, Messager and Broussan, that this would be a positive advantage. They had no easy task, but finally succeeded, and so the Diaghileff enterprise concentrated almost entirely on ballet from its second year.

While in Paris, Nouvel and Calvocoressi visited Diaghileff's very first French collaborator, Ravel, from whom he had commissioned *Daphnis and Chloe* in 1909. "I remember," says Nouvel, "that the composer lived near Fontainebleau, in a small cottage. The floods were very heavy that year, and, as we sat down to listen to what was ready of *Daphnis*, I noticed that the floorboards were curved by the water pushing up underneath. The ballet was intended for the following year, but it was not ready till 1911. The fact that it was commissioned the very first year of the ballet's existence shows that Diaghileff's policy of enlisting the very best talent, irrespective of nationality, was with him from the start, and was not forced upon him by circumstances, as so many have thought."

After weeks of feverish anxiety Diaghileff finally received a letter from the Imperial Treasury informing him that he had been accorded a subsidy of 10,000 francs. The money was needed urgently, much of it was already spent, but it was the week-end, and the Treasury was closed. Diaghileff rushed round to a private bank, and had no difficulty in borrowing the sum on the strength of his letter. Then came Monday morning, and with it an official letter from the minister saying that owing to unforeseen circumstances the subsidy could not be accorded. Frantically Diaghileff telephoned and interviewed the minister. There was nothing to be done, the veto had come from the Emperor himself, and on the margin of the letter, and in his own handwriting, that was reserved only for the most important occa-

sions, it was said, "Be careful, or he'll play you some trick yet."
Powerful enemies had been at work in an intrigue, the details of
which have remained obscure till the present day. Diaghileff had
enemies enough, and his method of obtaining money the previous year had caused considerable displeasure in court circles.
That, at any rate, was sufficient to influence the Emperor, whatever the interested person's motives may have been.

All that now remained was the balance of Nouvel's £1,000
soon due for repayment.

§ 2

This time a character as charming and fantastic as in any
ballet came to the rescue, and resolved all financial worries until
the War. Baron Dmitri Gunsbourg was tall, well built, handsome, and a great dandy—always dressed in the very latest
fashion. He had two passions in life—collecting antiques, and
the ballet. He had a luxurious flat, which he was always redec-
orating, and in consequence he often lived uncomfortably in one
room or at an hotel.

Valerian Svetloff has left a spirited account of his friend.

"A flat is such an intimate thing," he said, one night to Svetloff, "that it must reflect the personality, the moods, and tastes
of the owner. Moods and tastes change frequently—so must the
furnishing of the flat. I have just found some beautiful panelling. It was very expensive. I must use it; which means, of
course, that the whole room has to be changed down to the last
trinket. Come to dinner in two months' time. I think everything
will be ready by then. I have found some excellent workmen."

"I went," says Svetloff, "and found the whole room changed.
I approached the panelling, which was very beautiful, and
stretched out my hands to touch some oval silk medallions that
were inset in the wood. . . .

" 'Please, please don't touch those medallions, the silk is very delicate indeed'; and, with a beam of triumph, 'It is made from the dressing-gown of Alexei Michailovitch.[1] There was just enough material for the four.'

"I pulled up a chair, intending to sit down and smoke in comfort. . . .

" 'Wait a moment. Are your trousers quite clean? That silk is very light and fragile. It is made from the waistcoat of Louis Philippe.'

" 'To the devil with all silk, bring me a kitchen chair. I refuse to stand all evening.'

"He returned, bringing an uncomfortable wooden chair, with a low seat and a high narrow back.

" 'This is the *prie-dieu* from the monastery described by J. K. Huysmans in *L'Oblat.*'

"I sat down in some discomfort—at any rate there was nothing there that I could damage—and pulled towards me a non-descript-looking jar. For safety, I asked, 'Is it an ashtray?'

" 'Yes, but for God's sake don't use it for ashes or stubs! It is very fragile. I paid 7,500 francs for it in Cairo. It is a tear bottle from Cheops' pyramid.'

"He went out and brought me a penny saucer.

" 'There is, I suppose, one thing I must be thankful for: not having to take my boots off before coming in.'

"Finally we adjourned to Cubat's for a meal, because his new dining-room in the romantic style was not yet finished."

This was the man who saved Diaghileff at a critical moment. An arrangement was soon made between them. Gunsbourg was to be called *directeur-administrateur*, and to have a voice in all artistic questions. He took upon himself the settling of all small current expenses, which were to be refunded from the theatre cash-box the same evening. Finally the profits were to be divided

[1] The father of Peter the Great.—A. L. H.

and his capital returned intact, if and when he left the enterprise. Perhaps no one but such an unpractical *fantaisiste* of infinite charm could have worked in such close and harmonious collaboration with Diahileff. Like most thoroughly unpractical men he started out in a businesslike manner, bringing with him an expert bookkeeper.

"Where are the books?"

"There aren't any."

"The bills and receipts?"

"Somewhere in Diaghileff's pockets."

The bookkeeper left in disgust and amazement after a few days. It was quite impossible to keep track of expenses, since Diaghileff crumpled up all the bills and receipts and shoved them into the pockets of his suits, invariably having lost them by the time they were required.

For all practical matters Diaghileff referred people to the Baron, but it was always difficult to find him. Usually he would lunch at Henri's, drive in the Bois, tea at the Ritz, dine at the Café de Paris, and arrive at the theatre in time to assist the artists in making up, which was his great specialty. He was an amateur artist, and a costume designer of ability. Then after the performance he supped with Diaghileff, the artists, and friends; but before supper he always went to the cash-box to draw his expenses. Shaking out his cuffs from his irreproachable *frac*, he examined the pencilled figures. There were rarely any documents produced, and a lengthy argument always ensued. Once the Baron exacted payment for a certain sum:

"I don't know what it was for, as the stupid chambermaid has sent my shirt to the wash, but I clearly remember the sum was 670 francs."

He never received it.

One day, when driving with Diaghileff, they passed the Grande Maison de Blanc, where they saw the furnishings for a young girl's bedroom—white tulle portières, and a bed with a tulle canopy and a delicate rose-bud design.

"That is the very thing we want," said Gunsbourg. "It is *Spectre de la Rose* to-night, and this bed, with its hangings and delicate rose-bud design, just echoes the theme."

He went in and bought it for a large sum, carefully noting the price on his cuff. It was sent straight to the theatre, and substituted at the last minute for the regular set. But from the huge auditorium the delicate rose-buds could not be seen, and it was discarded after that one night on the stage.

Finance, as it was understood by Diaghileff and the Baron, led to continual excitement. An hour before curtain-rise one night, a bundle of essential costumes was delivered at the theatre —with, of course, a substantial bill. There was naturally no money available, and the messenger, not being susceptible to charm, refused to leave it without payment. Diaghileff was frantic. "Find the Baron at once." He phoned to every Paris restaurant, and finally ran him to earth.

"Come to the theatre at once."

"Let me finish my dinner first. It is a very good one. These partridges are excellent, and the wine is just the right temperature."

"Impossible. Leave it all and come at once. We need money for the costumes. The house is sold out. There will be a public scandal."

The unfortunate Baron raced through his dinner. The banks were closed, so he made the round of his Paris relations and the Rothschilds in search of the necessary money. The costumes were paid for a few moments before the curtain rose.

Gunsbourg was loved by the whole company for his unfailing good humour, and appreciated by Diaghileff as much for his artistry and charm as for his capital. Probably there was no half-share of the profits for him to receive; certainly he never saw his capital again, and many times the laundry must have obliterated all trace of his petty expenses; but he can never have regretted his share in the enterprise, and the ideal existence of pleasure and art, living the last years of his life in a perpetual romantic ballet.[1]

"When I went to the War," Svetloff continues, "he came to the station to see me off. His parting gift was touching and characteristic, an antique snuff-box, one of his favourite *bibelots*. I always have it with me.

"In the middle of the War he asked me to get him into my regiment, the cavalry of the *Division Sauvage*. I succeeded, and very soon he was wearing its picturesque uniform, in which he caused a sensation in St. Petersburg."

Gunsbourg was sent to the Caucasus with important papers. He never returned. No one knows exactly how he met his death. He was either treacherously murdered by the mountaineers, or killed by the revolting Cossacks. It was a tragic end to a life that had been a glorious light comedy. This is still another of those men who helped to make Diaghileff's dreams come true, asking nothing for himself but a share in the dreaming.

§ 3

The programme selected that year firmly established Diaghileff's success, and launched Leon Bakst on his spectacular career. No one knew better than he how to enjoy fame.

It was Leon Bakst who proposed the story of *Sheherazade*, and the first, second, and fourth movements of Rimsky-Korsakov's symphonic poem were selected. A committee, consisting of Bakst, Benois, and Fokine, with Diaghileff as *arbitre*, sat daily listen-

---

[1] So muddled and involved were the accounts that after Gunsbourg's death a certain sum was left outstanding. This Diaghileff had to pay by instalments whenever he visited Paris.—A. L. H.

ing to the music, marking on the score the dramatic action as it occurred.

Is it to be wondered at that there are disputes lasting till the present day as to the origin of each idea? Once again Ida Rubinstein was made the centre-piece of this exotic story. It was to be her last appearance with Diaghileff. Such rôles were hard to create, and Nijinsky's success as the slave eclipsed her own. When she left, she made some appearances at the Paris Olympia, with no marked success, but the triumphs of *Saint Sebastien* were not far off. *Sheherazade* launched a fashion, brightened the colours of shop windows and women's clothes, and has lightened the tone of every stage *décor* since. It spread to revue and music hall, till Diaghileff himself was forced to fly from it. In later years, when a revival was proposed, Diaghileff wisely demurred. "Memory has made all the colours seem brighter and more vivid. If I put it on now, everyone will say, 'How drab!' It would have to be intensified in colour in order to make any effect." When a ballot was held in London, in 1925, for the most popular Diaghileff ballet, *Sheherazade* headed the list, though it was not mentioned on the ballot paper. It would have filled the house, but Diaghileff was content to leave it as a memory of the youth of his Ballet.

Carnaval,[1] the next ballet, had already been presented at a charity fête, and so great had been its success that the Maryinsky Theatre acquired it, and it was performed there in an unsuitable spring landscape. At first Diaghileff was distinctly hostile to its presentation, and for a characteristic reason. It was too intimate, and he loved the grandiose. Bakst and Benois finally overcame his objections, and the curtained *décor* stressed that intimacy and gave a fresh note to the programme—a restful interlude after the orientalism of *Sheherazade*. The part of Columbine introduced to the Western public one of the most delightful and sub-

[1] See page 261.

sequently popular of the Diaghileff artists—little Lydia Lopokova, fresh from school; and the description of her first appearance, given by J. L. Vaudoyer, might have suited her throughout her career in the ballet:

"*Sa virtuosité est ingénue, et l'imperceptible gaucherie de
l'âge la tempère. Mademoiselle Lopokova II ressuscite les poupées
de Hoffmann et de Schwind; et sans doute mordait elle encore
l'an dernier, dans les tartines que distribue Charlotte.*"

She was the first Diaghileff "discovery" in the sense that he
fitted her with rôles and made her reputation abroad before she
was truly known at home.

For the sake of Nijinsky, it was decided to revive *Giselle*. He
had made a profound study of the part, and an admirable Giselle
was to hand in Karsavina, though the revival had originally been
planned for Pavlova. This ballet met with no real success. There
was still a marked hostility to classicism, and the Diaghileff successes had been made off the points. The romantic *décor* of
Benois, the art of Karsavina and Nijinsky could not compensate
for the weak old-fashioned music. In Russia there had been
regular ballet critics, while in France the Press was in the hands
of the musicians. Calvocoressi tells of the feverish hunt for the
holder of the copyright, and of how he finally tracked the happy
and astonished owner to a side street in Versailles.

§ 4

The big creation of 1910, the *Firebird*, was the first Diaghileff ballet proper, in the sense that the music was specially
commissioned, and that there was a close and perfect collaboration between composer, choreographer, and decorative artist—
Golovin. The very essence of a Diaghileff ballet was the fact
that there was never a gap between the three elements.

Diaghileff had heard *Feu d'Artifice* and *Scherzo fantastique* at the Concert Ziloti in 1908, and was so impressed that he commissioned first the *Sylphides* orchestrations and then the *Firebird*. Also, there now began a close friendship that lasted the whole twenty years of the Ballet's existence, and that must exempt Diaghileff from the usual charge of fickleness. As long as a collaborator had more and still more to give, he was welcome in the Russian Ballet, and Stravinsky gave richly for those twenty years; collaborating with Fokine, Nijinsky, Massine, Nijinska, Balanchine, and Lifar, giving each one an outstanding success, suited in style to the new vision of each.

From the very first Diaghileff believed in Stravinsky, not only in his actual creation, but in his musical judgement in general, and he listened to him as he would listen to no one else. Stravinsky, too, understood Diaghileff as few people did:

"Un autre attrait pour moi était la qualité de son intelligence et de sa mentalité. Il possédait un flair hors ligne, une faculté extraordinaire de saisir d'emblée la fraicheur et la nouveauté d'une idée et de s'emballer immédiatement pour elle avant tout raisonnement. Je ne veux pas dire qu'il manquait de raisonnement. Au contraire, celui-ci était très sûr chez lui, il avait l'esprit fort sensé et, s'il faisait souvent des fautes et même des folies, c'est qu'il était emporté par la passion et le tempérament, deux forces prédominantes en lui.

"En même temps, c'était une nature vraiment large et généreuse, exempte de tout calcul. Et quand il commençait à calculer, cela voulait simplement dire qu'il se trouvait sans le sou." [1]

They quarrelled at times, but so great was their appreciation of one another's intelligence that these quarrels rarely interfered with the work.

The subject of the *Firebird*—a Russian legend—greatly inspired Fokine, and he worked as closely with Stravinsky, as did

[1] *Chroniques de ma vie,* Igor Stravinsky.

Petipa with Tchaikovsky, going over it section by section, as it was written.

"They worked very closely together, phrase by phrase. Stravinsky brought him a beautiful cantilena on the entrance of the Tsarevitch into the garden of the girls with the golden apples. But Fokine disapproved. 'No, no,' he said. 'You bring him in like a tenor. Break the phrase where he merely shows his head, on his first intrusion. Then make the curious swish of the garden's magic horse's return, and then, when he shows his hand again, bring in the full swing of the melody.' " [1]

There was never any question in the Russian Ballet of giving a finished score to the choreographer, and saying to him, "Do your best with this." With the *Firebird* began an ideal system of collaboration, the true equality of the arts that it had been Fokine's whole desire to effect. The rôle of the Firebird had been originally intended for Anna Pavlova, but no one could have interpreted it more perfectly than did Thamar Karsavina. For her it was the ideal part, a combination of drama and classicism in which her remarkable beauty could be seen to full advantage, and her world fame dates from the *Firebird*.

Stravinsky himself finds the choreography "overladen with plastic detail," so that the artists have the greatest difficulty in co-ordinating their movements with the music. In any case it gained an instant success, and as a whole the success of the second year was far greater than the first. An annual visit became a certainty now.

[1] *Fokine*, by Lincoln Kirstein.

————CHAPTER XI————

THE EVENTFUL YEARS
1911–1914

*The season of 1911—Monte Carlo—Rome—Vassily—Paris
—Petrouchka—London début—The* Giselle *incident—Diaghileff and his company—La Kchesinska—1912:* L'Après-midi
d'un faune*—1913: Astruc's failure—*Le Sacre du Printemps
scandal*—The discovery of Massine.*

"Les répercussions des ballets de Diaghileff sur la jeunesse universitaire britannique
sont à peine croyables. L'influence de ces spectacles s'exerce sans relâche sur toutes
les activités intellectuelles, en Angleterre."

JACQUES EMILE BLANCHE

The year 1911 was to prove a highly eventful one in the life of
Diaghileff and of the Ballet; it included the first Monte Carlo
season, a brilliant Paris success again with Astruc at the Châtelet,
the first London season, and the separate existence of his company as a permanent institution.

The Monte Carlo contract was always greatly valued by Diaghileff. Not only did it have a certain cachet, but the cosmopolitan crowd that assembled in the small opera-house there was the
finest agent for international propaganda that existed, and since
everyone was out for enjoyment they made perhaps a more
indulgent audience than could a metropolitan public. "Monte
Carlo is the *répétition générale* for Paris," he always said; and
there yearly, from 1911 onwards, the new ballets were composed and the Diaghileff cabinet held its meetings. With three
performances a week the dancers could rest, they could perfect
their technique—and they could also on occasion lose a month's
salary, if they succeeded in penetrating into the Casino. It is

there that new recruits joined him and were "polished"; Sokolova, Dolin, Lifar, Markova, and many others began their careers at Monte Carlo, and to many generations of dancers to-day Monte Carlo means home and rest—the only one in a feverish life of trunks and station platforms. Certainly to the *balletomane* ballet is more enjoyable there than anywhere else, the theatre the most perfect for seizing every intimate detail, yet seeing the pictures as a whole. Each one of those six hundred spectators has the illusion that the spectacle is being given for his benefit alone.

Immediately after Monte Carlo the company left for Rome, where, for the International Exhibition, Diaghileff had arranged to give a series of ballets and fragments of opera at the Costanzi. Both Karsavina and Stravinsky, in their memoirs, speak of the delightful time spent there with Alexandre Benois—the finest of all guides, and able to make the past live before their eyes. Serov and Modest Tchaikovsky joined them there. The Ballet was always a second home for all Russian artists, and the Ballet now meant the travelling portion led by Diaghileff, and not the great institution that remained at home with his bitter enemy Teliakovsky at the head. Nouvel, before leaving for Rome, had to send on the material necessary for the Paris season. It was difficult to find anything in Diaghileff's flat, everything being always in most admired disorder. The faithful and indispensable Vassily alone knew the way about, and could be relied upon to despatch everything on time.

This invaluable Vassily deserves a paragraph to himself, since not only was he the perfect servant, but Diaghileff was always very much a hero to him. Of the same age as his master, he entered his service in 1894, and only left it at his death. He was intelligent and quick-witted, and he first proved himself in the time of the *Mir Isskustva*. The editorial disorder was notorious, but Vassily always seemed to know where everything was, and not only Diaghileff, but the entire staff addressed themselves to him when a book, an article, or a drawing was missing. He knew of every incident in Diaghileff's life, but he was discretion itself, and nothing would tempt him to gossip. Like the worthy Grimaud, he was taciturn, and his replies were always abrupt and to the point. Diaghileff was devoted to him, and frequently sought his advice when any practical help was needed, while Vassily, on the other hand, had studied his master, and understood his reactions as did no one else. He was respectful, and never permitted himself the slightest familiarity. He got on splendidly with the old *nynya*. At times she scolded him in motherly fashion, but was always ready to rush to his defence. Vassily had been unhappily married, and his wife died shortly before the War, leaving him with a son, who, through Diaghileff's influence, was entered in the Imperial School.

When Diaghileff began his foreign tours, Vassily accompanied him, making order out of chaos, and it was astonishing how a man who knew not a word of any foreign language could manage so well.

Later, when Diaghileff took an Italian valet, Vassily was heart-broken. The two servants could not agree, and Diaghileff gave Vassily the job of chief dresser to the men, a position he held till the end, though he could never get over the mortification of being separated from his master.

During the first seasons in Paris, Diaghileff had lent him to Nijinsky, and it was he who waited in the wings during *Le Spectre de la Rose*, with a towel and a cup of black coffee, first catching the dancer in his arms after the famous final leap.

Apart from the properties unearthed by Vassily, many of the goods needed for Paris demanded immediate payment in cash, and for this Nouvel put himself in touch with Gunsbourg.

"All right, I will be with you to-morrow at midday, without fail."

To-morrow came, and no Gunsbourg. Just a brief message: "Have been detained, arrange everything for the next day," and so it dragged on, day after day. It was not possible to suspect that anything was really wrong and "The Baron" unable to pay, but still Nouvel was worried. Then he discovered the reason. These delays were deliberate, occasioned by the little bit of business instinct this extraordinary character possessed. A few days' delay meant a few days' further interest in the bank. Gunsbourg was like that, and shared with Diaghileff an intense dislike for trifling payments. In a tram he would only pay his fare for one stage, remarking, "You never know what might happen before you reach the next stage," yet that same afternoon he would spend a fortune on his two hobbies—*bibelot* and the ballet.

In Rome, Stravinsky had been completing the score of his new ballet *Petrouchka*. It had come to him as a genuine inspiration, while waiting to begin *Le Sacre du Printemps*, which was already planned. He had conceived the idea of "*un pantin subitement déchaîné qui, par ses cascades d'arpèges diaboliques, exaspère la patience de l'orchestre, lequel, à son tour, lui réplique par des fanfares menaçantes. Il s'ensuit une terrible bagarre qui, arrivée à son paroxysme, se termine par l'affaissement douloureux et plaintif du pauvre pantin.*" [1]

He had also found for this the title *Petrouchka*, "the eternal and unhappy hero of every fairground and every country."

Diaghileff was enchanted, and this became the second tableau of the ballet. They agreed to entrust the *décor* and scenario to Benois, and together they elaborated the most moving drama that the ballet has ever shown.

The collaboration was perfect, but the preparations resulted in one of those frequent *ballet-russe* quarrels, only more serious in its results than usual. Benois was ill in Russia and late in arriving in Paris. The scenery was completed save for the portrait of

[1] *Chroniques de ma vie*, Igor Stravinsky.

the Astrologer, in Petrouchka's cell, an important feature in the story. Diaghileff became impatient at the delay, and told Bakst to proceed with it. He had just sketched it in in charcoal, when Benois arrived, and, naturally irritated at seeing his work in another's hands, started to upbraid Bakst bitterly. Diaghileff upheld Bakst, and the quarrel grew in intensity. It is said that as a gesture of peace Serov, who was older and respected by all, drew the Astrologer's portrait himself. Whether this is true or not the quarrel between Diaghileff and Benois lasted a year, and the following season every *décor* was the work of Bakst.

Petrouchka revealed Nijinsky in a new light—as an actor of intense power. *Petrouchka* was perhaps a little his own drama— the universal drama of every man who felt and could not realize himself fully—and Karsavina added to her fame as the *ballerina*. Stravinsky himself finds the set dances among the finest ever devised by Fokine, but regrets that the crowd scenes were improvisations rather than choreographic arrangements. Many dancers famous to-day have started in that crowd.

A small *divertissement* that season, suggested by the French writer, Jean Louis Vaudoyer, after Gautier's poem, *Le Spectre de la Rose*, won such instant success that it was encored and had to be repeated again. It entirely altered the French view of classicism. Through that they could now understand and enjoy *Les Sylphides*, and realize the use that Fokine was making of the old technique. It was in every way a contrast to the rest of the programme: a contrast for Nijinsky after the drama of *Petrouchka*; a contrast for Bakst after the exotic colouring of his previous works; a contrast for Diaghileff after the large scale of his usual creations. Nijinsky's leap has passed into history, and has often made the audience forget the true climax of the little drama—the awakening and the gradual disillusionment of the young dreamer. No one has ever rendered it so exquisitely as Karsavina. It remains hers for ever. The picture of Bakst wandering on the stage with his canary cage, to put the finishing touches to the young girl's room, is unforgettable. The remaining novelties, such as the submarine act of *Sadko* and *Narcisse*, left little mark.

§ 2

An appearance in London was now long overdue. Already after the triumph of 1909 Diaghileff had gone there with Calvocoressi, in response to an offer from a large music hall. He saw a performance there, and the idea of sharing a bill with performing animals and trick cyclists horrified him. During the last months of the War he was delighted to appear in that same house, and on the same bill as Lockhart's elephants, but much had happened in the interval. He was, however, able to secure an option on Drury Lane for an advance payment of £500. On return to Paris he soon found out that no £500 existed, he was snowed under by writs, and the London project fell through. Some of his artists, including Karsavina, found their way over alone, and gave the public the first taste of the delights to come.

When he did come, it was under the most favourable auspices —to Covent Garden, and at the time of the coronation celebrations. He came sponsored by the Marchioness of Ripon, who soon became a close personal friend both of Diaghileff and of his whole company, visiting their rehearsals, asking them down to the country to rest. Paris was all excitement, bustle, sensation, and taut nerves, while London, from the first, in its intimacy most clearly resembled Monte Carlo. But to reach London it was first necessary to cross the channel, an absolute ordeal to Diaghileff. A fortune-teller had once told him that he would meet death on the water, and he firmly believed it. When possible he postponed the crossing for a day or two, waiting for a calmer sea and calmer nerves. Diaghileff now settled in the Waldorf with his friends, soon to move to the Savoy, that became his permanent London home, the grill-room a nightly meeting place for his *entourage*.

The first performance was given on Wednesday, June 21st, the programme consisting of *Le Pavillon d'Armide*, *Le Carnaval*, and *Prince Igor;* and on June 26th one act of *Le Pavillon d'Armide* was given at the Coronation Gala—an occasion especially calculated to please Diaghileff, with the theatre decorated with pink roses and trellis-work, beautiful women, glittering jewels, fine uniforms, and oriental potentates that might have stepped out of his own productions.

London was a repetition of the Paris success, perhaps even a greater triumph, for it was not merely the exotic that appealed to English audiences. Adeline Genée, Lydia Kyasht, and Anna Pavlova, with her own company at the Palace, had already given them a deep love and understanding of classicism. Where Paris welcomed the sensational, needing novelty after novelty to retain its interest, London remained faithful from the very first year, understanding the quality of the dancing, and appreciating the dancers as individuals, from the *première danseuse* down to the *corps de ballet*.

Diaghileff himself never learned to speak fluent English, though he understood it far better than he made out. He had no wish to appear ridiculous in a language he did not speak readily, and there were also sound diplomatic reasons—much time to be gained in a business discussion.

As usual he gathered round him the most influential and interesting people, and the most interesting women of the day became his staunch allies, and he valued them above all others. "You can trust those English friends; with them absence makes no difference." What he valued especially in London was the respectful attitude and the discipline of the stage workmen.

In later years he changed his opinion of London many times;

sometimes grateful for the continued support, sometimes extremely irritated by the conservative attitude that prompted it. London could never have become his headquarters or have provided him with inspiration. It was his nature to enjoy the almost yearly fight to establish the new programme in Paris, and it was the new programme that counted there. He would always rather stake his all on a novelty than make certain and easy money through revivals. He appreciated the quality of fidelity in his London friends, but it was in Paris that he could plan, fight, and work. Although he was there for shorter visits than in London, it was his spiritual home from the first.

§ 3

Earlier that year (1911) occurred the incident [1] that was to give Diaghileff the control of a company of his own, where before he had taken artists belonging to the state theatres on tour. This account is taken from Walter Nouvel, who witnessed the famous performance.

"*Giselle* was given at the Maryinsky Theatre, with Nijinsky and Karsavina. All the costumes belonged to the theatre save those of Nijinsky, who had been given special permission to appear in those designed for Diaghileff by Benois in 1910. There were two costumes, one for each act. The first was made up of a brown *pourpoint* and tights in the Carpaccio style that revealed the lines of the body rather fully, since Nijinsky had omitted, for some reason or other, to wear the customary strap.

"The house was a full and brilliant one, the Empress Dowager being present with her daughter, the Grand Duchess Xenia.

"Following upon an article written by Svetloff a year ago (1934) upon this incident, he received an explanatory letter

[1] This is also related in Chapter XII, but from the point of view of the relations between Diaghileff and Nijinsky.

from Krupensky, *chef du comptoir* of the theatres at the time, and the adjunct of Teliakovsky. In this letter Krupensky explains the incident that ensued, in the following manner: Before the performance Nijinsky had shut himself up in his dressing-room, allowing no one to enter, only coming out just before curtain-rise. It was then that Krupensky saw that the costume was inadequate, and ordered him to change it for the one belonging to the theatre. This Nijinsky refused to do, and, since it was impossible to delay the performance, the curtain went up for the first act. Immediately an excited buzz of conversation began, and those in the public hostile to Diaghileff and Nijinsky did not conceal the fact that they were shocked. It was even said that the Dowager Empress expressed the wish to be warned the next time an indecent performance took place, but that I do not believe. Krupensky goes on to say that he came on to the stage during the second interval to order Nijinsky to dance in the theatre costume. In the second act he undoubtedly appeared in Benois's costume; that is why I believe that the version contained in a second letter to Svetloff, also from an eye-witness, is more accurate. This correspondent says that the Grand Duke Serge Michaïlovitch, who was hostile to Diaghileff, had been sitting in the Imperial box, and came on to the stage and asked to be shown Nijinsky's costume for the second act. Nijinsky was wrapped in a long black cloak. This the Grand Duke drew aside, and, satisfied with what he saw, told Nijinsky that he could appear.

"According to Krupensky, again, the court minister, Baron Fredericks, was not at the performance, but telephoned him from the Yacht Club afterwards, to ask for an account and to insist that Nijinsky be fined. A little later, after midnight, the minister telephoned again, and told him this time to dismiss Nijinsky. This is not altogether accurate, as the Baron Fredericks was undoubtedly there, since I saw him myself. After the first act he passed by me, red with anger, and made his way to the director's

office. What probably happened was that Fredericks himself
went to the Yacht Club later, the scandal being feverishly discussed there and his temper fanned by Diaghileff's enemies.

"The next day Krupensky sent for Nijinsky and dismissed
him. Nijinsky, he says, listened in silence, and then said : 'I shall
go to Diaghileff.' What is quite certain is that this occurrence
was totally unexpected both by Nijinsky and Diaghileff, who
had in no way provoked it. The next day we met in Diaghileff's
flat, to try and discover some means of changing the decision. I
wrote the text of a letter of apology, in Nijinsky's name, to the
Empress Dowager, but, whether she received it or not, the decision remained unaltered.

"This came as a bombshell to Diaghileff, who felt himself
responsible in some measure. He now had to employ Nijinsky
for the entire year, naturally with a full company of dancers—
an exceedingly difficult task. He was, of course, finally successful, but all his future activities arose out of this small incident."

§ 4

Actually to "own" a troupe was particularly suited to Diaghileff's essentially aristocratic outlook, and he took an immense
pride in that troupe, and a deep and active interest in the welfare of its members. He could always be as charming to sub-
ordinates as he was sometimes difficult with his equals. However,
he expected a very high standard of work, and this was immediately noticeable by the hush and the extra effort when he
walked into the rehearsal-rooms, and altogether his presence in
the theatre always meant a far better performance. It was for
him they always danced. The feelings they entertained for him
were mixed, compounded of infinite respect, fear, and hero-
worship. One well-known dancer has told me that she could
never speak to him without tears in her eyes, so greatly did he

impress her. There was never any intimacy between him and the average member of the company, and from the first it was out of the question to make any suggestions, to ask him for a rôle, or to seek praise. Even after a glorious success, he would say, "Not bad; you will do better next time," and the recipient was proud even of so much notice. He controlled the private lives of his artists rigorously, not morally—he was no hypocrite—but æsthetically. Once he had said, " 'Such company' is unworthy of a member of the Russian Ballet," the edict had to be obeyed, or the offending member would be forced to leave the troupe on the very first pretext. Generally he was faithful to his artists, and hated to part with them. Lydia Lopokova left him suddenly on more than one occasion, but he always gladly took her back, until the last time, when he said reproachfully, "We don't want grandmothers in this company," but yet she danced for him as an honoured guest artist. He could forgive much to a person of real intelligence.

On occasion, too, it pleased him to play the part of benevolent uncle. One of his favourite *premières danseuses* had had a disagreement with her friend, and he noticed that they were no longer talking. "If you really want him back," he told her, "I will arrange things"; and when, on the next day, a notice appeared on the board, "Mlle X will teach M. Y. the *pas de deux* from ——," the silence was very soon broken.[1]

Financially he was exceedingly generous, and took great pride in the large salaries that he paid. In times of difficulty—and there were many—full payment was never delayed for more than a few weeks at most, and then it upset him greatly. At the stage of forming his company, he seemed to realize the risk he was allowing them to take, and the sacrifices made by many of the artists when they left absolute security and abandoned their pensions. He deposited substantial sums in the accounts of many

[1] This was told me by the dancer concerned.—A. L. H.

—gifts that were unasked for and unexpected. Many of his artists, too, never had or required a contract—his word was always regarded as sufficient guarantee—and that is why perhaps on his death so many of them fell immediate victims to unscrupulous adventurers.

Favouritism, except in the case of his own particular friends, was unknown, and those friends invariably proved themselves worthy of rapid advancement. At one especially difficult moment in his career he was offered a large sum of money if he would advance a certain dancer. He admired her, but considered her unfit for the many rôles suggested, and refused without the slightest hesitation. He could forgive faults—as long as they were not faults of taste—more often and more generously than any other man. Perhaps because he knew his strength and accepted people as they were, he could even forgive disloyalty, and many who attempted to form or to join rival organizations were taken back as if nothing had happened.

Throughout the years discipline was absolute. An abortive strike for increased salaries led to the instant dismissal of the offenders, but the salaries were raised beyond the sum demanded. Such was his moral authority that he could even subdue an orchestra with its difficult union officials, over whom he had no formal authority. One dress rehearsal, by reason of constant repetition, having lasted until past midnight, the conductor turned to Diaghileff and told him that his men were getting restive and refused to play any longer. "You will give them ten minutes' rest, and then they must come back and play until we have finished—it may be till four in the morning." They came back before the time was up.[1]

Often he himself would sit in the theatre the entire night searching for some difficult lighting effect, trying perhaps the most difficult of all, to wash out the fold in the old backcloth of

[1] I assisted at this particular scene.—A. L. H.

Petrouchka. In the morning when his artists came to rehearsal they would find him still in the stalls, the only sign of fatigue being the heavy pouches under his eyes. It meant a fortune in overtime and tips, but every detail must be perfect always. He had an eagle eye for detail. Untidy hair in *Les Sylphides*, too florid a make-up or a safety-pin showing, invariably meant a hurried conference with Grigorieff and a list of fines on the rehearsal board. To work for Diaghileff was an education in theatre-craft that has left its mark even on the most unobservant.

Absolute authority—that is what the aftermath of the *Giselle* incident meant, and so Teliakovsky lost many of his finest artists to Diaghileff and the Russian Ballet became the Diaghileff Ballet in fact, if not in name.

§ 5

Later in the year (October), he returned again to Covent Garden for a long season of his own, with *Cléopâtre*, *Les Sylphides*, *Sheherazade*, *Le Spectre de la Rose*, and *Le Lac des Cygnes*. From the dancing point of view he had gathered more talent than at any time in his career. When Karsavina was forced to return to the Maryinsky, he "borrowed" Pavlova from Alfred Butt, and after that Kchesinska arrived from Russia— three great Maryinsky *ballerinas* in six weeks.

At last Kchesinska and Diaghileff were united. Two of the strongest personalities in Russia, they had met in many a stormy encounter, both as allies and as enemies, and each of them had great respect for the other, and the rare gift of never bearing rancour. In 1925, when Diaghileff introduced me to her in Monte Carlo, he said, "*Voilà un adversaire bien digne de moi,*" and that was their attitude throughout. Kchesinska was all-powerful in Russia, able to have everything her own way at the Maryinsky Theatre, with the result that more absurdities have been written about her by imaginative writers than about any-one else, identifying her with nearly every sensational happen-ing of her time—absurdities and identifications which she has never troubled to contradict. What emerges is a woman of infi-nite charm, wit, and intelligence, generous in instinct, a fighter, because one must be a fighter on the stage, whose greatest fault was never to lose her fights. If she and Diaghileff had been at daggers drawn the year before, there were no signs of it now.

In London she danced in the *Lac des Cygnes*, and a small note in the programme read: "The *adagios* in the first and second tableaux will be played by Mischa Elman." He was then at the height of his fame, and that very night was giving a recital at the Albert Hall, and what this caprice cost her will never be known, but it was the sort of grand gesture that Diaghileff could appreciate. She also danced in *Carnaval* with Nijinsky, whom she had largely discovered. She appeared again with Diaghileff the following year in Vienna, and in Budapest. Later, after the War, he tried his hardest to tempt her back to the stage, but he failed. She was one of those rare artists who have been wise enough to retire in their prime.

The following year, in London (1913), he engaged his first English dancers, among them the young Hilda Munnings, whom he subsequently christened Sokolova, after the great Rus-sian *ballerina*. From the very first she submerged herself into the atmosphere, and within a short period was as much a Russian dancer as any pupil from the Maryinsky. Diaghileff greatly valued her, and there was from the first a strong sympathy between them, increased by their common sufferings during the War. Sokolova's career has been unique amongst English danc-ers. She made her name at a time when Diaghileff had the whole Maryinsky to choose from, when Fokine was *maître de ballet*, Karsavina and Nijinsky in their prime.

"These English are fine dancers," said Diaghileff; "one day

they will form a school of their own," and throughout his lifetime they were the only foreigners admitted to the company.

§ 6

That following year (1912) led to a violent change of
method, to the first Diaghileff *succès de scandale*, and to the
stormy birth of a new choreographer. *Daphnis and Chloe*—
Ravel's masterpiece and one of the greatest compositions of its
period—*Thamar*, and *Le Dieu Bleu* inspired memories of the
Royal Siamese Ballet, and, representing Bakst at his most inspired, passed almost unnoticed beside the scandal that *l'Après-
midi d'un faune* [1] evoked, and Diaghileff revelled in the scandal.
He feared apathy alone, and this violent reaction proved to him
that his creations were still vital, besides being admirable publicity. Rodin and all advanced French opinion rallied to his side
against the attacks of the *Figaro*, and nightly the theatre was
filled. In his later years he sought for, and stimulated, such
attacks on occasion, but now there was no need to intervene.
Nijinsky's culminating gesture had proved sufficient. This storm
launched him as a choreographer, and started in him the struggle with creation that was to prove so unhappy.

At the end of the season Fokine left the company. The notice
given to *l'Après-midi d'un faune* had completely eclipsed his
own *Daphnis*, and he was never on the best of terms with Nijinsky, whose choice now as a second choreographer made his position intolerable. This was in no sense a rupture, and he was to
return in 1914, but meanwhile the echo of his successes made
him welcome at the Imperial Theatres.

That year, too, in Budapest, Nijinsky met Romola, his future
wife. Diaghileff was fully aware of her infatuation, mentioned
it to his friends, and thought no more about it. There was noth-

[1] For an account of the creation of this ballet see pp. 245 *et seq.*

ing new in a young girl falling violently in love with *le dieu de la danse*—such things were of daily occurrence, especially since *Le Spectre de la Rose*. They even went so far as to steal the petals of his costume.

There were two ballets left for Nijinsky to compose—*Jeux* and *Le Sacre du Printemps*. The idea of a primeval ballet had long been present with Stravinsky, and, together with the painter Roerich, he elaborated the idea. Fokine had left the Ballet, Boris Romanoff, the only available choreographer, was at work on Florent Schmitt's *Salomé*, so it fell to the inexperienced Nijinsky to tackle this difficult subject to exceedingly complicated music. Stravinsky was frightened of the collaboration. He realized Nijinsky's musical shortcomings, and found it necessary to teach him the very rudiments.

"Son ignorance des notions les plus élémentaires de la musique était flagrante. Le pauvre garçon ne savait ni lire la musique, ni jouer d'aucun instrument." [1]

To complete matters, the strain was proving too much for him. He did not realize his shortcomings, though the company did, and Diaghileff had hard work to maintain his authority. This made him highly irritable, and scenes were frequent. Diaghileff's dream of a happy union and a perfect collaboration were crumbling.

The *première* of *Le Sacre du Printemps* (1913) was to be the main event of the opening of the smartest theatre in Paris—Les Champs Élysées—under the direction of Gabriel Astruc; and the season included as well: *Boris Godounov*, *Khovantchina*, Nijinsky's second effort, *Jeux*, and a revival of *Daphnis* that had not received its due the previous year. Once again a scandal robbed it of attention.

Diaghileff, a business genius in such matters, had driven a hard bargain.

[1] *Chroniques de ma vie*, Igor Stravinsky.

"I had said to Diaghileff," says Astruc, " 'This year no more Opéra, no more Châtelet! You are coming to me.' "

"But my dear friend, the directors of the Opéra want me."

"So. And how much are they offering you? Doubtless twelve hundred francs, your usual price."

"Yes, but you must understand that for six years now people say that Astruc invented the Russian Ballet. That, my dear friend, must be paid for."

"How much?"

"At least 25,000 francs a performance."

"Even for twenty performances?"

"Even for twenty performances."

The signing of this contract, Astruc goes on to say, meant his death warrant, for to those 25,000 francs it was necessary to add as much again for incidental expenses, and no success could cover such a strain. Gallantly he says, "That mad act, that I had not the right to commit, allowed the creation of *Sacre*, and cost me the life of my management."

The new theatre could have received no finer advertisement than the outcry that followed upon the production of *Le Sacre du Printemps*. Its details have become too well known to need repetition. The music was of a kind unheard before, the choreography muddled and over-complex. The smart crowd behaved like hooligans, and pandemonium was let loose. Stravinsky, in the wings, hung on to the frantic Nijinsky's coat collar to prevent him rushing on to the stage, while Diaghileff, in a frenzy, ordered the lights first off and then on, and Astruc shouted, "First listen, then hiss." The Dowager Comtesse de Pourtalès informed Astruc, as she swept out, that if he repeated such foolery it was the last time she would be seen in his theatre.

Jean Cocteau has described the scene after the storm:

"At two o'clock in the morning Stravinsky, Nijinsky, Diaghileff, and I crowded into a cab, and got it to take us to the Bois

de Boulogne. We were silent; the night was cool and pleasant.
. . . When we arrived at the lakes, Diaghileff, muffled in opos-
sum, began to mutter in Russian; I felt that Stravinsky and
Nijinsky were listening, and, as the cabby lit his lantern, I saw
tears in the *impresario's* face. He continued to mumble slowly
and without tiring.

" 'What is it?' I asked.

" 'Pouchkine.'

"There was a long silence, then Diaghileff uttered another
short phrase, and the emotion of my two companions seemed so
great that I could no longer resist interrupting them to ask the
reason.

" 'It is difficult to translate,' said Stravinsky, 'really difficult;
too Russian, too Russian. . . . It means, approximately, "Will
you make a trip to the Islands?" That's it; and it's very Russian,
because, you see, with us we go to the Islands, just as to-night we
go to the Bois de Boulogne, and it is while going to the Islands
that we first conceived *Le Sacre du Printemps.*'

"For the first time they had referred to the scandal. We came
back at dawn . . . and, whatever Diaghileff may have done after,
I shall never forget him in that cab, reciting 'Pouchkine' in the
Bois de Boulogne, his plump face wet with tears."

§ 7

In 1913 Diaghileff presented a season of ballet and opera
under Sir Joseph Beecham's management at Drury Lane, and
the hundredth performance of the Ballet in London was celebrated (July 25th). *Le Sacre du Printemps* passed without a
repetition of the Paris scandals. London was amazed, but polite.
The previous year *l'Après-midi d'un faune* had registered an
instant and amazing success, the most conservative of the illus-

trated papers publishing a "Faun" supplement with a series of Greek bas-reliefs to show the origins of the work.

It was his last appearance with Nijinsky. After the season they went for a holiday to Baden-Baden. Nijinsky was restless, capricious, and irritable after his efforts as choreographer, and already their relations were a trifle strained.

The company had been engaged for a tour of South America, and up to the very last moment Diaghileff could not make up his mind whether to go or not.

The company left from Southampton, with Baron Gunsbourg in charge. Nijinsky under the special care of Vassily. The sea journey had proved too formidable, and Diaghileff remained behind, waving a final farewell at Cherbourg.

§ 8

The sailing of the boat meant the end of a friendship and a collaboration. There was now an important gap to be filled.

Fokine had rejoined the company both as choreographer and *premier danseur*, but the rôle of Joseph in Strauss' *Légende de Joseph*, which had been written for Nijinsky, required a very young man. Diaghileff returned to Russia and made a prolonged search. Finally in Moscow, at the Imperial Theatre, he found a seventeen-year-old boy who had been studying at the dramatic and ballet schools, and who had just graduated. He was slim, exceedingly beautiful, with his large brown eyes, the very embodiment of the Joseph that Diaghileff had in mind. He was engaged for the rôle, and immediately placed under the care of Cecchetti. From the *corps de ballet* he became a *premier danseur* within a few months. Only Diaghileff would have had the daring and the confidence to present a novice in Paris and London in an important rôle, with his own magnificent and highly experienced company. Paris at once acclaimed him: "The little

Massine looks like a poet, and his dancing is poetry." London called him "The Russian wonder boy." But Diaghileff knew, Cecchetti knew, and Massine himself knew how far it was necessary to travel in order really to deserve such praise.

The programme that year was uninteresting, and none of it has survived save the brilliant memory of *Le Coq d'Or*, presented as a ballet. *Joseph* and *Midas*, both studies in the exotic, and *Papillons*, an attempt to reproduce *Carnaval*, left little mark. All that remained was this startling new discovery, Leonide Massine.

The London season that summer, again at Drury Lane, was a brilliant one, with Chaliapine at his finest in *Boris Godounov*.

Nijinsky had proved beyond doubt the strength of the company as a whole. Last year its brightest ornament, this year his absence made no difference to the general success. "Nijinsky has not yet been missed," wrote the *Daily Telegraph*, "for his successor was altogether demoniac as the lovely Sultana's negro lover." While on his own he had been a failure—for the first time. It was the beginning of his tragedy.

DIAGHILEFF AND NIJINSKY : FACT AND FICTION
1909–1917

Nijinsky till his meeting with Diaghileff—The meeting with Diaghileff—The Giselle *incident—Nijinsky's marriage—The war years—The American season—Nijinsky in charge—Nijinsky as choreographer—The last tours—The end of the tragedy.*

It should not be necessary to be on the defensive when dealing with such a man as Diaghileff. To attempt even in a remote degree the task of whitewashing him would be impertinent in the extreme. In his feverish existence he committed many petty actions and some unworthy ones, but they are more than balanced by the greatness of his achievements, and by the many large and generous deeds that are known only to his friends and immediate *entourage*. Unfortunately, through the recent publication of Romola Nijinska's life of her husband before any biography of Diaghileff had appeared, Diaghileff has become known to a very large public, who care nothing for art or for the things that he represented, as the villain of a highly coloured episode. A more impartial survey shows us the events in their real proportions, and they are simpler and far less dramatic than common report has made them, and, if they do not redound entirely to his credit, they cannot by any stretch of the imagination make him into a convincing villain. When the evidence has been fully sifted, he can be seen as the victim of a drama of human relationships with no hero and no villain.

Nijinsky's importance in the whole pattern—both artistic and

224

mara Karsavina as The Slave in *Cleoparta*   Ida Rubinstein as Cleopatra, Paris, 1909

Lubov Tchernicheva as Cleopatra

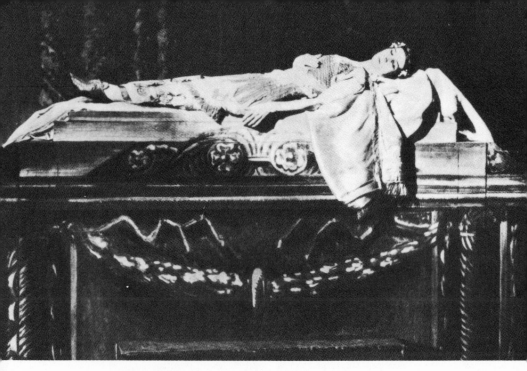

Vera Trefilova as the Sleeping Beauty, London, 1921

Ida Rubenstein by Serov

private—of Diaghileff's life has in this manner been exaggerated; but it is well to follow the story of their relationship in the closest detail, even to stress it beyond its importance in the general scheme, as we have now been able to gather and to sift all the evidence with so much exactitude that it helps us to build up our full portrait of Diaghileff, the essential aim of this book. It is often necessary, where rumour has been at work, to destroy a false impression before the accurate account can readily be received.

We do not lay any blame on the biographer of Nijinsky. The great love that she professes for her husband, and the fearful strain of living with a man going slowly insane, whose most terrible symptom was a mania of persecution, cannot fail to have coloured her views, which must from the start have been unfavourable to Diaghileff, and very understandably so from the moment that she learned the true nature of their friendship. It would have required a consummate, almost unearthly detachment, quite impossible in an impulsive young girl very madly in love, both with an individual and a highly coloured view of that individual, to sift truth from falsehood, and to see Sergei Pavlovitch as he really was. It is not surprising if, in these circumstances, she has not always been strictly accurate in details of fact, both small and large, that were actually ascertainable; and her whole romantic story is, moreover, too intensely subjective, too lacking in light and shade, to be in any way plausible.[1]

From the outset it must be made quite clear that it is impossible to fix anywhere the blame for Nijinsky's insanity—the culminating point of the tragedy. It was an unfortunate accident that has subsequently distorted our attitude to the three principal actors in the drama. Nijinsky carried it in him from the start,

[1] Adolf Bolm, who has been presented by Madame Nijinska throughout her book as the kind friend, and who therefore cannot be considered hostile to her, writes to me (New York, April 5th, 1935) that he considers the book highly distorted, and that he regrets it as much for Nijinsky's sake as for Diaghileff's.—A. L. H.

and it is idle speculation to seek the cause. I have asked several well-known psychiatrists about this particular form of insanity, *dementia præcox*, and the reply is always the same:

"It is possibly glandular in origin, possibly mental; but whether the mind causes the glandular disturbance, or vice versa, no one yet knows. It is also impossible to say definitely whether an absolutely calm, unemotional existence could save someone so threatened. It is possible. One thing is certain—people do not go insane through certain unfortunate or harrowing circumstances unless they already have the seeds of insanity in them.

"Mania of persecution is generally one of the first symptoms, when the subject is otherwise balanced, so that this feeling of persecution can seem highly plausible to the victim's *entourage*, who are often the last to notice that anything is the matter, they themselves thus easily becoming victims of it too. Many people remain on the borderline, with an extreme haunting sense of injustice, and their own attitude towards the world may eventually make them victims of mistrust, while others in a short time topple over the edge into unmistakable insanity."

With that in mind, let us leave the psychiatrist's study for the theatre, and follow the story of the man who had every gift save that of mental stability. Mania of persecution, chief symptom of his illness, must not be allowed to colour our views as we judge this episode in the life of Diaghileff.

Nijinsky was one of those rare favoured persons who literally leap into fame. At school he worked hard in the ordinary manner with his teachers Legat, Obouhof, and Fokine. He suffered none of the long periods of misunderstanding through which so many advanced artists have to go; at the same time he lost all the advantages of the struggle which acclimatize the artist bit by bit and prepare him for fame.

226

We can have no conception of what fame meant to the dancer in Russia. It cannot be measured through any parallel with the great film star or prominent athlete of our day. Life in Russia then was spacious and extravagant. Money flowed like water, and the wealthy spent a fortune to satisfy some whim—to recompense the *tsiganes* after a night's carousing, to make champagne flow from a fountain, to eat a banquet of meats and fruit out of season. The favourite pleasure of the slightly inebriated *nouveau riche* was to smash the crockery in the restaurant, and then to foot the bill without a murmur.[1] Everything that we knew in the height of prosperity must be multiplied a hundredfold. Fame, to a dancer, did not merely on occasions offer the *entrée* into moneyed circles, but also a certain familiarity, however remote, with the court and the aristocracy that money itself could not always buy. The dancer was an expensive luxury maintained at the court's expense, and its most especial pride. Sudden success was enough to turn the best-balanced head, and to convey a set of entirely false values.

Nijinsky's time at school was a happy one. There was no foreboding of misfortune, yet, when we look at the register of those who graduated with him, nearly all met with disaster: Rosai died of tuberculosis; Babitch was killed by a jealous husband; Yakimov committed suicide; Fedorov was "killed by error" in the revolution.

Nijinsky was from the first brilliant in his dancing, dull and slow-witted in his school work and, while already something of a celebrity in ballet circles, only able to graduate a year after his time, failing twice in his exams, and being admitted the third time—probably out of charity. His début in a dance with Schollar at the graduation ceremony was a triumph. The critical Svetloff acclaimed him without hesitation, just as he had acclaimed

[1] This was so current that a moaern Russian joke tells of two *émigrés* in a Lyons teashop: "Don't let's wreck the table; they mightn't understand it."

Anna Pavlova a few years before. Then Kchesinska, the unique, the all-powerful, chose him as her future partner—and he had arrived.

Between May and September the Imperial Theatres were closed, and many of the artists sought work abroad or found temporary and highly paid situations teaching the daughter of the merchant, the prince, or a combination of the two, how to curtsey or dance a drawing-room waltz. During these months of Nijinsky's first vacation La Kchesinska took him with her for a series of special performances to Krasnoë Selo and there, as her partner, his fame spread throughout Russia.

It is certain that Diaghileff must have known of him and admired him since his schooldays, but the exact date of their first meeting is not known, and their names were not linked together till the great enterprise of 1909. That enterprise was already well advanced when Nijinsky came on the scene, and it was not he who suggested it, or even determined Diaghileff in his resolve. As we have seen, it was the logical result of what had gone before.

It is more than probable that the meeting took place at the house of Prince L. or at the Restaurant Cubat, the usual rendezvous of the *élite* after the ballet. It was there that the performances were discussed in detail, heated arguments took place between partisans of the great stars, the *débutante* was made or damned for ever, as Svetloff wrote his *communiqué*.

Prince L. was a wealthy aristocrat of medium intelligence and considerable charm, but of dissolute and degenerate tastes. I use the word degenerate where he is concerned—although his tastes were the same as Diaghileff's—with intention. Amusement was his aim in life, and amusement that manifested itself in a somewhat vulgar and ostentatious manner, in veritable orgies of extravagance, with men masquerading in fantastic travesty and the like. Nijinsky was flattered by his attentions, became a frequent guest, and was loaded with expensive presents of jewellery from admirers of both sexes.

This was no more the right atmosphere for Nijinsky than it was for Diaghileff. Nijinsky was a god on the stage, but dull-witted and something of an oaf in private life, and these early impressions must have been bewildering and harmful to him in the extreme. Also they initiated him into a certain mode of life the responsibility for which has been wrongly ascribed to Diaghileff. From the very moment he left school Nijinsky was protected by a wealthy purse, his every wish satisfied. Where a woman can, and invariably does, adjust herself to a sudden change of environment, and wear even unexpected fame with grace, as if it were an inborn right, a man, and a dull-witted one at that, is speedily submerged.

For some reason that is not clear, the meeting with Diaghileff and the subsequent friendship was engineered by Prince L. himself, who repeatedly told Diaghileff's friends what an advantage it would be to both men. Diaghileff had admired Nijinsky on the stage since 1907, but he was suspicious of a meeting on account of Prince L. He could not bear the idea of any scene, and the possibility of sharing the young man with another was abhorrent to him. As things worked out, it seems as though Prince L. was genuinely concerned with Nijinsky's welfare and realized that he himself could not advance his artistic future.

§ 2

Nijinsky's meeting with Diaghileff was an immediate success. Here was someone who understood and appreciated his art, and, whatever amusing diversions there were in life, art was the main, the absorbing interest. However lacking in book-learning and general culture he may have been at the time, it is a mistake to imagine that Nijinsky was, on the stage, merely a beautiful physical specimen, a highly trained athlete, and nothing much else besides. He may have appeared so to the average person, but certainly not to Diaghileff. Such a type would never have appealed to him. It is true to say of Diaghileff that it was essentially the mind, and not the body, with which he fell in love—the undeveloped mind that he could form and guide according to his own ideas. Nijinsky was always an artist, with deep feelings about his art that he was struggling to express consciously. The story of that struggle is largely the story of his tragedy. At the time of that meeting he was at the crossroads, and only some external event that would provide the right atmosphere could make it possible for those feelings to become thoughts. The meeting with Diaghileff was that external event. Diaghileff did not seduce him—Satan-like, taking him on to some lofty mountain and promising the world in return for his soul and his body. That is the picture that so many would like to see, and it is dramatically obvious—Nijinsky's Trilby to Diaghileff's Svengali— but it is a definite contradiction of the characters of both the men. Diaghileff certainly loved him, and expected entire devotion, but he saw and understood the artist, who could help him to turn certain dreams into reality. Nijinsky, on his side, loved and admired this man, who could help him to find himself, give him the opportunity to work, and who seemed to know and to understand everything. Nijinsky was no child; he fully realized the immense advantages that were to be had in exchanging Prince L. for Diaghileff.

I no more desire to glorify their relationship into a beautiful idyll than to pass moral judgement upon it. Psychologically it was wrong, and could give no permanent happiness—if permanent happiness is a proper aim in life—but while it lasted the light shone brightly and the results were brilliant. Without Diaghileff, Nijinsky would have been just another great male dancer, more partner than individual, known in his own country but not beyond it. A normal friendship and collaboration might have produced similar results; it might possibly have endured longer, though by the end Nijinsky had given his all and was a spent force artistically; but the principal actor would not have been Diaghileff, and we must be content to accept events as they actually occurred.

§ 3

For the first two years Nijinsky, the star of the Russian Ballet on tour and the sensation of Paris, is still a comparatively unimportant member of the parent body in St. Petersburg. These two years, perhaps as a dancer his greatest, are years of intensive education. Diaghileff throws Nijinsky into close contact with the finest thinkers of the day, watching him carefully so that he may study and guide the reactions of those interminable, stimulating mealtime conversations. Certainly Diaghileff is jealous, but he does not keep Nijinsky caged up or in isolation. He selects his company with the greatest possible care. He educates him, and tries hard to teach him languages, but, as in former days, Nijinsky does not prove an apt pupil. Their names are linked together everywhere, the Boulevard papers make jokes in doubtful taste, but Diaghileff himself is scrupulously correct, and from his public conduct nothing can be guessed. It is certain that this relationship between them, known to the company, keeps Nijinsky from his comrades—the price that had to be paid for this artistic paradise; but Nijinsky, as long as he was sane, was always a good comrade, and did not arouse jealousy or antagonism in others. All who saw him at the time speak of him as taciturn, glum, and a little bewildered, but a being completely transformed when he was dancing. A man so greatly flattered, with whom feminine conquests would have been so easy, may well have been disgusted at the open manner in which women courted him. At any rate, he seems to have been well content in the society with which

231

Diaghileff surrounded him. Nouvel speaks of Nijinsky as a being never fully sexually awake, as someone who poured all his emotions into his work, and to whom the active adventures of love meant absolutely nothing.

Then in 1911 came the incident that cut Nijinsky away from Russia and from the necessary discipline of the Maryinsky Theatre.

This incident has already been related in detail, so that it is only mentioned here in so far as it concerns the relations between the two men. It has often been suggested that Diaghileff engineered the whole episode, but that is scarcely consistent with the facts of the case. Diaghileff could not have foreseen, when the costume was designed, that a member of the Imperial family would be present on that occasion, nor could he have foreseen the extent of the scandal that would ensue. He may well have taken advantage of what occurred, but even that is somewhat contradicated by the fact that, with Nouvel, he helped to draft a letter of apology addressed to the Empress Dowager. What is most likely is that Nijinsky, after two years in a freer artistic atmosphere, and aware of the powerful support of his friends, himself revolted against the official prudery of the theatre. There had already been signs of such an artistic revolt a short time before.

"For some period of time, even if Nijinsky and I were not in the cast of a performance, we were made to appear on every ballet night in a *pas de deux*. We had gone through many, preparing dances for every occasion till it came to one on the music of Sinding. We rehearsed it at the orchestra rehearsal on Friday. On Saturday I rang up either Benois or Bakst, I do not recollect which, to ask for some details about my costume. I was told that there would be no *pas de deux*, as Nijinsky intended to refuse to dance that night. If I remember rightly, the explanation was that for some time the Direction objected to the music of Sinding being introduced into that particular ballet. The directions from

Diaghileff or his group were that Nijinsky must not compromise on music. From that you can see that Nijinsky's attitude had been one of defiance for some time already." [1]

This particular incident, unlike that of *Giselle*, had no serious consequences, but it shows the widening of the breach between Nijinsky's two managements, and it suggests artistic diversion rather than a carefully laid plot. If in fact Diaghileff did take advantage of it, he was well within his rights.

In writing of the immediate sequel, Madame Nijinska falls into a grave error of fact when she states that the Imperial Theatre made offers to Nijinsky, culminating in a proposal of the highest salary ever paid, even to such singers as Chaliapine. Actually he was in his fourth year of service at the theatre, and his salary reached at most 1,500 to 2,000 roubles per annum, while Chaliapine's salary was 36,000 roubles for a very limited number of performances. Walter Nouvel, who at the time was serving in the Chancery of the Ministry of the Imperial Court, to which the Imperial Theatres were subordinated, and who was of course vitally interested in the whole question, would have heard of any such offer. Actually it was impossible, as the theatres did not bid for an artist in open competition with commercial managements, and the loss of Nijinsky, though they might regret it, was no great misfortune to them.

Financially at any rate there could be no doubt as to the great extent he benefited in following Diaghileff, who then formed his own permanent company as a result.

§ 4

The whole story of Nijinsky's marriage is difficult to understand. Mr. Drobecki, a friend of Madame Nijinska's, to whom she so frequently refers, says:

[1] Tamara Karsavina to A. L. H., October 23rd, 1934.

"The story of Nijinsky's betrothal resembles an episode from the *Arabian Nights*; it was so sudden and unexpected that one could only explain it by admitting that Nijinsky *had lost his head* [italics are his] on board during the trip."

Mr. Drobecki clearly does not mean to imply that Nijinsky had *lost his head* simply because he married a young and attractive woman, but because of the manner in which the whole thing was done—his sudden decision to marry someone with whom he could not exchange a word, and the frantic rushing through with the marriage. It is most logically accounted for, perhaps, as a subconscious act of defiance against the domination of Diaghileff; the feeling that something must be done—and very quickly too—while he was still free.

But what of Diaghileff in all this? That is our main concern. He is not consulted, not warned; in fact, he is the very last person to be thought of. He, the director of the Russian Ballet and Nijinsky's true friend, is left in complete ignorance of everything until he receives a cable sent by his valet, whom he had loaned to Nijinsky.[1]

Whatever the relations between the two men, this was an undoubted affront. If, at the time of his own sister's marriage, Nijinsky felt he was losing a comrade, what must Diaghileff's feelings have been on losing someone of whose affection he felt sure, someone whom he had for more than four years formed, educated, and guided, whose genius he had brought forth, whose triumphs he had sponsored?

It was only natural that he should have been deeply wounded by such disloyalty, for not until some days after his marriage did Nijinsky himself inform Diaghileff of the event, and try to explain his reasons, in a letter which took three weeks to reach Europe from the Argentine.

[1] Diaghileff received the cable in Venice and not in London, as Madame Nijinska states.

Diaghileff was far too clever not to realize that Nijinsky's marriage would put an end not only to their friendship, but also to any further possibility of a close artistic collaboration. He knew Nijinsky and fully realized his limitations. His was a one-track mind. From that moment—whatever else happened—his artistic career was at a close, and no action on Diaghileff's part could have changed that fact. The first impulse of his violent nature may well have been to revolt, to avenge himself, to inflict punishment, and it is then that he may have uttered the melodramatic sentence which has become the basis of so many fantastic charges: "As high as Nijinsky stands now—so low am I going to thrust him," though there is nothing but hearsay evidence even for this.

At all events, Diaghileff for the moment held his peace, and, as is the case with most quick-tempered people, his anger was soon followed by acute moral and physical depression. Drobecki writes:

"I remember, when the ballet returned from South America, Diaghileff, suffering from his breach with Nijinsky, called me to St. Petersburg and begged me to replace him in the organizing of a tour, and the signing of the contracts with the theatres for the following season, as he was incapable of doing it himself. His conversation bore no trace of hatred for Nijinsky; there was only a feeling of affliction and of love, quite incomprehensible to me."

In fact, it is clear that Diaghileff decided to dismiss Nijinsky only after long and sufficient consideration. Two months elapse after the marriage before he informs Nijinsky that their collaboration is at an end. It is difficult in this to see an act of vengeance. No one can expect Diaghileff to go on with an association that was not only painful to him, but that could no longer be expected to produce any artistic results.

This decision was not merely the result of a personal vendetta;

it was discussed with artists, friends, and intimates, and all were agreed that Diaghileff should send the cable. Subsequent events, abortive attempts at collaboration, show plainly that Diaghileff was well advised when he made his first decision.

Nijinsky's first trial alone at the Palace Theatre is a tragic failure. "We seemed to be pursued by bad luck, or more truly by Diaghileff," writes his wife, but without any real justification. What exactly are the concrete charges? That he sought to retain Bronislava Nijinska in his company, and that he egged on Fokine to take out an injunction to restrain Nijinsky from dancing in his *Spectre de la Rose*.

The first is too trivial to deserve serious attention. Bronislava Nijinska was a valuable artist, and there could be no possible reason why Diaghileff should not make every possible effort to retain her in his company. The second charge is inaccurate. Fokine denies that he took out such an injunction on that occasion, and anyone who knows the man cannot for a moment imagine him as either a tool or a conspirator.[1]

To face facts, Nijinsky failed because without Diaghileff and the organization he could not succeed, but from now on everything is laid at Diaghileff's door. It is alleged that he commenced a campaign of slander—"Nijinsky is greatly changed under the influence of his wife; *Sacre* is too modern, etc." That Diaghileff —who sacrificed everything to be modern—should have uttered such a thing is obviously ridiculous.

Then comes the story of Nijinsky's next meeting with the company, thanks to the kind offices of the Marchioness of Ripon, who was trying to effect a reconciliation between the two. There is no truth in the assertion that she delivered an ultimatum to Diaghileff that without Nijinsky there could be no season. All the details were settled a considerable time ahead, and the ballet was too popular and too well established for any one member,

[1] Interview with A. L. H., Paris, 1934.

however great a dancer, to make any real difference as to its success. Nijinsky came of his own accord, was never billed to appear, and there was no meeting with Diaghileff. Serge Grigorieff writes [1]:

"It is quite natural that the Marchioness of Ripon, a great admirer of Nijinsky's, should have done everything within her power so that he should dance some performances with us. Either she wished to rehabilitate him after his London failure, or she simply hoped that a reconciliation would take place. I must tell you, however, that such a return was not possible at the time, not merely because Sergei Pavlovitch did not wish it, but also because Fokine, who had come back to us both as choreographer and dancer, was to replace Nijinsky, according to contract, in all the latter's rôles."

Nijinsky never came to the theatre with Drobecki, as Madame Nijinska states; the artists did not turn away from him, and no announcement was ever made of his possible participation.

"You will probably remember that this was the most brilliant pre-war season for us—we were giving operas and ballets, *Joseph* with Massine; *Le Coq d'Or*, and Chaliapine was singing. We had no need of Nijinsky." [2]

I am pleased that Grigorieff refutes once and for all the story of Nijinsky's bad treatment by his former comrades. Such a happening would have been more than a reflection against Diaghileff, a charge against the whole company at that time.

Since Madame Nijinska was not herself a direct witness of that episode, could it have marked the beginning of this mania of persecution?

At no time did Diaghileff's friends cold-shoulder Nijinsky. Both Bakst and Benois received him amicably on many occasions.

[1] To W. N., April 5th, 1934.
[2] Grigorieff to Walter Nouvel.

They found him altered—garrulous where he had been taciturn, full of plans which would have been incapable of realization.

§ 5

During the early years of the War, Nijinsky suffered a very genuine persecution, removed from his beloved work, suspected, a prisoner of war in an enemy country; and then Diaghileff intervenes, stretches out his hand and saves him from this.

Madame Nijinska acknowledges the help of the Marchioness of Ripon and the Comtesse de Greffulhe, but she does not know that all these efforts were made at Diaghileff's initiative and insistence. Thanks to his numerous acquaintances in diplomatic circles throughout the world, he had succeeded in interesting the King of Spain, and even the Pope, in this dancer's fate. Such a struggle would appeal particularly to Sergei Pavlovitch. Russia had no further interest in Nijinsky, since he had severed his connection with the Maryinsky, and had not Diaghileff been organizing a season with the Metropolitan Opera in New York the Nijinskys would probably have remained in captivity till the end of the War. Ansermet, one of Diaghileff's greatest musical collaborators, writes:

"Having joined the troupe while Nijinsky was in Austria, and being a close friend of Diaghileff and Massine, I was obviously ranked by Nijinsky amongst the suspects. Diaghileff had spent all the summer and autumn of 1915 at Lausanne, where I was living at the time, paying for his company's keep, and rehearsing it in view of the approaching American season. I saw him almost daily, and was a witness to all the pains he took to obtain Nijinsky's release from his internment in Austria, and I even took some part in it. All the attempts mentioned by Madame Nijinska in her book, as well as some others that failed, were initiated by Diaghileff. He spent on these attempts, let it be mentioned, considerable sums, as certain intermediaries demanded large compensation. His plans and projects for the American season were based on the return of Nijinsky as well as on that of Karsavina."

These facts are confirmed not only by Walter Nouvel's own experience, but by Serge Grigorieff: "Had Diaghileff not existed, never would Nijinsky have obtained his release or gone to America." [1]

Diaghileff does more than that: through his influence and prestige he obtains for them a diplomatic passport, which greatly facilitates the difficult wartime journey, and which seems to have been a special source of pride and satisfaction to Madame Nijinska.

Whatever the situation in the past, there can be no doubt who is the debtor at this stage in the story. How is the debt repaid?

Ansermet continues:

"To allege that Diaghileff could have thought of dispensing with Nijinsky and Karsavina from the beginning is a calumny needing no refutation. Why should he have played this comedy to himself for so many months and invested his money in it? When it became known that neither Nijinsky nor Karsavina would be able to come on the date appointed for the beginning of the tour, it was too late for Diaghileff to abandon it. There was too much money and too much preparatory work invested there. Whatever the Americans themselves may have thought, Diaghileff had the right to insist, since he was bringing with him *Petrouchka*, *l'Oiseau de Feu*, and the rest of his programme— all first performances there. Thus we left for America, after having given a charity performance at the Opéra, Paris."

Here, as always, Diaghileff and his ballet, even a ballet of anonymous performers, was more important than any soloist, and when at times that fact was forgotten the soloist invariably

[1] Letter to W. N., March 20th, 1934.

suffered in pocket and prestige. Never at any epoch in the whole history of the art did one man, and a non-dancer, so entirely dominate his period, and the whole tragic story of Nijinsky— the greatest dancer in the world—is a vivid illustration of this fact.

Now, thanks to Diaghileff, Nijinsky was at last free to rejoin the company, and the time for the longed-for reconciliation had come. Diaghileff had held out his hand, advancing more than half-way, but apparently Nijinsky refused to take it—a fact difficult to reconcile with his whole previous conduct and utterances. Something had occurred to occasion this change of heart.

We come now to the long and involved question of the financial dispute between the two men. Nijinsky claims the sum of *half a million gold francs*, alleged to represent unpaid salary. It would be easy to reply that owing to the relationship between the two men Nijinsky had had everything paid to him, had received his entire keep as well as a generous allowance and lavish presents, but such an answer is inadequate, such a defence quite unnecessary here. What strikes one immediately is the enormous total of the sum—*half a million gold francs!*

Mr. Drobecki, admitted by Madame Nijinska to be a close and faithful friend, and manager of the Russian Ballets over a number of years, writes: "I cannot admit that Diaghileff owed Nijinsky half a million gold francs; I only know one thing— that he was keeping Nijinsky entirely, paying for his first-class hotels, first-class tailor's bills, and generally assuring him a life of luxury. Besides, *he paid important sums to the artist's current account at the bank*, where Nijinsky owned a considerable fortune. On one occasion, when Diaghileff was short of money to pay the salaries of the artists, he borrowed from Nijinsky seventeen thousand francs, which I personally reimbursed."

All who have known Diaghileff will realize that his undertaking was not commercial, that it did not at any time pay its

Karsavina and Nijinsky in *Giselle*

Nijinsky and Dolin in *Le Train Bleu*

Olga Spessivtseva in *Les Sylphides*

way, and that it relied for its existence on subsidies that Diaghileff succeeded in obtaining and which frequently proved insufficient. It is therefore possible that, before Nijinsky departed for the Argentine, Diaghileff borrowed from him a certain sum, and that it remained due. That this sum should have been anything approaching half a million gold francs is fantastic and incredible. In fact, as we see later in New York, when Madame Nijinska succeeds in causing certain sums to be deducted from Diaghileff's profits, the debt is completely paid off, and she does not refer to the subject again. It is of course impossible that during a three weeks' season Diaghileff should have been capable of paying so considerable a sum, half a million gold francs, as a mere deduction from the net profits!

If Diaghileff never gave Nijinsky any money, how did the couple live after their marriage?

We are given accounts of lavish expenditure, gowns, jewels, hotels, and journeys, and, in addition, when the expensive London season was a failure, we are told that Nijinsky paid his thirty artists for a whole year out of his savings. Nijinsky's reply to his parents-in-law when they suggest he should work and earn money is that it is not necessary. Indeed, Nijinsky's savings must have been considerable, for they were still in existence when he was released from captivity, and the Spanish Embassy in Vienna advanced him money on a letter of credit. At this period Nijinsky is certainly far better off than Diaghileff, and it is Diaghileff who has been the source of his whole fortune. Nijinsky must have owned, at the time when he broke with the Russian Ballet, and shortly before his illness, a fortune of at least a million gold francs.

Diaghileff was exceedingly scrupulous in money matters, and, like the scrupulous man, often expressed a rather grudging admiration for the business-man rogue. Nothing would cause him more worry than unpaid salaries; it was a point of honour with him that, however difficult the situation, his artists should always have the first claim; he was proud of the salaries he paid them; and this whole question of the half-million francs may just as easily have come innocently from the imagination as the reported conversation between Stravinsky and Nijinsky, in which the composer is supposed to have discussed his *Mavra,* which was only conceived five years later, and a quintet, which has not yet been written.

The meeting of the two men after a lapse of two and a half years since their break is marred by his financial question, and, when we realize Diaghileff's financial situation, it cannot be wondered at if he is annoyed by this fantastic bill.

With the declaration of war his entire enterprise was crumbling; he had signed a series of engagements for the 1914–15 season with a group of theatres in Central Europe. His company was dispersed, and most of the artists were obliged to return to Russia, while Baron Gunsbourg, his financial backer, had had to enlist. It was obviously impossible at the time to obtain any backing for ballet. Diaghileff had retained near him but a small group of artists, freed from military service, and made his headquarters in Switzerland and Italy in an attempt to continue the work and to arrange new creations. He was on the verge of ruin, when suddenly this American contract reached him with a welcome advance payment. His strength was renewed; he tried to collect his old artists and to engage new ones. In spite of untold difficulties, he succeeded in reconstituting the company and in rehearsing his entire repertoire, complete with scenery, costumes, and settings. When he arrived in New York, the advance payment was completely spent.

Nijinsky then, as a first step towards reconciliation, presents his bill! In fact, ever since landing in New York, the Nijinskys had been hostile in their attitude towards Diaghileff. M. Grigorieff writes: "Nijinsky came to us as an enemy in the full

acceptance of the word"; and M. Ansermet shows that this hostility was evident from the very beginning: "On our return from
a provincial tour we found Nijinsky had just arrived in New
York. His first action was to grant an interview, in which he
isolated himself from the rest of the company with the exception
of Bolm, throwing suspicion on the new elements of the troupe,
and denigrating all that had been done in his absence. In spite
of this behaviour the company received him with the greatest
courtesy and affection. Everybody knew against whom these
arrows were aimed. I called on him and spoke immediately about
Stravinsky. This name froze the air. Ever since meeting him in
Switzerland, Nijinsky imagined him to be an enemy, and it was
obvious from the first that all those who were, or appeared to
be, with Diaghileff were hostile." This certainly is the beginning of insanity, and not long afterwards yet another accusation
was put forward. There were rumours that Nijinsky was a de-
serter. His wife states that he was exempt from military service
as soloist to the Emperor, but this is inaccurate, as at no time had
Nijinsky been soloist to the Tsar, nor had he ever been exempt
from service, so that it is only natural that the question should
crop up. It is a little difficult to see what interest Diaghileff could
have in circulating rumours of desertion against his *premier
danseur*, a celebrity whose co-operation could only be advantage-
ous to him. We have seen what efforts Diaghileff made to secure
his services. The part played by Diaghileff in the matter is the
exact opposite. Mr. Drobecki writes: "I remember perfectly conversations with Diaghileff concerning Nijinsky's exemption
from military service—in fact, Diaghileff moved heaven and
earth in the matter, and once again succeeded in arranging the
matter satisfactorily."

There are many other trifling disagreements, but it is in the
arrangement for the next year's season that Diaghileff is the

most ill used, and his hard work to preserve the company dangerously menaced.

§ 6

For the following year, in America, Mr. Otto Kahn, as head of the Metropolitan Opera syndicate, had conceived the plan of a coast-to-coast tour. Nijinsky was popular, his European prestige was immense, and, with the enforced absence of Karsavina and Fokine from the troupe, he was in a position to dictate to the American management, who wanted a star at all costs—and the costs in this case were to be heavy. Nijinsky makes it an express condition that Diaghileff is not to accompany the tour. To complicate matters still further, he also decides to do without Grigorieff, most experienced of stage managers. He is to attempt to run the machine without the inventor and without the chief engineer. The artistic management and supervision of the whole tour is to be entrusted to Nijinsky, a dancer of genius certainly, but a man who is lost every time he has to buy himself a railway ticket or book a room at an hotel, who almost died in attempting to organize the disastrous London season, and whom the doctor had expressly forbidden to do anything but dance and rest. This is the man who is now to organize, to create, to dance, and at the same time be fêted and lionized. No one could perform such a feat; even Pavlova herself never attempted anything of the kind.

Diaghileff does not resist. He appears to be perfectly satisfied with the solution, since other projects—the building of the future—attract him much more. He is in a hurry to join his friends, above all Stravinsky, as well as his new collaborators, Picasso, Derain, Larionov, and Gontcharova.

Exiled from his own enterprise, Diaghileff sails for Europe, leaving behind him two managers: Mr. Drobecki, the Nijinskys', and Mr. Barocchi, at that time married to Lydia Lopokova, *ballerina* of the company, with the dancer Kremneff in Grigorieff's position as stage manager.

The tour is of course a complete failure. It was doomed from the start. Nijinsky has done everything to render himself helpless, and it does not require the acts of any enemy to bring disaster.

The important creation of the season, *Tyl Eulenspiegel*, is a fiasco. On the first night it is not fully composed and the company is forced to improvise. It is only given for a few performances and then dropped.[1] Its failure proves the great part played by Diaghileff and his *entourage* in Nijinsky's work—a part that Diaghileff never at any time claimed either in speech or writing. It was, in fact, his habit to give his artists the entire credit, and his pride to point out that he had not been mistaken in his selection of them.

Ansermet writes:

"Nijinsky's first ballets, which he carried to a successful conclusion, were born in that atmosphere of Diaghileff's, where a certain collaboration was always at work, however difficult it may be to analyse."

§ 7

It is not my object to belittle Nijinsky, but merely to arrive at the truth, and to remove him from a false position that he himself would at no time have been prepared to assume.

In this connection the true story of his first creation, *l'Après-midi d'un faune*, is illuminating. It shows the actual process not merely of the creation of a ballet, but of the creation of a choreographer.

It is only natural that Diaghileff should wish to make his

[1] Interview with Lydia Sokolova, London, 1934.

favourite into a choreographer, especially as he realized that the régime of Fokine could not last for ever.

After a trip to Greece, Diaghileff, and still more especially Bakst, were haunted by the recent discoveries at Knossus and by Greek archaic art. Bakst dreamed of interpreting these things on the stage. They discussed the matter at length, searching for a subject and music that would be adequate. Finally they agreed on Mallarmé's *Eclogue*, of the existence of which Nijinsky was not aware till the work was completed, and Debussy's music. They decided too that they would give Nijinsky his first chance with this work, but they kept the strictest supervision of detail in their own hands, and, as far as the central idea was concerned, they resolved to make of the ballet a moving bas-relief, all in profile, a ballet with no dancing but only movement and plastic attitude—the inspiration for all this being solely Bakst's. There is no truth in the assertion that Nijinsky conducted his rehearsals in private, only admitting Diaghileff when the work was complete.

As Bakst has said on many occasions, after having explained at length to Nijinsky the character and style which they wished to give to the work, Diaghileff and he followed each rehearsal with care, correcting and guiding Nijinsky at every step.[1] Indeed, they had the greatest difficulty in making their meaning clear to him, and he in his turn found it difficult to explain it to the dancers. Finally, after the superhuman difficulties of the three concerned and with the goodwill of the whole company, the work was achieved. This is the explanation of the unheard-of fact that the choreography of a ballet lasting but ten minutes,

[1] This is fully confirmed by Igor Stravinsky: "*A la suggestion de Bakst, qui était emballé pour la Grèce archaïque, ce tableau devait figurer un bas-relief animé, avec sa plastique de profil. La part de Bakst dans ce ballet, l'Après-midi d'un faune, était prédominante. Sans parler du cadre décoratif et des beaux costumes qu'il avait créés, c'est lui encore qui indiquait le moindre geste de la chorégraphie.*"—*Chroniques de ma vie.*

and taking eight artists in all, should have needed a hundred and twenty rehearsals.

M. Ansermet confirms all Bakst's statements: "As an instructor in ballet-dancing Nijinsky was entirely lacking in pedagogical gifts. When we resumed performances of *l'Après-midi d'un faune* in Rio, I recall that he forced me to go over the beginning of the second movement, where the 'cellos have a *motif en triples croches*, twenty-three times, because he could not make it clear to the artists what he wished them to do. This man, who had the most beautiful visions of movement when he had to express them himself, was, when he tried to create, tied to the details, and unable to liberate himself from them in order to recapture the general theme."

Ansermet goes on to give an admirable summary of Nijinsky's character:

"I have been able but rarely, and only intermittently, to converse with Nijinsky. Observing him from a distance as well as at close quarters, I have always thought that he suffered from a latent conflict between his genius as a dancer—that grace which nature had bestowed on him—and his critical faculties. Had Nijinsky been left alone, he would as a born dancer have limited himself to the interpretation of music according to a rather accurate feeling for it. His sole aim would have been his own plastic perfection. In short, he would have done what Pavlova was doing with more taste and inventiveness, and he would have been perfectly happy. But he lived when all traditions were being questioned. Diaghileff wished him to submit his art not only to an æsthetic theory, but also to a constantly changing æsthetic theory. As long as he was under Diaghileff's influence, he materialized the latter's ideas, unconsciously and without realizing that what he was doing was, to say the least, half suggested through an atmosphere where several creative brains were working ceaselessly under the stimulus of this insatiable man.

"Once away from this influence, Diaghileff's ideas were capable only of upsetting him, and of contradicting his true nature. The latter was all too simple, one might almost say even too healthy, for æsthetic speculation.

"Therein lay the real conflict between Diaghileff and Nijinsky, as also, probably, Diaghileff's only fault towards him. Diaghileff's weakness in general consisted in thinking that he could make choreographers out of artists who were not born to it, though otherwise richly endowed.

"The illusion of culture, which had enveloped Nijinsky while he was at Diaghileff's side, gave birth in him to aspirations which his intellect was incapable of realizing. He was ceaselessly a prey to thoughts which held him a prisoner and within which he moved as in a vicious circle.

"The deficiency of the intellectual control of this instinctive nature is apparent in a thought which he once tried to explain. It was the notion that, since his family had acquired the faculty of exceptional leaps, he expected that his grandchildren should be able to fly. He considered it a logical result of the Darwinian principle of the evolution of species.

"I should here like to mention another instance of Nijinsky's queer logic. One of the dancers had a taste for learning, and one day, when I was walking up and down the deck with Nijinsky, we met her reading attentively. 'Always books,' exclaimed Nijinsky; 'what is this one? Ah, Newton. Isn't that the man who, standing under a tree, saw an apple fall—and this gave him the idea of electricity?' He said this with a mischievous smile, as if he did not believe it himself. One would be wrong to dismiss it as mere nonsense. No doubt he knew that it was the law of gravitation which was in question; but when he was about to find it in his memory he considered the relation too simple. He wanted something more eminently genial, more surprising. He conceived the striking or the admirable only in what was completely irrational. It is a kink of the brain fertile in art, because it is a guarantee against the conventional, but even there common sense is sometimes a necessity.

"In my opinion Nijinsky's tragedy is as follows. He was endowed with a personality which on its irrational side possessed a marvellous power of communication with the world, of self-revelation, in dancing. On the rational side, however, it had remained in an infantile state, and closed. Had he been able to express his personality solely by means of that part of his being open to the exterior, he could have been perfectly happy, but he was ambitious, and life led him to make use of that other part of his personality—incapable of self-expression. He wished to raise both poles of his being to the same level. *The tension between them both was too strong*—and his being was wrecked."

Nijinsky was an instinctive choreographer. Every other choreographer of note has arrived on the scene of rehearsal with a mental ballet almost fully worked out, that is only slightly modified when it is united to, or expressed by, the artists, though the last-minute details, as in *Les Sylphides*, may be the making of the ballet as a whole. Nijinsky was essentially the dancer, conceiving movement experimentally in terms of his own body. He was accustomed to sit for hours in a darkened room, visualizing movements and then working them out bit by bit. A whole morning's work might give him but one instant that really mattered. The movements he devised were worked out in the rehearsal room by actual experiment on the dancers themselves, a method that it is uninspiring to follow, but that can give certain remarkable though limited results in a novel direction.

I believe that Diaghileff himself was disappointed in Nijinsky as a creator of ballet, and hence his lack of interest whenever Nijinsky wished to discuss his future plans with him. This would account in full for Diaghileff's decision to return to Europe, leaving Nijinsky in charge. He was, as we know, sufficient of a fighter to have resisted these absurd and humiliating conditions had he had the slightest inclination to do so. Massine was at hand, his gifts were beginning to be revealed, and it was there that the future clearly lay.

Diaghileff never allowed personal questions to interfere with the work he had planned, never bore a grudge for any length of time. One day he might quarrel bitterly, violently; insult and be insulted by his opponent; but a week or two later the whole matter would be forgotten, and he would greet him with the remark, "What about our collaboration?"

This ballet of Diaghileff's was no fixed business run on commercial principles, with a regular board of directors; to carry on with a business simile, there was a new deal, with a new board, for every single work undertaken. The accusation that Diaghileff made and then promptly unmade his collaborators in order to leave himself in a strong position will not bear investigation. He had no need of such a device. His own position was unassailable because the particular liaison work that he did could only be carried out by a lay expert in every branch of art. He created the position, and, when he died, it died with him—although magnificent ballet, of a different type, continues.

These dates of various collaborations show Diaghileff's fidelity :

Alexandre Benois: 1909, *Pavillon d'Armide* and *Les Sylphides;* 1911, *Petrouchka;* 1914, *Rossignol;* 1924, *Médecin malgré Lui* and *Philémon et Baucis.*

Leon Bakst without interruption from 1909 to 1917, and again with *The Sleeping Princess,* 1921.

Jean Cocteau: 1912, *Le Dieu Bleu,* 1917, *Parade,* and 1925, *Le Train Bleu.*

Michael Larionov: 1915–22, and again in 1929.

Stravinsky: 1910, 1911, 1913, 1914, 1920, 1922, 1923, 1924, 1927, 1928, 1929.

Prokofiev: 1921, 1927, 1929.
Fokine: 1909–12, 1914.
Massine: 1915–21, 1925, 1927, 1928.

In fact, Diaghileff, as this list so clearly shows, always returned to his old collaborators after a brief separation. He did not exploit them, but paid them handsomely for their contributions, and encouraged them to give of their very best. Once they had left him, without exception they longed to return to the stimulating atmosphere of his presence. It would be to misunderstand the nature of his work completely to expect him to accomplish his long career with only one set of artists. Had such a thing happened, not only would his enterprise have been doomed, but Nijinsky himself would never have had the opportunity to create.

From this record we can clearly see that, if Diaghileff did not persist with Nijinsky, it was because for one reason or another Nijinsky had nothing new to give to the ballet as Diaghileff conceived it. It is consistent with Diaghileff's whole character to sacrifice a friend for the work in hand, but not to sacrifice friend or enemy while there was still something worth while to be shown. His gift was not passive—merely to hold the peace among creative artists. Had that been so, there might be something in the charge that at times he deliberately kept them apart. But such an action would have been negative, and there was never anything negative in his character, as his whole achievement shows.

The only reason that after the War he called his company "Les Ballets Russes. Saison de Serge de Diaghileff" was the urgent insistence of his friends because, following his success, many mushroom companies had sprung up under the name *ballets russes,* which no longer had any meaning. Diaghileff himself objected to this for many years. With him the quality of the work always counted, and not his personal reputation.

§ 8

The difficulties of the American tour hastened the climax of Nijinsky's dreadful malady. He became morose, saw plots everywhere, and soon fell under the influence of two fanatics, who attempted to ruin his art and his domestic life. There were occasions when a distracted stage manager had to go to his hotel to beg him to dance, while he dreamed of the peace of the simple peasant life as a reaction from the difficulties that were fast crowding in upon him.

Actually this American tour based on Nijinsky's name and reputation, to which Mr. Otto Kahn had been forced to sacrifice Diaghileff, caused the management of the Metropolitan a severe financial loss which reacted on Diaghileff, who was never able to reimburse himself.

Grigorieff writes [1]:

"You know only too well how this enterprise ended. It was a complete fiasco, and Otto Kahn remained indebted to Sergei Pavlovitch to the amount of several hundred thousand francs."

Nijinsky, of course, had his salary paid in full.

The next meeting with Diaghileff was in Spain, with the same clouded mind that makes understanding impossible. Diaghileff had wired to invite Nijinsky for another South American tour, and Nijinsky had accepted in principle, and then imagined that he had been tricked into appearing, when he was told that in Spain an exchange of telegrams is a binding contract. The simple way out, if he had wanted one, would have been to demand an exorbitant fee, since no terms had yet been mentioned. This evidently did not occur to him.

[1] To W. N., March 28th, 1934.

Once again the two religious maniacs have him completely under their control, and Nijinsky's intuitive nature, always inclined towards a dreamy and obscure mysticism, makes him promising soil for all influences of this kind.

It seems a pity that Madame Nijinska in her difficulties did not confide in Diaghileff. He would have been a powerful ally, and their interests this time were at any rate identical. Diaghileff severely reprimanded the two men concerned, but his influence over Nijinsky was by now a thing of the past.

Of the unhappy incidents on this tour Grigorieff writes [1]:

"In spite of Sergei Pavlovitch's sincere desire to collaborate with Nijinsky, good relations between them could only be reached with difficulty. Nijinsky now wanted to play the part of a director, to manage everything and to guide the enterprise as he wished. Certain divergences occurred, petty intrigues as regards the participation in different ballets, the alternation of artists in their rôles, the billing and publicity. When after the Madrid season we left for Barcelona, realizing that he could no longer direct as in America, Nijinsky decided to leave, greatly harming our enterprise." [2]

"It is by pure chance that the flight was discovered. We lived in the same hotel, Diaghileff, Nijinsky, and I. At six p.m., when Sergei Pavlovitch was by chance leaving the hotel, he noticed Nijinsky's luggage in the entrance-hall in charge of the hall-porter, who was about to send it to the station. On his enquiry, the latter informed him that the Nijinskys were shortly leaving for Madrid."

Diaghileff had no other course but to prevent this irresponsible flight, by force if necessary, since the consequences to him and to every member of the troupe would have been serious, starting with the scandal of a countermanded performance, the

[1] To W. N., March 28th, 1934.
[2] Barocchi confirms this. Letter to W. N., August 3rd, 1934.

irretrievable compromising of the Barcelona season, and the annulment of the South American contract.

Diaghileff immediately went to the Governor of Barcelona, laid the situation before him, and orders were given to prevent the flight.

"The situation was explained to Nijinsky," says Grigorieff; "and he submitted, and the same evening a special agent of the Government was appointed to watch over him; he was not arrested, but this surveillance was continued until the close of our season."

In the middle of July, Nijinsky and the troupe left for South America, while Diaghileff, with Massine and sixteen dancers, proceeded to Italy.

It was the final separation. Six years later, when they met again, the being whom the world acclaimed as Nijinsky, the greatest of all dancers, was no longer there in fact; the photograph that shows us the two men together mercifully conceals the terrible tragedy of Nijinsky's end.

§ 9

On receipt of the tragic news of Nijinsky's complete breakdown, Diaghileff was heartbroken, and the whole unpleasant stage of their relationship was forgotten. Explained by what had happened, it could be forgiven. Diaghileff's one thought now was to find some means of restoring the broken mind. He visited Nijinsky, took him to rehearsals, chided him gently for not dancing, and on one unforgettable occasion took him to see Karsavina and Lifar in *Petrouchka*, in the hope that this would awaken one little spark of interest. It was of no avail. Whether Nijinsky recognized him or not one does not know. Once, frantic with joy at the news that there was some improvement, Diaghileff journeyed to Paris, only to meet with disappointment. There he shared with Romola Nijinska her great sorrow. Before the immensity of the tragedy there could be no recrimination on either side. Perhaps at last, in his passive state, Nijinsky had found peace.

For me, the pleasantest ending and the most generous was in a conversation that I had with Nijinsky's daughter, Kyra.

Nijinsky had wanted a son to carry on the great tradition of his family, but Kyra, his daughter, may do so. She is very much Nijinsky—the same slanting Mongol eyes, the same feet and legs, and with a nature that is sweet, understanding, simple, and forgiving. She can truly speak for her father.

After telling me of her early memories of him, before his brain was clouded, of all her love for him "whom she worshipped like a god," she went on: "I remember one day Diaghileff coming to our flat in Paris. I must have been about nine at the time. Father was already very ill, and Diaghileff hoped to awaken something in him. He came up to father, spoke a few quiet words, but father only stared into space beyond him, looking at nothing. There was no trace of recognition. I could see how Diaghileff suffered, and I felt infinitely sorry for him. Then he spoke to me, just some conventional phrases of the kind one speaks to a child. At once I felt all his charm, and I loved him.

"Now that I am old enough to understand, I am infinitely grateful to this great man for my father's sake. I honour and respect his memory. He understood him as no one else ever could, he gave him the chance to develop and show his wonderful creations to the world—yes, I am truly grateful."

It is in that spirit that we must look on this story of the complex relationship between these two unusual men, who together gave so much positive beauty to the world that it seems a tragic thing to see in it nothing more than a rather sordid melodrama.*

* It is only just to state that Nijinsky's sister, Bronislava, disagrees with this version, as with Romola Nijinsky's.—A. L. H.

──CHAPTER XIII──

DIAGHILEFF AND THE BALLET
1909–1914

THE STORY OF AN EVOLUTION: PART II

The new element in dancing under Diaghileff—Music—Painting—Choreography—Diaghileff and Fokine—Diaghileff on classicism.

"Classicism like everything else evolves."

DIAGHILEFF

"The art of dancing is the most difficult, delicate, and refractory art. It never condones mistakes."

DIAGHILEFF

"It is from this time that the Russian Ballet began to annex the music of Chopin and Schumann and Greek costumes; some ballet dancers even went as far as to discard their shoes and stockings."

ISADORA DUNCAN

We have followed Diaghileff as an individual up to the War, which marks the close of the first phase of his activities, and we have tried wherever possible to trace his own share in each creation, but often that has been lost, immediately the voices died away over the supper-table. It has never been possible to take Diaghileff completely away from the many who surround him, and now more and more he is only to be found in his work. It is important, therefore, to study that work in some detail, and to estimate the actual development of dancing and of the ballet under his control. If it is not of Diaghileff himself that we are now talking, it is of the Diaghileff Ballet. From what we now know of the man we shall not easily lose sight of him.

In these five years the actual dancing itself has undergone

very little change, though the whole conception of the functions of the dancer have been altered, and dancers now earn their applause from a different public and for different reasons. Till 1911, as regards personnel, Diaghileff's Ballet is still the travelling branch of the Imperial Theatres, and, even after that date, there is no need for him to form dancers of his own with the Imperial School at the end of the wire. Only the accident of war and revolution ever made that necessary.

Though he employs the same dancers as the Maryinsky, his actual use of them is entirely different, and those that he selects are not necessarily the same who will enjoy the greatest success at home. From the moment of the Paris triumph there is a wide gulf in taste between Paris and St. Petersburg. The most popular works in his repertoire, though later shown in Russia, are never in any sense a general success. The proof of that lies in the fact that Soviet Russia in its ballet taste has not altered since pre-revolutionary days. The same ballets are given—only without the creative and supervising genius of Petipa.

Under Diaghileff, the dancer who might have been overshadowed at home has a greater chance of revealing herself. There are three ballets in the evening, there is a daily performance, so that fresh dancers are constantly in demand. The influences at work on them are educational—travel and meeting with leading European artists must have its effect. It was never Diaghileff's desire to change the accepted technique. He admired it, and saw in it the perfect instrument for his requirements. He engaged Cecchetti from the Imperial Theatres to coach his company. Cecchetti was never at any time capable of understanding Diaghileff's aims, but Diaghileff appreciated the classical system and wished for no other. Any subsequent change of policy in the training of his dancers was forced on him by external circumstances, and then he tried to develop a new system that should most nearly approximate to the old. At this particular period he could discover artists who were already trained and reveal to them their true bent—later, it was necessary not only to discover them, but to have them taught as well.

In dancing, this period is intimately associated with Karsavina and Nijinsky. Both are known in Russia, but both are in some respects his discoveries too. It is in the case of Karsavina, *ballerina* in his company and at the Maryinsky at the same time, that this is best seen. Meet a Russian *balletomane* who has never left his country. He will know Karsavina, and admire her as we do; but it will be a completely different Karsavina, and only rarely will the rôles overlap, and only someone who has travelled between Paris and St. Petersburg knows the full extent of her artistry. Russia saw a brilliant solitary star, one of some half-dozen in the whole country, a dazzling virtuoso of the old repertoire—Western Europe saw her as part of a company, perhaps the finest part, but definitely linked to the whole, with the emphasis on expression rather than on execution. Such a double personality is unique in theatrical history. In detail of make-up and interpretation Diaghileff definitely influenced those who danced for him.[1]

In music this period definitely follows the line struck out by Duncan, dancing to ready-made music, not because Duncan had done so, but because it was natural for a young organization, and the only manner in which the original composer could learn the requirements of ballet. Diaghileff did not commission music haphazard. He brought the composer into close contact with the ballet and its *entourage*, and waited for the idea to take shape; and some of the composers whose works were subsequently performed had their first experience of ballet through orchestrating these early works. Stravinsky's first work for Diaghileff was the

[1] " 'Omission is the essence of art . . . livid face—eyebrows in a single line' (from Diaghileff). Nothing more, yet that was enough to touch the spring that made me see all *Thamar* in a flash."—Karsavina, *Theatre Street.*

orchestration of a portion of *Les Sylphides*. In this first period, too, Diaghileff's own practical knowledge played a very large part in the selection and preparation of the music. Many of the works were a patchwork that only a skilled hand could have directed without complete disaster. To this day there are many who assail the taste of orchestrating Chopin at all—perhaps they are justified, though the actual manner in which it was done was highly skilled. *Les Sylphides, Carnaval, Le Spectre de la Rose, Sheherazade, l'Après-midi d'un faune, Cléopâtre, Thamar* are all examples of the adapting of already existing music to ballet, which after this period becomes comparatively rare, and is only adopted in the case of arranging ballets from older works: *Pulcinella, La Boutique Fantasque, Les Dieux Mendiants*.

This first period is more definitely the painter's period. The group surrounding Diaghileff was plastic in outlook, and the most urgently needed reforms were decorative. Vsevolojsky had already begun the musical battle when he enlisted Tchaikovsky and Glazounov.

Bakst and Benois, painters, both play a very large part in inaugurating choreographic ideas, which are then adapted to suitable music.

For the first time in its history Russian art was influencing the whole of the rest of Europe, turning its leading artists towards the theatre, teaching them the *métier*. Bakst, who did his finest work in these years, was of all artists most close to Diaghileff and his ideas. He identified himself absolutely with the spectacle—so much so that his easel work suffered. In its *décor* this period is exotic; in its music and theme, romantic; in its choreography, neo-classic.

The three important new creations musically are: Stravinsky's *l'Oiseau de Feu, Petrouchka,* and *Le Sacre du Printemps*. They mark the beginning of the Diaghileff Ballet, with its complete fusion of the arts.

259

§ 2

It is on Fokine, of all his choreographers, that Diaghileff had the least direct influence, for his neo-classicism was already evolving. Fokine was a man making the same journey as Diag-hileff, and one cannot doubt that he was the richer for such a travelling companion.

Prince Igor, more than any other ballet, was calculated to cause a sensation in Paris. Not only was it Slav, savage, exotic, but it made full use of the male dancer, and Paris was unused to male dancing of any kind. Its savagery even made some of the Russians doubt, but the horde of savage warriors completely conquered Paris. It still remains his most perfect work, the one in which he would wish to see nothing altered.

Les Sylphides,[1] originally *Chopiniana,* was in its first version given a romantic story in which Chopin figured, but later that was dropped, and the suite of dances we know so well was carved out of it. Fokine's orientation can clearly be seen in the costumes—long ballet skirts *à la* Taglioni instead of the exaggeratedly small fringe that was the fashion. It was this skirt, symbol of a return to romanticism, that prompted Diaghileff to rename the ballet after Taglioni's *La Sylphide.* This ballet, like so many of Fokine's works, was first designed for a charity matinée, and proved so successful that the Imperial Theatres purchased the rights, and, as *Chopiniana,* it was performed in Russia by every great *ballerina.* Diaghileff always maintained that there was no *corps de ballet,* only *premières danseuses,* and that so important is the dancing of each member that one faulty movement can spoil the whole romantic reverie. The inspired grouping was actually arranged at the last minute before curtain-

[1] Some account of the origins of these ballets is given in this chapter, strictly out of its place, since it is necessary to establish the manner in which they were created in order to do full justice to Fokine.—A. L. H.

rise. Diaghileff as a musician fully realized the artistic pitfalls of orchestrating Chopin. He laid himself open to fierce criticism, and actually received it from musical purists. One cannot doubt that in principle they were justified, though in this particular case so close is the mood of the action to the spirit of the music that it is pedantic to invoke principles. However, Diaghileff took every possible precaution in having the music entirely reorchestrated by the finest musical talents available. Throughout the twenty-five years of the Ballet's existence *Les Sylphides* remained in the repertoire, rehearsed almost weekly under the careful supervision of Grigorieff and Diaghileff himself, whose favourite work it remained. Since then it has been given by every company, changes have crept in, but the magic of the original remains, and it has been the contact between the dancers of yesterday and to-day. A volume could be written on its various interpretations, on the correct make-up and style of hair-dressing, but even without all that it lives as does no other ballet.

Carnaval, another romantic ballet, was also conceived for a charity entertainment. The humorous magazine *Satyricon* was organizing a dance in a large public ballroom, and the whole festival was to be called *Carnaval*. Schumann's music immediately suggested itself to Fokine, and he read up the period at length. Leon Bakst seemed the ideal decorator, and Fokine himself paid him part of his fee, for which he was presented with a picture. The actual choreography was composed in three rehearsals, so spontaneously did it arise out of music and *décor*. At first Diaghileff hesitated about taking the work into the repertoire, but at last gave in to the insistence of Bakst and Benois. Again the musical difficulty presented itself, and the piano music was entirely reorchestrated by Glazounov, Rimsky-Korsakov, Liadov, and Tcherepnin, and the work transferred from ballroom to stage. The original Harlequin created by Leontiev became very much Nijinsky's own, and later it was possible to revive it with the brilliant Stanislas Idzikovski. Though it has been given many times since, the difficulties of Harlequin, especially in the Paganini variation, have always marred the performances.

§ 3

In these ballets Diaghileff came nearer playing the part of *impresario* than at any other time in his career, but even that is not a fair statement. He cut them drastically and cleaned them up, especially musically, so that they would stand the most searching criticism in every detail, and Grigorieff has assured me that the difference in them after Diaghileff's work upon them was considerable. Even so the ballet of the first few years, until the collaboration over *Petrouchka* and *l'Oiseau de Feu*, is more fairly called the Fokine ballet, the manifestation of his successful revolt against the academism of the Imperial Stage. He was assisted by Diaghileff, and ably so, but never in any sense discovered by him, any more than were Bakst or others of the early collaborators. In his later utterances Diaghileff would seem to have resented this somewhat, and he never gave to Fokine the generous acknowledgment that was his due. As a result Fokine was perhaps the less willing to admit Diaghileff's great artistic achievement, so that in their remarks on one another neither man's contribution to art stands out clear, and it is necessary to examine the history of these early years with considerable attention, and to weigh carefully the statements made by both the men.

If Fokine carried the ballet to glory with the indispensable assistance of Diaghileff and his advisers, Diaghileff himself was able to continue it, and to make it his own beyond all dispute, so that Fokine—the initial phase in a cycle—is not the "phase" that made that "cycle" into a practical possibility.

Diaghileff realized from the first that the greatest difficulty that confronted him lay in the selection of choreographers. He saw that it would be impossible to rely always upon Fokine, not through any shortcomings on his part, but because a change from time to time was essential. He could not send to Russia for a ready-made *maître de ballet* in sympathy with his ideals, so he set out to create one. At the back of this there must have been the natural desire to play a closer part in the creation of ballet and to express his own ideas more concretely. Nijinsky was the obvious selection, and his brief interlude, in the midst of Fokine's reign, assumes a larger importance in the history of ballet than the small number of his works or their actual importance merits. It proved to Diaghileff that a choreographer could be formed by him; it removed the ballet from classic influences; and even the sensations that ensued upon the production of *l'Après-midi d'un faune* and *Le Sacre du Printemps* were welcomed by him not merely as publicity, but also as showing both to the public and to himself that he was in advance of the times.

His own position with regard to classicism is interesting and always consistent. He loved it, seemed to turn his back on it, yet returned to it again and again as a source of inspiration and strength. On the question of classicism in training he was quite positive. He admitted no other system. It created the dancer who could perform both *Les Sylphides* and the Dance of the Chosen Virgin in *Le Sacre du Printemps*—the perfect exponent of his ideas.

There may undoubtedly have been some exaggeration of modernism, as the real reasons for this departure are three, not only the logically single one as explained by Diaghileff himself. We must reckon with accidental and psychological factors as well. At the close of this first period the War cuts him off from the *Mir Isskustva*, his friends who provided the initial inspiration and the ballast of the enterprise. They had developed him and developed with him, so that progress at first was gradual.

Cut off from them, uprooted, he must educate a new group of artists unfamiliar with the tradition, and therefore more boldly experimental. The other reason, the psychological, is more important still. As a young man Diaghileff could remain close to tradition without the fear of being considered a back number. He was known as the leader of a successful revolt against academism, and that label could suffice him for years. When he grew older, leaving behind him the scenes of his early triumphs, he was not so secure. With him it was a crying need to be considered ahead of his time; with *Petrouchka*, *Le Sacre du Printemps*, and *l'Après-midi d'un faune* he had aroused a storm which greatly pleased him and convinced him that he was still a very young man and on the right track. The fear of death and decay was all the time urging him on. It is the unconscious mainspring of each one of his moves.

He made a very clear distinction between classical training and the classical mode of expression—a distinction that has not been understood by so many of those who have sought a new direction for the dance and, for all their revolutionary ardour, have never travelled the distance of Diaghileff but have remained in a backwater. In the first part of his argument, the necessity for change, they would follow him whole-heartedly.

"Life doesn't stand still—it changes. Even nature seems to change its aspect. Where will you find to-day the classic landscape of the Romantic period, with its willows, its lake, the marble figures, and the sluggish clouds?

"The lake has been filled in and the trees cut to give way to signals, stations, and rails. The physical organism gets old, and is destroyed, but art itself must have a permanent youth, change, and be renovated.

"When I am accused of going to the Left, it is a great compliment. I am growing younger. I have always loathed habit and routine.

"I am accused of treating classicism with neglect and contempt. Rubbish! Classicism, like everything else, evolves. We must make up our minds what is classicism. There were outcries, at first, about the music of Igor Stravinsky—now it is classic. In Vienna, in 1911, when I produced *Petrouchka*, the orchestra wished to resign, and the oboes declared that they could not play such poisonous music.

"Yes, first one must find new music. Every year it becomes more difficult, but it is ridiculous to say that there is a poverty of talent. The greatest difficulty lies in discovering choreographers. The real choreographer must be a man of culture, he must remember Noverre. A new *maître de ballet* is a great event. I have been singularly lucky in this respect.

"The science of our theatrical dance is very young. While classical painting and sculpture were created centuries ago, ballet classicism was created in the eighteenth century and developed in the nineteenth with the ballet skirt, the dancer's uniform of last century. Classicism is the university of the modern choreographer, but to develop theatrical creation we cannot remain academic. We have all learned Algebra and Greek, but not to solve problems or to speak Greek. The dancer and ballet master of to-day must matriculate, just as Picasso must know anatomy and Stravinsky his scales.

"Duncan, Dalcroze, Wigman and Laban—all these are creators looking for new schools. But their struggle with classicism has taken Germany into a *cul-de-sac* from which it cannot escape. Germany can move beautifully, but she has forgotten how to dance. Yet from all this we must not conclude that the path of modern choreography lies exclusively in being in love with the *tutu*. Those who believe this belong to societies for the preservation of ancient monuments. Creators of skyscrapers could easily add arms to the Venus de Milo, because they have had a classical education, but the Greek doors of the Carnegie

Library and the Doric columns of New York railway stations offend our eyes.

"Skyscrapers have a classicism of their own, they are the palaces of our time. Classicism is a means—but not an end. When it becomes merely a restoration, we must destroy the poison that affects the whole organ. That is how classicism appeared to me in Ida Rubinstein's recent performances. I can say so, because twenty years ago I brought into the dance the mysterious, extravagant, biblical Rubinstein. How could she spoil the impression that seemed unforgettable?"

That is the sense of his direction throughout the twenty years. In the time of which we are speaking the signs of an approaching change are evident only in the Nijinsky interlude, but shortly it will be here for good.

To many this first period is the richest and most perfect of all. When we have discounted the sentimental memories of the past, there is much to support that view. The work of the first five years endures to the present day, when revivals of more recent ballets are impossibly dated. The link with Russia was closer, the collaboration between Diaghileff and his friends had been carefully tested, and they worked in natural harmony. Diaghileff was young, and the feverish quest for a lost youth that marred so many of his later efforts was yet to come.

It is only natural—remembering his dictatorial instincts— that he should be prouder of the later years in which his discoveries were greater and his indebtedness to his friends far less. It is a sign of his greatness that he did not persist in the work of these years and reduce it to a formula. There was never such a thing as a Diaghileff formula.

——CHAPTER XIV——

THE WAR YEARS
1914–1918

"The War was nothing else but a struggle between two cultures that cannot be decided by force of arms."

DIAGHILEFF

The London season ended on July 25th, and the outbreak of the War found Diaghileff in Venice, whither he had gone as usual. He went immediately to Rome, and then settled in Florence, where he had taken a villa so small that when any more than three sat down to table it was necessary to open a door leading into another room.

There seemed little possibility of his being able to continue the work. The holidays, and then the War, had scattered the whole company, and the majority of the dancers were home again in Russia. All his engagements for a prolonged autumn and winter tour of Central Europe had naturally fallen through, leaving him in a desperate financial situation. It would have occurred to no one but Diaghileff that, war or no war, his Russian Ballet must continue its activities. The Paris Opéra was closed, travelling was a tedious and risky business, and there were not enough neutral countries in Europe to keep a company in work the whole year round. At the moment, too, there was no company to keep, or, to be exact, only one member— Massine.

Although he had formed his own troupe in 1911, the main strength of the company was still "borrowed" from the Maryinsky. Now it was necessary to start an entirely new enterprise,

267

to keep alive a whole group of artists, entirely cut off from their homes—something more complex than 1909 or 1911.

Only a man of one idea would have persisted, only a fighter could have succeeded. What is more, during these war years he did not mark time. They were years of intense creative activity, in which he began to develop a totally new æsthetic. He prepared the young Leonide Massine, both as dancer and choreographer, and through him he produced many of his most outstanding works, the mainstay of his post-war programme. Today it seems scarcely possible to credit such an achievement. The Russian Ballet remained almost as a small independent state, a world of art under its king, Diaghileff, respected by the belligerents on both sides, with powerful allies, when they were needed, in the Pope, the King of Spain, and President Wilson. It had taken but five years to establish himself thus; five years on top of the *Mir Isskustva* experiences and his stepmother's lessons in Perm—"When you want to you can."

Round Massine he started to rebuild a company. The great *maestro* Cecchetti was there, working daily to create still another *premier danseur*. Now he worked with Massine as he had done with Nijinsky, giving him the knowledge that he himself had acquired from Giovanni Lepri, and that went right back to the very origins of the classical system. The intelligent restless mind of Massine was to give it a new lease of life in the years to come, to add to it the vitality of the Spanish national dance and the richness of museums, for the "art of ballet is but three hundred years old, while man's plastic knowledge is ageless." [1] Never did Diaghileff send more telegrams than in these few months. From the famous school in Warsaw he secured two magnificent new recruits: Stanislas Idzikovski, whom the lack of two inches robbed of the fame that was Nijinsky's, a dancer of truly prodigious classical technique, and Leon Woizikovski, later

[1] Massine to the author, a conversation, 1934.

a pillar of strength in every rôle assigned him—Bolm's, Nijin-sky's, Massine's, and his own. From a private school in Moscow —Nelidova's—he found a young dancer, Vera Nemchinova, later to be his *prima ballerina*, and from the Maryinsky he en-gaged the brilliant Olga Spessivtseva, since then one of his very favourite artists. Lydia Sokolova, too, rejoined the company. It was young, raw, but never had there been more promising mate-rial, and Cecchetti was there.

Diaghileff also succeeded in reuniting a "cabinet." As always, he was surrounded by his group of "geniuses"—the word is his. Stravinsky was living close by in Morges (Switzerland), unfit for military service on account of his eyesight. More and more he was entering into the future programmes, and now in their isolation, the two were able to form a close collaboration that lasted till the very end, and an enduring friendship. Stravinsky also brought the brilliant conductor, Ernest Ansermet, into the family.

Larionov, the latest artist to be associated with the ballet, after a few weeks at war, was invalided out of the army. Once again Diaghileff spent a small fortune on telegrams, becoming more and more insistent, and Larionov and Natalia Gontcharova soon joined him.

Diaghileff had first met Larionov in Russia, during the last *Mir Isskustva* exhibitions, and had been immediately interested by his novel ideas.

Larionov was the son of the local chemist in the small town of Tiraspol. He had won a scholarship to the Academy. Always a revolutionary, his career there had been brilliant and chequered. His modernism had caused a sensation—his conduct too. One day, to attract attention, he had gone round Moscow with a bright picture painted on his face. This farce delighted Diaghileff, and he sent the young man to Paris with the exhibi-tion of 1906. There Larionov saw plenty to interest him, and soon found inspiration among the advanced French artists, the *école de Paris*—within two weeks the collecting fever had taken so firm a hold of him that he was forced to cable Diaghileff for his return fare. Larionov introduced Diaghileff to Natalia Gontcharova, and was again invited to Paris on the occasion of the *première* of *Le Coq d'Or*. Larionov was intensely interested in the theatre, in dancing in particular, and in the circus and fairground. His army service had had a profound influence on him, and had turned his attention to popular art, the scribblings on walls and the various methods of expression of the illiterate Russian soldier.

Larionov's whole orientation was towards buffoonery and the grotesque, and it is in that direction that he influenced Diaghileff, now cut off from his former *entourage*.

Diaghileff had long planned to produce a ballet by Prokofiev, with whom he had been in touch, through Walter Nouvel, from the early days. Once again the wires were set humming, and Prokofiev made a long and difficult journey from Russia through the Balkans for a few weeks' conference. The first projects of *Chout* were discussed.

The first scheme to be actively considered was a ballet called *Liturgie*, based on the Passion of our Lord. The ballet was to be danced without music, but Stravinsky was to compose incidental music for the intervals. Here for the first and last time Diaghileff tried his hand at choreography, only to abandon it in impatience.[1] He knew exactly the effects he wanted to produce, but he was no dancer, and could not explain them to the dancers. His explanations became more and more involved, and more and more incomprehensible. All that now remains of *Liturgie* is a series of very beautiful designs by Natalia Gontcharova, a combination of modernism with the old Russian religious manner.

[1] This may be apocryphal. Though I have heard it many times there is no direct evidence.—A. L. H.

Meanwhile Massine's education was proceeding rapidly. Diaghileff renewed his youth in revealing the museums and monuments to his highly receptive pupil, while Larionov also played a large part in his development, introducing him to Jacques Callot, a mine of choreographic suggestion.

In 1915 Diaghileff came to settle in Switzerland, at the Villa Bellerive, Ouchy, thus becoming a close neighbour of Stravinsky's, and there they discussed the idea of *Noces* that was only completed a few years after the War.

It was becoming increasingly difficult not only to keep the Ballet alive, but for Diaghileff himself to live, when an offer from Otto Kahn on behalf of the Metropolitan Opera, New York, saved the situation. Diaghileff was cabled a handsome advance, and set to work mobilizing his resources. Adolf Bolm, who happened to be in Geneva, now joined him, and rehearsed the company in the whole of the old repertoire, twenty ballets in all, a gigantic task. America had insisted upon those names that had become famous in Europe. Karsavina was no longer available for domestic reasons. Fokine was *maître de ballet* at the Maryinsky, so Diaghileff set to work with all his energy to obtain the release of Nijinsky.

Massine had just produced his first work, *Soleil de Nuit*, a suite of popular Russian dances to the music of Rimsky-Korsakov's *Snegouroutchka* and with Larionov's *décor*. Diaghileff had but recently proved himself totally incapable of producing a work directly, but he had succeeded in making a very young man, only two years out of school, produce a work so mature that it bore frequent revival in after years. This contrast shows, better than anything else, Diaghileff's particular strength—his ability to discover talent and to develop it. He himself had failed in one ballet and abandoned it, but immediately after he had educated a Massine, who would produce twenty or thirty mag-

nificent ballets, and among them an unusually large percentage
of enduring works. If in the case of Fokine we can doubt the
extent of his influence, if Nijinsky was a comparative failure,
with Massine we can have no doubts. "Massine," Diaghileff
once said to me, "is the most brilliant mind I have ever met
with in a dancer. Why, he knows things before one explains
them to him."

The first performance of *Soleil de Nuit* was given in Geneva,
and the programme was made up of *Carnaval* and *l'Oiseau de
Feu*, as a symphonic suite conducted by the composer himself.
Felia Litvinne opened the performance by singing the Russian
national hymn. This performance was the first at which Ansermet conducted for the Russian Ballet. From Geneva the company
went to Paris, and gave one brilliant charity performance at the
Opéra, specially opened for the occasion. Stravinsky made his
Paris début as a *chef d'orchestre* with *l'Oiseau de Feu*, and
Massine's first ballet was also presented. The receipts were 400,-
000 gold francs.

The next day they embarked on the *Lafayette* at Bordeaux
en route for New York.

§ 2

It can be imagined what an agony this long and dangerous
wartime journey was to Diaghileff, who feared the hour that
separated Calais from Dover. Always intensely superstitious, he
had taken every possible precaution. While he paced the deck
moodily with Massine, Vassily, the ever faithful, was delegated
to pray for him before the ikon in the cabin. He was not in any
sense a religious man—but one never knew. After many days
of intense strain and false alarms he heard a terrifying sound of
sirens. At last the worst had happened. He rushed to the boats,

Spessivtseva and Lifar in *Le Lac des Cygnes*

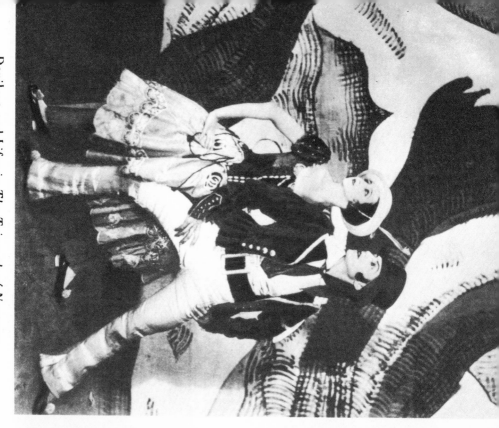

Danilova and Lifar in *The Triumph of Neptune*

Premier of *Triumph of Neptune*, Lifar—Lord Berners—Danilova

life-jacket on, but the journey was over. The *Lafayette* had reached New York in a dense fog.

That was Diaghileff; his moral courage superb, keeping his company, creating beauty while the whole world went destruction mad, his physical courage almost nil, teeth chattering, knees knocking at the very thought of some distant danger.

In New York, Lydia Lopokova returned to the fold. Nijinsky was still a prisoner, but the company was a strong one, and the repertoire that had captured Western Europe totally unknown. The tour was a huge success. They visited forty towns, with full houses everywhere, but Diaghileff did not enjoy his experiences. He appreciated much that was American, but he bitterly resented their democratic ways, the good fellowship, the hand-shaking, back-slapping, and other familiarities. He could not be "a good fellow" according to the American formula. He was essentially a European, a pre-War Russian, the upholder of a rigid caste system, as far as his own conduct in life was concerned. It was not a matter of carefully thought-out principle, but an instinct. It was part of his code, his conception of the æsthetics of life. The bluff, straightforward American stagehand upset his composure by not understanding his methods of command and giving him unquestioned obedience.

What he did understand and admire without reserve was America's important contribution to contemporary art, her architecture, her jazz music, and her well-trained teams of vaudeville girls. I remember his really immense enthusiasm for the Gertrude Hoffman girls, whom he went to see on many occasions in Paris.

"America will have a lot to say in the art of the future. Already her influence is to be felt everywhere—in painting, the theatre, and music. French composers have picked up the jazz idiom, and America has had her say even in the old and conservative institution of ballet; if only she would recognize classicism as the basis of dancing, she would rapidly form her own school." [1]

These words he said in 1926, when *Matelots, Le Train Bleu,* and *Pastorale* were among the most popular numbers in the programme, and already in 1917 the setting of *Parade* had been an American music-hall. He never produced an American ballet, though many projects were discussed, but the influence was there, and he recognized and welcomed it.

Back in New York he met Nijinsky, after the long separation. He was delighted to see him again, all rancour had gone, all that mattered was the work in hand. But his welcome met with an immediate rebuff. A contract for the following year was signed, without him, and in the circumstances he was pleased. He saw that the future lay with Massine, and there was work to be done in Europe with Stravinsky, Larionov, Gontcharova, and Bakst, who was now in Switzerland. He returned to Europe after another nightmare voyage, zigzagging in an Italian cargo boat, dangerously loaded with munitions.

§ 3

In Spain, where he gave a few performances, Stravinsky joined him, and he then settled in Rome with Massine and a skeleton company of sixteen, with Lubov Tchernicheva as *ballerina*—the advance guard of the future. There were planned those ballets that were to be the mainstay of the post-War programmes, and that are still popular at the present day.

Diaghileff had long wished to do a ballet to music by Liadov, but the composer was so dilatory that it was never safe to commission anything. The Russian suite, with its fantastic subjects, gave him an admirable opportunity, and Larionov's render-

---

[1] To-day one of Diaghileff's collaborators, Balanchine, is attempting to found an American school on a basis of classicism.

ing of this folklore seen through peasant—not child—eyes makes a delightful entertainment. The tales that compose *Contes Russes* were produced singly, and only given as an entity after the War, the last number being Lubov Tchernicheva's unforgettable Princess Cygne, where she hides her retainers under her long train, as she walks proudly to be sacrificed to the dragon. Another ballet of this time (1917) is *Les Femmes de Bonne Humeur*, to music of Scarlatti, discovered by Diaghileff himself. For this ballet Massine came under the influence of Hogarth and Longhi, at the suggestion of Bakst, who designed one of his most beautiful *ensembles*. It is difficult to believe that this quiet old-world ballet was produced in the midst of war. Not so with *Parade*, the remaining ballet of that year. It is almost prophetic in its forecast of the immediate post-War upheaval in painting and ballet. A violent cubist manifesto, relieved only by flashes of real humour, Massine's Chinese juggler remains a masterpiece of subtle observation. There is nothing to show that these are early works—no groping or uncertainty.

La Boutique Fantasque, only presented in 1919, was also planned in Italy. Diaghileff, who had been making further finds, decided to make a ballet out of certain pieces that Rossini had composed in his old age for the entertainment of his guests. Three artists designed the *décor* and costumes: Larionov, Bakst, and Derain—and it was the last-named who was finally chosen. He had originally conceived the ballet as a game of cards, and the magnificent costumes of the kings and queens alone remain of the original idea. Derain, perhaps more completely than any other easel artist of the French school, has entered completely into the spirit of the theatre. His designs are not merely pictures *à la* Derain, but a part of the music and the choreography itself.

During this time the company made two tours without its inspirer—the second American and the second South American tours. The American tour under the artistic direction of Nijinsky was a lamentable failure, both artistic and financial, and it was during the South American tour that the unfortunate man's persecution mania became acute. He imagined every conceivable plot around him, even simple accidents beings construed as attempts at assassination. His dancing days drew rapidly to a close. Poor *dieu de la danse!* His name had become synonymous with dancing; he had grown into a legend in the first years of his career, and now madness had separated him from the one man who really understood him, finally to leave him a pitiful wreck.

Meanwhile Diaghileff visited Naples, Madrid, and San Sebastian. In Rome once again, he had attracted a brilliant circle around him, and it is there that he met Lord Berners, who was to compose the first English ballet, *The Triumph of Neptune.* Picasso, Jean Cocteau, Bakst, and the futurist Balla also joined his *entourage.* His interest in the new painting was at its height. Futurism was the topic of the hour, cubism waiting to be born. Just at the outbreak of the Russian Revolution he gave a Russian gala performance at the Costanzi, and was faced with the dilemma as to what should be played in place of the national hymn. Finally he hit on a popular melody that has since gone round the world, "The Volga Boatmen," and Stravinsky hurriedly orchestrated it. For that one night it became an official anthem. Little did he realize at the time that the "peaceful revolution" meant that he was never to see Russia again; that he and his little group were now representatives of all that remained of the old order of things. The prophecy of his Palais Tauride speech had come to pass; his hope that the amenities of life would remain undisturbed was left unfulfilled.

§ 4

The last year of the War was the hardest of all. The company arrived in Portugal for a season in a city of darkness. A revolution was in progress, and the streets were being swept by machine-gun fire. It was even risky to make the short journey from the station to the hotel. No one had either time or inclination to think about ballet. There they were—stranded—and the company had to fend for themselves as best they could. Diaghileff found his way to Madrid, and then there followed a period of actual starvation. He was literally without a penny. All hopes of a season in Barcelona—the one thing that could save him— had fallen through, and matters were further complicated by the fact that some impostor had taken his name and turned up with a group of dancers.

Sokolova, who was in Madrid at the time, and herself in a desperate situation with a baby to look after, has told me of his courage. Diaghileff, always self-centred, always an extreme physical coward, always a sensualist who attached enormous importance to the comforts of life, now thought only of others. He was always devoted to children, and could not bear to think of the little one's suffering. One day, when rummaging in a trunk, he found a heap of foreign coins. He immediately sold them to buy food and medicine for Sokolova's child. He himself was growing thin and weak from hunger and anxiety, anxiously awaiting some news from Sir Oswald Stoll in London. Once he walked into Sokolova's lodging in the middle of the night, and awoke her with a telegram to translate, but still the news remained vague and unsatisfactory. At last a satisfactory telegram came, and with it a substantial advance. Then only did he break down and sob with the accumulated weakness and worry of months. The company was saved. He had succeeded in the gigantic task of keeping it intact throughout the War.

CHAPTER XV

RECOVERY AND FRESH TRIALS
1918–1921

*Bakst and elephants—The "buffer state"—*Le Chapeau Tricorne—*The tragedy of Felix—Return of Nouvel—*Astuzzie
Feminili—Pulcinella—*More difficulties—Chanel to the rescue—The rupture with Massine—*Chout—Cuadro Flamenco.

"Were the world run on right lines, Diaghileff would be appointed International
Minister of Arts by all the countries to whom he has brought beauty with his
Russian Ballet, for that wonderful combination of artistry, talent, and beauty has
done more to improve the taste of the world in colour and in music than any institution ever founded. Its influence has extended far beyond the Theatre."

C. B. COCHRAN: *Secrets of a Showman*

On September 18th, 1918, Diaghileff began his season at the
Coliseum. The very idea of appearing in a music-hall, however
famous, had always horrified him, but on this occasion there was
no choice, and he had to welcome the opportunity which had
arrived just in time to save the existence of the company. His
friends, still faithful after the lapse of four years, followed him
there for their meagre fare of one ballet a performance, and,
though the arrangement cannot be said to have been a happy one
artistically, many a person who came for Lockhart's elephants
must have left the theatre an enthusiastic supporter of the ballet.

The programme consisted of revivals and of ballets produced
during the War. The company was a strong one, and it was Massine's London début as choreographer. The interval had also
brought him forward as a dancer, and there were new names to
applaud—Sokolova, Woizikovski, and Idzikovski. Lydia Lopokova, also, had fulfilled all the expectations of the St. Petersburg

278

balletomanes, and, while retaining all her childish charm, had added a new authority and attack. She was particularly suited to interpret the composers of the Italian eighteenth century, and her partnership with Massine was one of the most successful in ballet.

As soon as he arrived in London, Diaghileff telephoned his old friend, Edwin Evans. They had been associated since 1911, though only unofficially, and now Diaghileff proposed a closer and more permanent collaboration. Evans's exact tasks were never clearly determined, although he has always described himself as "the buffer state," and one of his main functions was to keep disgruntled artists as far away from Diaghileff as possible. From the first this was not an easy task. One day at the Coliseum an angry *ballerina* proved too much for him, and marched straight into the lion's den, staggering under a load of posters and handbills of a size that only the Coliseum could use.

"Look here—and here—and here"—dumping them down on Diaghileff's desk. "It is disgraceful. I am a star, and yet my name is in very small print—under X's, who has never danced any important rôles. I want to know at once what's going to be done about it."

Diaghileff did not explode, as might have been expected, but screwed his eye-glass firmly in:

"This is interesting. I have never seen so many posters. I didn't even know that we had them, did you, Evans? Tell me, how did you get hold of them? Who gave them to you?"

"My husband."

"Your husband? Hum—it's a pity—a great pity, then—that he couldn't give you any other signs of his affection."

Usually Evans, supremely tactful, succeeded in avoiding all such collisions, and so greatly did Diaghileff appreciate his advice that he began to ring him up at all times of the night, and nothing that Evans said could put a stop to this, until he suggested, with a smile, that there might be reasons why this was particularly inconvenient, and Diaghileff, as a man of the world, understood. The idea that anyone could want a quiet night's rest could not be expected to appeal to him. When there was work to be done, any and every hour of the twenty-four was waiting to be used.

Although it was merely in an administrative capacity that Evans joined "the cabinet," his advice in musical matters, and the liaison work that he was able to accomplish with English opinion, proved invaluable, and continued with but one interruption until the end. During the last season Evans was obliged to go to America, but he returned just in time for the very last night of the Ballet's existence.

This visit was enlivened by a violent controversy with Ernest Newman, and it would be difficult to find two men of greater culture but more opposed in outlook. Diaghileff had given an interview in the *Daily Mail:* "The soldiers are coming back to London to find the old German idols being worshipped here just as stupidly and uncritically as ever. . . . Brahms is nothing but a putrefying corpse. . . . Beethoven has been imposed on you by German propaganda. Beethoven, my dear Englishmen, is a mummy. . . . Listen for yourselves, and you will realize that in a work like the Beethoven violin concerto, which goes on and on for three-quarters of an hour, there is not to-day one spark of living interest. It is a horrible huge mummy. As for Schumann, I see in him nothing but a homesick dog howling for the moon. . . . Elgar is a composer paralysed under the effects of the poison gas of Brahms and Wagner."

This was dramatic and violent, but not as it might seem, and must have seemed at the time, inspired by any blind war hatred. For a long time Diaghileff had disliked the Teutonic in music— the manufactured element that he called "the saliva." Ernest Newman was immediately drawn to a witty and vitriolic reply in the *Sunday Times,* in which he challenged Diaghileff's knowledge of Elgar, defended English taste as being not uncritical, but, on the contrary, too critical.

"With all respect," he wound up, "having at last shaken off the German yoke, we are not going to submit to that of France or Russia. We prefer to do our own thinking for ourselves; and in the most friendly way we beg our latest foreign mentors not to imperil the new *entente* by adopting a patronizing attitude towards us that only its naïveté saves from being an impertinence."

If Newman is at times deaf to French and Russian music, Diaghileff's views were certainly a little naïve in their expression. He replied in a further interview in the *Daily Mail:*

"If a stay of a year in London gave me cause to say that the English public is Bochefied, the controversy of the last few days has brought me complete conviction—I would say more—I have observed that German art has in London not only innumerable admirers, but also a well-organized police, ready to punish any 'foreigner' who utters a protest against established and unshakable Boche authorities. . . . *The War was nothing else but a struggle between two cultures,* and this struggle is not concluded by the victory of arms. . . .

"Every one of us has loved his father, but none of us had the idea of keeping his father's dead body in the room. If the music of Beethoven and Brahms is dangerous, it is not because it represents a corpse, but because flies feed upon it, and will infect the public with their poison. . . .

"Let us introduce into our programmes works which were artistic events, samples of German classicism, if only to serve as a contrast to the brilliance and life of Latino-Slav art. But if we are invited during a whole year to funeral services such as a Beethoven festival or a grand Wagner concert, we can no longer breathe, work, or create."

This was the narrow viewpoint of the active man and not the leisured critic, but German music differed from the *Ambulant* movement, and he was tilting against a windmill—pleasurable exercise to such a fighter.

London's welcome proved so warm that for the following year it became an almost permanent home. The Coliseum season ran well into the new year (1919), while in April the company moved on to the Alhambra, and in September to the Empire.

At the Alhambra, Diaghileff produced one of the most perfect and important ballets of his career—*Le Chapeau Tricorne*. He had long been an admirer of Spanish dancing, and on his frequent wartime visits had applauded the magnificent art of Pastoria Imperio, and he had now also come into close touch with Picasso and Manuel da Falla. Spain, too, had had a marked influence on Massine, since much of his most formative period had been passed there, and he had already produced various small works in the Spanish manner, in San Sebastian and Madrid.

One day, in Seville, when Diaghileff had gone with some members of the company to see a festival of gipsy dancing, he noticed a boy who outshone all the others. His name was Felix, and his friends called him Felix "Loco," the loony. He was strange and glum till he danced, and then he seemed transformed. He lived only for his dancing, sitting restless while the others performed, waiting to excel them. With his plan of a Spanish ballet in mind, Diaghileff realized how useful he would be, and engaged him to teach Massine and Sokolova and Woizikovski his native dances. This he did, but the unfortunate boy, always unbalanced, and now suddenly transported from his everyday surroundings to the mad life and atmosphere of the theatre—a life that only a completely sane man can support—imagined that he was to be the centre of all these impressive preparations. He could not conceive that others would perform his own beloved dances, leaving him to be a mere insignificant looker-on. Then he found out. For a few days he acted in a strange and terrifying manner, and when the day came for the performance he was nowhere to be found.

In the theatre the applause was tremendous—but it was not for poor Felix, who, late that night, was found by a policeman dancing frenziedly, like the Jongleur de Notre-Dame, upon the altar of a dark and deserted church. He still lives in an asylum near London.

It has frequently been said that Felix was ill used, and that he actually created *Le Chapeau Tricorne*. The first part of the statement is certainly true. To take this simple fellow away and to make use of him, however well he may have been paid, was an act of unthinking cruelty. He was useful at the time, and his meeting with Massine gave birth to a masterpiece—but to say that he actually created *Tricorne* is absurd. *Tricorne* is something highly complex, a translation of Spanish folk-dancing into the sophisticated terms of the theatre—whereas Felix's movements were entirely spontaneous. It could only have been created by an experienced choreographer—by one who knew the respective merits of Picasso and Da Falla and was fitted to be their partner. The unfortunate Felix, innocent victim of this experiment, was no more than the raw material.

Karsavina, who had just succeeded in making her escape from Russia, joined the company this season, and, as the Miller's Wife, secured one of the triumphs of her career, while Massine's own dancing in the *farucca* remains a major contribution to the dance.

The following year, 1920, after a season at the Opéra Paris, there was a return to Covent Garden, with *Astuzzie Feminili*, an opera by Cimarosa, with a danced *divertissement*, that alone survived as *Cimarosiana*, and one of the most perfect works produced by the Ballet, *Pulcinella*.

Diaghileff, ever since the success of *Les Femmes de Bonne*

283

Humeur, had had the idea of producing another work by a classical Italian composer. On each of his journeys he was accustomed to add to his artistic experience, and during his long stay in Italy he had found many manuscripts of works by Pergolesi, and in London he completed his collection. Knowing Stravinsky's admiration for this composer, he handed the material over to him, and decided upon Picasso as being the artist who could best render the Spanish flavour of this Neopolitan composer. The actual work was then done in the closest collaboration, Massine making frequent visits to Stravinsky and Picasso, while Diaghileff, as usual, was the final arbiter. There were the customary dramatic disagreements, but on the whole the collaborators were single-minded. Stravinsky, the hardest of all critics, where any of his own work is in question, says:

"*Pulcinella* is one of those spectacles—and they are exceedingly rare—where everything holds together, and where all the elements—subject, music, choreography, and decorative scheme —form a coherent and homogeneous whole."

How much this was the case, one could only fully realize when, after Diaghileff's death, it was revived with new *décors* by Chirico, and new choreography by Romanoff; and then it was that one could fully appreciate the meaning of a collaboration under the critical eye of Diaghileff himself.

Meanwhile Diaghileff had got into touch once again with his old friend Walter Nouvel.

"At the end of May 1919 I left Russia. In Helsingfors I read in the papers that Diaghileff had a season at the Alhambra in London. Immediately I wrote a long letter to him, and he replied, as usual, by telegram, proposing to me to come at once to work with him. For family reasons I was unable to leave Finland till a year later, but, as I was in a difficult situation financially, of his own free will he sent me a certain sum of money that I gratefully accepted.

"In June 1920, when he was back in Covent Garden, I was at last able to join him. He left the theatre to meet me at the station, accompanied by Prokofiev, who had just come from Russia. I found him scarcely changed at all, only a little stouter. He was gay, pleased with life, and more energetic than ever. My reception was cordial. He took me with him to the Savoy, and we talked unceasingly of the last six years. He proposed to make me general manager of the Ballet at once; but, since I had as yet no experience in that direction, my previous collaboration having been purely artistic, I wanted a brief period of apprenticeship— time to look around.

"Then he initiated me into his new artistic tendencies, told me of his great friendship and admiration for Picasso, his collaboration with Derain and Matisse, and of Massine's extraordinary gifts as choreographer; and it was then that I really got to know Massine, who had been so young when I had seen him before, during the 1914 season, that I could form no opinion of him. Now that I saw his work for the first time, I was deeply impressed with his gifts both as creator and dancer, though with certain reservations concerning the extremes of grotesqueness that characterized some of his work."

Musically, at this time, Diaghileff was most enthusiastic about the Italian composers of the eighteenth century, and Massine fully shared his enthusiasm. He had just produced, with a company of Italian singers, Cimarosa's opera, *Le Astuzzie Feminili*, which was concluded by a danced *divertissement*. The composer had passed several years at the court of Catherine II as *maître de chapelle*, and had called this *divertissement* "Ballo Russo," having introduced many Russian themes that were Diaghileff's especial delight. The opera itself had little success, but the ballet survived, and, as *Cimarosiana*, was a permanent feature of the repertoire.

Diaghileff was optimistic. Back again in Covent Garden he

imagined that the difficult times were gone for ever. He had met with success in both Paris and Rome, and it gave him immense satisfaction that, for the first time since the War, instead of having to look for engagements they came to him unsolicited. Alas! he was soon disillusioned.

The season at Covent Garden did not come up to his expectations; the programme was not well chosen, and there were ominous gaps in the stalls. One day the management found it impossible to meet their obligations, and the affair was put into liquidation. In order to obtain his money, Diaghileff was forced on the day itself to cancel the last performance, and the innumerable last-night baskets of flowers and bouquets were forwarded from the theatre to the Savoy Hotel—an ironic tribute. The company was paid in full, but Diaghileff did not receive the sum due to him, and now followed tedious legal proceedings, with innumerable visits to Sir Charles Russell, his advocate. It was only some years later that he received a part of the sum.

Once again he was penniless, and the unexpectedness of the shock made it still more difficult to bear. He borrowed money for the immediate needs of the next few weeks, and went to his beloved Venice with Massine and Nouvel, and there, in the company of the Serts and a new friend, Mlle Gabrielle Chanel, passed an agreeable fortnight. Whatever difficulties existed, Venice was always to prove a rest and a consolation. Then to Rome for a few days, for a series of conferences with Emma Carelli, Director of the Costanzi, about the season in January. He tried to persuade her to produce Rimsky-Korsakov's *Snegouroutchka*, playing it over on the piano, but it was of no avail, and it was decided to limit the season to ballet.

From Rome they went to Naples, where they stayed a month. While Diaghileff and Nouvel remained in the city, Massine took up his residence in an old mill at Positano, a place that he loved particularly. Already then he had the project in mind of buying one of the little rock islands off the coast and building a house on it—a project that he subsequently realized.

Lack of money never prevented Diaghileff from developing his artistic schemes, and now he had the idea of producing a ballet to music by Paisiello, an idea that delighted him, for his composer also had passed many years at the court of Catherine II, and Diaghileff hoped to find some Russian echoes. Daily he went with Nouvel to the Conservatoire, where a pianist played the score to them, but the result was disappointing, since in all the material there seemed to be nothing sufficiently interesting out of which to make even a one-act ballet.

Meanwhile the financial situation was becoming more and more disquieting, and once again it became necessary to solicit engagements, which were not at all easy to find. There was nothing in prospect till January in Rome, and, although it was essential to keep the company in work, schemes for a tour in Spain, a tour of the English provinces, and immediate work in Italy, fell through, one after the other.

In despair they returned to Paris. A hasty English tour was fixed up, at the last moment, by a former employee who lived in England, and from the first it proved a disaster. Not only were the financial conditions bad, but in one town the box-office manager vanished with the receipts. The only result was another lawsuit that meant time and money, but that never brought in a penny.

Back again in Paris, it looked as if the Ballet, which had survived the terrible years of the War, would have to be disbanded, and at a time when there were so many interesting projects, and when Massine was gaining daily in creative skill and knowledge. It was at this critical moment that a new friend, Mlle Chanel, came to the rescue. She was a great lover of the ballet, and had a strong personal sympathy for Diaghileff himself, but it was especially Stravinsky whom she knew and admired. He it was who explained to her all the difficulties, and she thereupon placed a very large sum at Diaghileff's disposal, helping him also with the renewal of costumes. Almost at the same time an engagement was forthcoming, so that once again he could feel that he had weathered the storm.

Rolf de Maré had recently become lessee of the Champs Élysées Theatre, which he intended as the permanent home of his newly formed Swedish Ballet, and he had given the management to Jacques Hébertot, who was on friendly terms with Nouvel. It was arranged, since the Swedes were not ready, that the Russian Ballet should open his management for a three weeks' season, the special attraction to be a revival of *Le Sacre du Printemps*, which had now become popular in the concert hall, with a new choreography by Massine. This was brilliantly worked out by him on entirely different lines from Nijinsky's, and Sokolova made a considerable success as the Chosen Virgin.

The performances were a success, but not as great as had been expected. The closing of the affair again led to complications and unpleasantness, but this time Diaghileff had backing and there was no immediate danger.

§ 2

The Rome season (1921) opened pleasantly, with the usual *entourage* of friends, and Diaghileff was germinating the idea of a new collaboration with Derain. At last all his troubles seemed over. Then there came a catastrophe that for a time made everything else appear insignificant. Money troubles he could face with courage, but what happened now seemed to threaten the very heart of the work itself; for Massine, on whom every project centred, left the company.

Perhaps, like many parents, Diaghileff did not realize that his artistic child was fully grown, with friends and ideas that were

Lubov Tchernicheva in *The Good Humored Ladies*

Diaghileff, Stravinsky, Prokofiev, Massine and Gontcharova listening to Chout, 1918
Caricature by Larionov

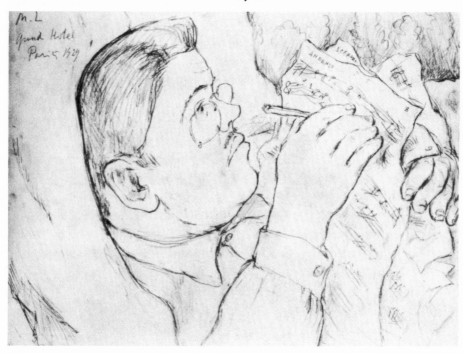

Diaghileff working in bed—Grand Hotel, Paris, 1927
Caricature by Larionov

his own, and with an intense longing for independence. Many of his *entourage* had foreseen that a break was imminent, since Diaghileff expected a subservience that Massine was not prepared to give, once he had felt the full extent of his power and had reached artistic maturity. Scenes and disagreements had been frequent of late, and now, in Rome, matters came to a climax and Massine left.

This was the worst tragedy that Diaghileff ever had to bear, and his every plan for the future, his every creation, seemed to have collapsed and disappeared. He was ever a man of one idea, and, now that the idea had failed him, nothing remained. For a time his friends feared for his health, and even for his reason, and they watched him anxiously day and night.

Matters were further complicated by the fact that this had happened in the middle of the Roman season. In one day he had lost not only his choreographer, but his *premier danseur*. The necessity of making an immediate effort, and of thinking of the present in a practical manner, saved him, and he soon had himself in full control—at any rate as far as he revealed himself to his friends. Woizikovski was rehearsed in Massine's rôles, and made an instant success.

Massine's departure, looked at in retrospect, was to prove a blessing both to the Ballet and to him. He had been working ceaselessly for six years, with such concentration that there was a danger of his losing all contact with reality. His work was rapidly developing certain mannerisms and had become angular and jerky. *Le Sacre du Printemps* had been his last great effort, the work a tremendous strain. Now he was able to look about him, take stock of all that he had done, and the easy, graceful *Beau Danube* was the first fruit of his new independence, a work of relaxation. When he returned to the Ballet three years later, he had found fresh strength, and Diaghileff was able to look at him in a new light and with a newly found respect for his authority and independence.

Diaghileff's immediate worry was as to how his friends would take this rupture, with the sudden shifting of plans that it entailed, and he was so anxious that Nouvel went to Paris, and was soon able to reassure him on that point. On his return he found Diaghileff resigned, already looking for some way out, and once again thinking of the future.

They returned to Paris by way of Lyons, where there was a week's season. And now it became necessary to look for engagements. For the future only Monte Carlo had been decided upon, a season of a few weeks, and much time remained to be filled in. An engagement was arranged in Madrid; Barocchi left with the troupe as advance agent, and Diaghileff then joined them with Stravinsky, whom he had invited to conduct *Petrouchka*. Spain was a success, the King himself, a great *balletomane*, coming to every performance, and even trying at times to imitate some of the steps. In Seville, where Diaghileff had gone for Easter Week, he met Cochran, and a contract was decided upon for a season at Prince's Theatre. At this time contract followed contract in the most haphazard manner, always with enough difficulty to cause anxiety, yet just in time to save the situation.

The arrangements for the Paris season gave anxious work. The Opéra was impossible that year, and at the Champs Élysées the Swedish Ballet was installed, so, through his old friend Astruc, he engaged the Gaieté Lyrique for the season. In Massine's absence the preparation of the programme presented innumerable difficulties. For Paris, more than anywhere, novelty was essential. *Chout* had been planned, with Prokofiev, Larionov, and Massine, since the first days of the War, and now a new choreographer had to be found. At first he hit upon Woizikovski, who proved to have no ambitions in that direction; and then Larionov suggested Sokolova, but could not convince Diaghileff.

Finally it was decided that Larionov himself should do the work in association with Slavinsky. He had a wide theoretical knowledge of dancing, and had guided Massine in his early days.

This one novelty was not sufficient—Paris required still more. Always a devotee of Spanish dancing, Diaghileff then engaged a whole troupe from Spain, and in an amusing setting by Picasso presented them in a *Cuadro Flamenco*. Further to strengthen the season he engaged Lydia Lopokova to dance in a revival of *l'Oiseau de Feu*.

In spite of all these attractions the Paris season was not a triumph. *Chout* was a failure—of the type that Diaghileff subsequently termed a "magnificent failure." Perhaps it had come at the wrong time. It was over-long, highly grotesque, rich in material, but it needed an experienced choreographer to give it true style and unity. The Spanish dances aroused a certain interest, but any commercial *impresario* could have brought them over. They did not exhibit the "Diaghileff touch," which was what his public wanted above all. By his previous efforts he had made all ordinary success out of the question—it had to be splendid triumph or utter failure.

Diaghileff was depressed, and seemed to have lost all his usual buoyancy, and it was in that state of mind that he left for London, where his old idea of reviving *The Sleeping Princess* took concrete form.

The season at Prince's was a comparative success, in spite of the fact that to Diaghileff's horror a black cat had found its way on to the stage. Like Paris, London rejected *Chout*, was a little suspicious of *Le Sacre du Printemps*, though it was amused by the *Cuadro Flamenco*. One of its leading dancers, a legless man who performed wonders on his stumps, was banned by the authorities from appearing; and this was unfortunate, since he was an artist and gave great character to the spectacle. A little more official kindness of that sort, one sadly reflects, would have put an end to his livelihood. Maria Dalbaicin, a beautiful girl of fourteen, afterwards remained with the company and appeared with them in *The Sleeping Princess*, but her beauty was all that she had to offer. Later she was a dismal failure in the balletized Spain of *Le Chapeau Tricorne*. She made a few appearances in French films, and died before she came of age.

The season lasted ten weeks, Cochran lost £5,007, and, like all Diaghileff's backers, was well satisfied with the result. It was becoming more and more apparent that a limit in modernism had been reached—the end of a phase—and *The Sleeping Princess* came as a restful interlude while the next step forward was being evolved.

CHAPTER XVI

"THE SLEEPING PRINCESS"
1921

The original production—A link with the past—Finding the cast—Trouble with Bakst—Mechanical difficulty as an omen—Failure and bankruptcy.

"It is a great satisfaction to me as a musician to see produced a work of so direct a character at a time when so many people, who are neither simple, nor naïve, nor spontaneous, seek in their art simplicity, 'poverty' and spontaneity."

"Tchaikovsky's music is quite as Russian as Pouchkine's verse or Glinka's song."
IGOR STRAVINSKY, *in a letter to Diaghileff*, 10th October, 1921

In 1921, with the production of *The Sleeping Princess* at the Alhambra, Diaghileff appeared to make a sudden artistic *volte-face*.

The original *The Sleeping Princess* (1890) had been perhaps the greatest event in the life of the Imperial Ballet, and the lavish *décor* and costumes caused a sensation even at the Maryinsky, home of splendour. Special designs were prepared by the director, Vsevolojsky, himself, and the necessary silks and velvets were imported at great expense from Lyons. Tchaikovsky, best loved composer of the day, worked in the closest harmony with Petipa, accepted his suggestions readily, and expressed his unrestrained admiration for the resulting choreography. The rôle of Princess Aurora was created by Carlotta Brianza, and Enrico Cecchetti took the part of the male Blue Bird.

The ballet was an immediate success with the public, but at first the Press was hesitant. "This is not a ballet at all, but a fairy-tale, a whole *divertissement*"; "Tchaikovsky's music would be more at home in the Dvoranskie Sobranie.[1] It is for the concert hall, serious and heavy." Thirty years and another country could make a startling change: when *Aurora's Wedding* was produced at the Opéra, Paris, in 1922, the musicians practically refused to perform—"This is for the Folies Bergères, quite unworthy of an orchestra of repute." Diaghileff had to bully them into playing it, and then the Press described it as "du pire Massenet."

Diaghileff usually listened to the opinion of Paris with respect, but this time he had a variety of reasons for going in an opposite direction—reasons both practical, personal, and æsthetic. Now that Massine had left him, there was no modern choreographer available, and the reception of *Chout* showed that extreme modernism, unless created by a master hand, was a certain failure. Stravinsky, who was Diaghileff's inseparable companion at the time, and who also loved Tchaikovsky, felt that the time had come to rehabilitate him. Diaghileff agreed, and counted heavily on the prestige and authority of Stravinsky in accomplishing this. Also there must have been more than an element of nostalgia in his decision, for Diaghileff, in spite of his modernism, was deeply sentimental at heart, and this ballet was a part of his youth. The Revolution had scattered many great dancers who were now available; it was the first and last opportunity of reviving the work on a grand scale. At first the fantastic idea even came to him of engaging Carlotta Brianza for some of the performances—a sentimental gesture in the grand manner. She was teaching in Paris,[2] and he went with Svetloff to invite her. She was fatter, but still very young in appearance, and full of energy.

"Could you, Carlotta, dance Aurora?" Diaghileff asked cautiously.

She laughed, and then paused a little to think.

[1] St. Petersburg equivalent of the Queen's Hall.   [2] She still is.—A. L. H.

It was, she explained, quite impossible for the present; it would take her some time to prepare for such a rôle.

"But I want the name of Brianza associated with this great revival."

She offered to take the part of the wicked Fairy Carabosse.

"What, after creating Aurora herself?"

This was unexpected, but it delighted Diaghileff, and the contract was signed on the spot.

Then with the aid of Nouvel, who made several journeys throughout Central Europe, he put himself in touch with the various artists, engaging Bronislava Nijinska, who had just come from Kieff, as choreographer and dancer, Wilzak, Schollar, Spessivtseva, Egorova, Vera Trefilova, and Vladimiroff. The choreography was to be reproduced by Sergéeff, who had taken an exact notation of the original according to a special system of his own.

Diaghileff was never content to leave well alone. In every revival some improvement occurred to him, so that now Nijinska was asked to add some extra numbers in the grand *divertissement* —a perfectly legitimate thing, as in Russia the *divertissement* was elastic. "The Three Ivans," by Nijinska, which became one of the most popular numbers, was admirably composed, but the peasant blouses seemed out of place in the court setting. In his efforts to improve by cutting, Diaghileff was less successful, and, rare thing for him, he soon gave in to the arguments of his *prima ballerina*, Trefilova, though in the most gracious manner.

"MY DEAR VERA ALEXANDROVNA,—According to the saying, '*Ce que femme veut, Dieu le veut*,' I have ordered the twelve mermaids' dresses that you so insisted upon, and will add them in the act of 'Visions.' I hope that this will now be finer and more complete, as you are convinced that it will be.

"I am always pleased to give satisfaction to your wishes."

295

Diaghileff had the greatest respect for a great classical *ballerina* who had made such a revival possible.

When first the idea came to him in Rome, immediately after Massine's departure, he had tried hard to interest Derain in it, but had failed. Then he thought of Benois, the greatest expert of that period, but it was not yet possible to secure his release from Russia, so finally he decided upon Bakst, who was just recovering from another bout of physical and moral depression. Part of the cause at least was due to a violent quarrel with Diaghileff over the *décors* of *La Boutique Fantasque*. He felt that it had been promised him, and unfairly withdrawn at the last moment, but, as usual when there was a new collaboration in view, the peace was soon made, though Bakst retained a hidden grudge.

Through the good offices of Wollheim a contract was signed with Sir Oswald Stoll for a long series of performances at the Alhambra, and a large sum advanced for the production, which was to be on a lavish scale, a private enterprise emulating the Imperial Ballet at the height of its fame. This sum was to be repaid, week by week, from the receipts.

Diaghileff threw himself into the work of preparation with energy, but from the start there were difficulties and unforeseen expenses: the entire orchestra parts needed recopying, since the material could not be found; then Bakst delayed with his sketches from day to day, always giving an evasive reply. The situation was becoming desperate when Diaghileff demanded them in his usual incisive manner; and then Bakst explained. He would only deliver them if Diaghileff entrusted to him the *décor* of Stravinsky's *Mavra*, then also under discussion. He had been caught once, he said, with *La Boutique Fantasque*, and felt himself fully justified. He produced a contract ready drawn up, stipulating that, if Diaghileff failed to give him *Mavra*, he should pay him as damages double the sum agreed upon for *The Sleeping Princess*. There was a violent scene that lasted all through one morning, Bakst rushing in and out of the room to put cold compresses on his head. Diaghileff was horrified, Bakst obstinate. Finally Diaghileff gave in and signed, warning him that in any case he had not the slightest intention of abiding by the contract, since it was extracted by force. Bakst finally delivered the designs. One might imagine that after this their relations would be strained to breaking-point, but not at all. They left for London together, and continued their work in the most complete harmony.

The date for the first night underwent many postponements, owing to difficulties with the machinery in the scene where the enchanted forest grew. The London machinery was much more primitive than in Russia, where the effect had been an enormous success.

§ 2

Finally the first night arrived, and with it a catastrophe. There was a sound of cracking, creaking wood, and the enchanted forest refused to grow, ruining the curtain of the second act. This spoilt the reception of the work to a certain extent, but its effect was still more far-reaching. After the performance Diaghileff broke down completely and sobbed. He was exhausted by the struggle, and saw in the mishap an omen of ill fortune. From that moment, perhaps for the first time in his life, he was a beaten man, with no confidence in the success of his great creation. He was surrounded by friends—he had even invited, as his personal guests, the leading French critics to witness his triumph—but no one could console him. He was a pitiful sight, and it marked the beginnings of his illness. Also, his forebodings were soon fulfilled. After the third week the receipts dropped lower and lower. In December, Barocchi, who had been general manager, left, and Nouvel took charge. He says: "It was a nightmare; every day matters grew worse and worse. As it was agreed, the management deducted the production expenses, so that scarcely anything remained for Diaghileff. Yet there was the company to be paid and various running expenses. For that it was necessary to beg the management to retain less. They understood our situation, and often agreed to this. Finally they proposed that we bring from Paris the materials of the other productions, which could be relied upon as a certain success and would have helped pay expenses. But Diaghileff was unwilling. He had his contracts with Monte Carlo and Paris, and could not risk having the material seized in the event of failure. There were interminable discussions between Diaghileff and Sir Oswald Stoll, with the tactful Edwin Evans as intermediary."

To complicate matters still further, Diaghileff had greatly exceeded his production estimates. Stoll was generous, but he could not run a theatre on such fantastic principles, and Diaghileff from the first was quite incapable of appreciating his point of view. He could not see that he was doing anything wrong or even out of the ordinary. His whole attitude was, "I have spent more than I said I would, admitted, but then I have also given far more beauty." It was strictly true, but it could not be expected to appeal to the director of any commercial undertaking. Diaghileff was also up against his imperfect understanding of the English mind and English business methods. In his dealings with artistic collaborators he was scrupulous, but with tradesmen not at all. Evans continually urged him to be prompt in his payment for goods, pointing out that by establishing a sound credit he could save at least 40 per cent, but he would never see it. Tradesmen had always tried to take advantage of him in Russia and elsewhere, so that it must be the same here.

Finally it was decided to close the season at the beginning of February. There was no money left to pay either company or tradespeople. His only resources were £1,000, borrowed from an eccentric millionaire, who was clamouring for repayment. A week before the end, he left for Paris, in the hopes of finding some money, leaving the unfortunate Nouvel in charge.

"I shall never forget that dreadful week alone in London. Some of the artists who had not been given their full pay threatened to ruin the last performance by a general strike. Thank goodness, with the help of Grigorieff and the reasonable artists, I was able to ward that off, and the last night, at any rate, was a triumph. Never did I return to Paris with more pleasure. But, if I awoke from a nightmare, the reality was scarcely more pleasant. The company was left behind without resources. Any moment it might split up, and already some of the artists had joined Massine at Covent Garden. Grigorieff had the heroic task of keeping things going—and without the means. In Paris neither Diaghileff nor I had enough to pay even for our modest meals in a small restaurant. Things were as bad as that. He had already been forced to sell his black pearl stud, a highly valued present from Lady Ripon, and one of the very rare personal effects he prized."

It is then that the Princesse Edmond de Polignac came to Diaghileff's rescue. As he was preparing to produce Stravinsky's *Renard* at the Opéra, a work written for her and dedicated to her, she put a certain sum at his disposal that enabled him to save the company and proceed with the strictest economy. Once again an admirer of the great composer's had saved the situation.

The Sleeping Princess was an artistic triumph. It was sensational, but not in the customary Diaghileff manner. To discuss it over the dinner-table it needed a real knowledge of dancing, and the usual descriptive adjectives for the latest music and *décor* were meaningless here. Originally, according to Fokine's ideals, the three elements of dancing, painting, and music were to be equal, but in some recent productions the dancing had been completely overshadowed. *The Sleeping Princess* redressed that balance. It gave the ballet public rigid standards, and to-day in England its influence in retrospect is tremendous. No one who saw those performances could ever think the same about dancing again. This seemingly light entertainment was one of Diaghileff's most profound lessons in ballet and stage-craft.

CHAPTER XVII

IN SEARCH OF LOST YOUTH
1922–1929

Boris Kochno—Mavra—*The break with Bakst*—Le Renard—
A lean time—Ballets Russes de Monte Carlo—*Unexpected
arrival of Serge Lifar*—Les Noces—*Success again*—Bakst's
vengeance—*Reviving Gounod*—Anton Dolin—*Return to
London*—Massine back again—*Bakst's death*—The emergence of Lifar—*Kochno as intermediary*—The scandal of
Romeo and Juliet—*Le Pas d'Acier*—Diaghileff's favourite
dancer—*Le Fils Prodigue*—Bal—*Le Renard*—Collecting
books—*Breakdown in health*—Nouvel's adieu.

"Il s'est trompé souvent et ses erreurs l'honorent. Il a tout essayé. 'Omnium curiosi-
tatum explorator.' Il a bravé toutes les difficultées. Ce pétersbourgeois décédé à
Venise consacre la victoire de l'esprit humaniste."

WALDEMAR GEORGE

It was necessary now to arrange for the forthcoming season at
the Opéra with the most rigid economy—never a strong point
with Diaghileff.

A work that had already been decided upon was Stravinsky's
opera, *Mavra*.

On the recommendation of the painter Soudeikine, Diaghileff
had taken as his secretary a young Russian, son of an officer in
one of the leading Moscow regiments. He had succeeded in
escaping from Russia, via Constantinople, with his mother and
half-sister. From a very early age Boris Kochno had been deeply
interested in literature, had read almost everything, and poetry
was his special enthusiasm. He was something of a poet himself.
His gifts were exceedingly varied: while an amateur in everything, he drew quite well, had an excellent ear and understand-

ing of music, and was receptive in everything concerning art. Though he was a fervent disciple of modern poetry, Pouchkine always remained his idol, and he knew much of his poetry by heart. Diaghileff encouraged the boy's own poetic talent, and with his strongly developed pedagogical sense began to develop his general culture and to guide his taste. He welcomed his arrival not only for the congenial company, but he saw here a young man who could keep him in touch with youth, and with what was going on in advanced artistic circles.

At the same time Stravinsky, who had been gradually receding from the spirit and mentality of the "Five," found himself more and more attracted by Glinka, Dargomijsky, and Tchaikovsky, whose musical thought was so much closer to his own, and it was precisely these three composers who had the best rendered in music and understood Pouchkine's poetry, which also delighted Stravinsky. It was in this atmosphere that *Mavra* was born. Kochno wrote a libretto on a Pouchkine subject, and Stravinsky composed the music.

Bakst, who took part in these deliberations, was equally enthusiastic about the Russian 1830's, and was convinced that he would be entrusted with the mounting of this little opera. But Diaghileff, who had just commissioned from him the grandiose *Sleeping Princess*, did not wish to show still another Bakst. It was a fixed principle with him to allow a monopoly to no one artist, and Stravinsky supported him in this. Then followed Bakst's London outburst which had forced Diaghileff's hand and compelled him to sign the contract. Had he once considered Bakst in this connection, he was far too much of a fighter to give in now, and he entrusted the *décor* to Survage, an action which led to the final breach with Bakst that lasted till his death.

The next novelty was Stravinsky's *Renard*, a plunge once again into modernism, with *décor* by Larionov, and choreography by Nijinska. The director of the Opéra was not yet fully satisfied with the programme, since he had been greatly counting on *The Sleeping Princess*, which was now impossible with all its material forcibly detained in London. Diaghileff then hit upon the idea of composing out of it a one-act ballet—*Aurora's Wedding*. He had thought of Benois's costumes for *Le Pavillon d'Armide* that were of just the right period. Fortunately they were in an excellent state of preservation, and with the addition of some new fairy-tale costumes by Gontcharova this ballet became one of the most economical that he had ever shown, and in London one of the most popular.

The season was not a big success, and again he was confronted with a serious problem. It was essential to keep the company at work, even if it meant accepting engagements at a loss. London, since the War a safe home for so many months in the year, was closed to him, and Paris was never able to support a long season. But now he was compelled to play again in Paris almost without interruption. At the end of his second season, the situation remained unchanged, and then followed a series of engagements, many of them under the most deplorable conditions: in Marseilles for the Colonial Exhibition, Geneva, Biarritz, Bordeaux, and finally Belgium. The company was growing stale, and in this way it was becoming impossible to think of producing new works—for Diaghileff the worst trial of all. Then came an idea: Monte Carlo had a small permanent ballet troupe that took part in the operas, and he suggested lending the greater part of his dancers to complete their company during the entire winter, and then, as in former years, giving his own season in April. The management accepted, and in this way he was safe till the Paris season in the spring, and the company became, "Les Ballets Russes de Monte Carlo, direction Serge de Diaghileff." This contract was renewed yearly till the end.

§ 2

Once again there was time to think and plan for the future. Diaghileff had always been on the look-out for young talent, and Nijinska now told him of four young pupils, whom she had left in Kieff, and of how useful they would be. He had the greatest confidence in her, and immediately took the necessary steps to secure their services. In January 1923, they arrived in Paris: Lapitzky, Unger, and the brothers Hoyer, but to the amazement of Diaghileff a fifth boy turned up, of whom he had never even heard—Serge Lifar. This boy was strikingly handsome and beautifully built, but as yet he knew literally nothing. Diaghileff was bewildered and disappointed, and despatched them to Monte Carlo to take classes with Nijinska.

For a very long time he had had the idea of putting on Stravinsky's *Noces*, of which he was passionately fond. Stravinsky had begun the work before the War, and in Switzerland, in 1915, when he played the first two scenes, Diaghileff was so enthusiastic that the work had been dedicated to him. By 1917 the music was almost completed, but the orchestration remained to be done. Now he decided to make up the *ensemble* with chorus and solo singing, four pianos and percussion. To conduct the choir an excellent musician, Kibaltchikh, former *maître de chapelle* of the Russian church in Geneva, was selected; the *décors* were entrusted to Gontcharova, the choreography to Nijinska.

Its first performance at the Gaieté Lyrique was a triumph of a kind that the Ballet had not enjoyed for a long time, and people were being turned away in their hundreds. Diaghileff was jubilant, but his pleasure was now spoilt by Bakst, who, acting on the contract that he had forced Diaghileff to sign in London, had obtained a writ to seize the receipts. This action profoundly disgusted Bakst's old friends, who without exception broke with

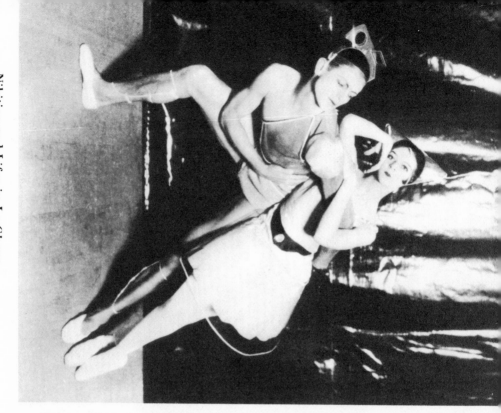

Nikitina and Lifar in *La Chatte*

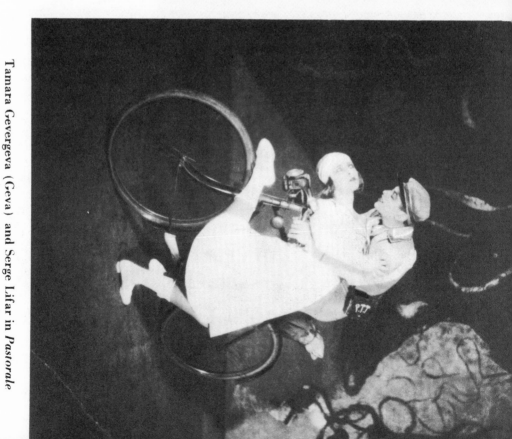

Tamara Gevergeva (Geva) and Serge Lifar in *Pastorale*

Tchernicheva, Nikitina, Danilova, Doubrovska, and Lifar in *Apollon Musagetes*

Serge Lifar and corps de Ballet in *La Chatte*

him, but in justice to him it must be said that he was not completely balanced then, carried away by the notion that he had been badly treated and must seek revenge. He wrote letter after letter of hysterical abuse to the whole group. The sum was finally paid.

A more pleasant result of the success was the organization of a *grande fête* in the Galerie des Glaces at Versailles. Diaghileff, a modern Louis XIV, composed a lavish programme of singing and ballet, and such was its success that at the last moment it was impossible to obtain a seat even for three thousand francs. Once more he was on top of the world, enjoying the triumphs he had known before the War.

§ 3

These last few years of Diaghileff's life resolve themselves more and more into a list of new productions and new collaborators, with an almost feverish hunting after novelty, made more acute by the first Soviet activities that found their way to Paris, and from time to time a return to the calm of early loves; into artistic successes and the recurrence of financial worries with long and disquieting lawsuits as the result.

For his novelties Diaghileff came largely to rely upon the "Six" grouped together by his early collaborator Cocteau (who almost alone among the friends of 1909 could keep pace with every fresh activity), and gravitating round Satie. Poulenc gave him *Les Biches*, with *décor* by Marie Laurencin; Auric *Les Fâcheux*, with *décor* by Braque—each a pure expression of French painting, Nijinska the choreographer alone remaining of Russia.

But it was in opera that he turned back to an old favourite and made a bold attempt to resurrect Gounod; and this craze for Gounod was of the same order that he had for Tchaikovsky, and was characteristic of his musical tastes at the time—an absolute necessity to plunge himself once again in the atmosphere of an early love, that had always remained with him somewhere in the background, and that now came as a natural reaction against the recent musical ideology with which he felt himself saturated.

That winter *Philémon et Baucis* had been revived at the Trianon Lyrique. He went several times, and even took with him Stravinsky, who was equally delighted. This turned him to a search among Gounod *partitions*, and to his joy he unearthed a little masterpiece, *Le Médecin malgré Lui*, belonging to the same period as *Faust*. At the same time he selected, as well as other operas, *l'Education Manquée* of Chabrier, a small work full of grace and verve.

Then began a hunt for singers. Diaghileff was exceptionally hard to please, more so with the human voice, perhaps, even than with dancers. He loved especially the Italian *bel canto*, and was rarely satisfied with French singers. He left with Nouvel on a journey of discovery to Italy, and in Milan gave innumerable auditions, finally he made his choice, among them, Barrientos, De Angelis, Des Paolis. With the exception of *Philémon*, the other operas were to be given in French. According to tradition there is always in French *opéra comique* a spoken portion, and this Diaghileff detested. He decided to replace it by sung *récitatifs*, and he commissioned French musicians to compose these *à la manière de* Gounod: *Le Médecin malgré Lui* to Satie, *Philémon et Baucis* to Auric, *La Colombe* to Poulenc, and *l'Education Manquée* to Milhaud. Benois had just returned from Russia in time to undertake the *décors* of *Médecin malgré Lui* and *Philémon et Baucis*, while the remaining *décors* were entrusted to Juan Gris.

This 1924 season in Monte Carlo was a brilliant one, but it was the ballet, and especially *Les Biches*, that had the greatest success, while the attempt to revive Gounod was a failure, which turned Diaghileff from opera for good.[1]

What was now needed to strengthen the company was a young *premier danseur classique*, and that year he made an important new discovery. Seraphine Astafieva, a former member of his company, who was teaching in London, wrote to him continually about a young English boy, Anton Dolin, who had been in *The Sleeping Princess ensemble*, and who had now improved beyond recognition. He gave the boy an audition, was delighted with the result, and sent him to Monte Carlo. Dolin was something new in the ballet, a magnificent *premier danseur classique* who was at the same time the embodiment of the modern athletic spirit, and through him it became possible not only to revive great works, but to treat of contemporary life. *Jeux* had failed before the War, but now, round Dolin's personality, it was possible to make a striking success of another *ballet sportif*, *Le Train Bleu*.

One day Jean Cocteau saw Dolin ragging in a theatre corridor, doing the most complex acrobatics with a pure classical *plastique*. This gave him the idea of a contemporary ballet round the athletic hero of the pleasure resorts, and Diaghileff suggested to Milhaud to treat it as a "ballet musical comedy." The scenery, by the sculptor Laurens, was of the very latest constructivist pattern, and the bathing costumes by Chanel. It was original, chic, amusing, and an immense success. Almost overnight Dolin became a star of the first magnitude. This ballet influenced dance production for a time in a way that many great works have failed to do, and it came at an opportune moment during the Paris Olympic season. However, in spite of a triumph, the books once again showed a deficit, and resulted in the inevitable and unsatisfactory lawsuit. At the same time another company

[1] The only other opera he produced was Stravinsky's *Œdipe Roi*, but in concert form.

was appearing in Paris—Les Soirées de Paris, organized by the Comte Etienne de Beaumont with the collaboration of Massine —a fact that Diaghileff bitterly resented, especially since they employed many of the artists whom he had first launched in the theatre, including Picasso, whom he had long hoped to interest in another project, without success. This was a bitter blow; his favoured artist now working with the enemy, Massine. He concealed his irritation, but for a time their relations were affected. Les Soirées de Paris were not a great success, and later Diaghileff himself took over the Picasso-Massine *Mercury*. He was certainly jealous under all circumstances when any artist who had ever worked for him took part in other activities; in this particular case, perhaps, there was more reason than usual. When one of his former dancers said to him, "But, Sergei Pavlovitch, how can you possibly be angry? We must all live, and you have no monopoly of ballet," he replied, "That is true, but I am a barman. I have invented and launched a certain cocktail according to a recipe of my own. You cannot expect me to be anything but annoyed when others come and try to combine the same ingredients."

And however many attempts those other "barmen" made, during his lifetime they were unable to meet with success, although the ingredients seemed so very much the same. The secret lay in the shaking—and that was the Diaghileff touch.

Paris was followed by a lengthy tour of Germany, with successes everywhere, but a bad contract left him with another hole in the budget and a difficult problem to face. Monte Carlo meant temporary safety, Paris under almost any circumstances a certain loss, while London, the one source of profit, had been eliminated. London alone could save him. For many months, through the skill of his agent Wollheim, negotiations had been carried on with Stoll, and finally the matter was settled, and once again the Coliseum came just in time. The first season there liquidated a large part of the debt, while he was able to live and create on an advance for a further season there the following spring.

§ 4

During this first Coliseum season three events occurred that profoundly affected the life both of the Ballet and its director.

He had heard of the arrival from Russia of a young choreographer, Balanchavadze, considered too revolutionary and advanced for Red Russia, together with three dancers, Danilova, Gevergeva, and Efimov. He immediately engaged them, and whether the fact that Balanchavadze was a choreographer or not affected the matter, Nijinska, who had already disagreed with Diaghileff on many small points, turned up one morning at the Savoy, and announced her intention of leaving the company. He tried his best to retain her, and failed. Once again he was left without a choreographer upon whom he could rely. Balanchavadze, now renamed Balanchine, was there, but without the chance yet of being initiated into the atmosphere.

For some time Massine had been seeking to rejoin the Ballet, and Diaghileff found that it would now be wise to make the peace. Nouvel and Wollheim were entrusted with the negotiations, and they proved almost interminable, for Massine had learnt the value of independence. Finally a contract was signed by which he was engaged as choreographer only, and entrusted with the novelties for the next Paris season. A link with the past was forged once again, and his most brilliant discovery back in the fold.

On the evening of December 28th there was still another vivid reminder of the past. During the performance some journalists came to the Coliseum, and asked to see Diaghileff; they had come to note a dramatic reaction, and they were not disappointed. "Bakst is dead. Have you anything you can tell us?" There was nothing that he could say. He rushed out of the theatre in tears. All quarrels were forgotten, and only the memory of a long and fruitful friendship remained. While Bakst was alive, there was always the chance of a reconciliation. Now this was final. It brought home to him vividly the terrors of death, reminded him that he was no longer young, that the days of the *Mir Isskustva* already belonged to history. Diaghileff cried, and could not be consoled.

Back in Monte Carlo (1925) he began to prepare a new programme. Deaths, quarrels, and separations must not be allowed to interfere with his annual struggle. Many slipped out with the years, but there were others, fresh young talents, wanting to be established. In Berlin he had noticed the remarkable gifts of young Serge Lifar, the uninvited dancer, and he sent him, during the vacation, to Cecchetti in Turin. There his progress proved so great that it was time to entrust him with a work of importance, and also to intensify that education with the great *maestro*, who again joined the company as *professeur de dance*.

Lifar's first ballet was also Massine's first under the new arrangement. Kochno had developed the theme, the music was entrusted to a young friend of his, Vladimir Dukelsky, and Braque did the *décors*.

Zephire et Flor was not an outstanding success, but it launched Serge Lifar on one of the most notable careers that any dancer has ever known, and a well-deserved success, for he worked as I have never seen a dancer work. He was Cecchetti's last great creation as a dancer, Diaghileff's as an artist, and no one in this whole story has been more faithful to his memory or has paid more constant tribute to his discoverer. Lifar to-day is one of the very few who is pleased to admit all that he owes to Diaghileff, and as *premier danseur* and *maître de ballet* of the

Opéra, Paris, so often the home of the Russian Ballet, he pays him daily homage.

He rehearsed his first rôle like one possessed, sometimes working ten hours a day, till overstrain pursued him, and on the night of the orchestral rehearsal both his ankles gave way and he collapsed in agony on the stage. Diaghileff was in despair. "It is my fault. I should not have boasted. It was all too beautiful to come true." Yet another disappointment, and when fortune at last seemed to have turned. Lifar was in plasters, and the *première* postponed. Then in Barcelona, according to contract, it had to be given, and Lifar saw his great chance vanishing. Diaghileff promised to make it up in every way possible, but nothing could console him; Lifar also attached a superstitious importance to the rôle that had been designed for him and talked of suicide. Against doctor's orders he danced, Diaghileff watching, terrified, in the wings. He succeeded, created the rôle, began his great career, and then went to bed again for some weeks. In Massine's next ballet, *Les Matelots*, he made a still greater impression, and his progress was so rapid that soon he took the lead in every new creation, as well as dancing in many revivals of famous works, steadily gaining a knowledge of music and painting, even sharing in his mentor's cult for Pouchkine.

The arrival of a new star had throughout Diaghileff's life meant the setting of a former one, not because he wished or engineered such a thing—on the contrary it made his plans more difficult to realize—but because it was inevitable, and, with Lifar in the ascendant, Dolin left. He was perhaps in any case too independent to remain any length of time in the company, and he was not prepared to undergo the intensive hot-house education that was required of him, so that disputes became more and more frequent. Diaghileff could not understand the English boy's outlook on life, and was shocked by a hundred small trifles. It was a complete mystery to him how anyone could wish to play tennis or go for a picnic with friends when he might be listening to an improving conversation with Stravinsky or Picasso. Later, when Dolin returned, he was older and better able to appreciate the great advantages of dancing with the Russian Ballet.

A London season, backed this time by Lord Rothermere, followed Paris, and revealed Balanchine's first ballet—*Barabau*—and then a short stay in Berlin, with an immense artistic success, and, aside from London, the almost inevitable loss.

§ 5

Diaghileff felt only too keenly that the distance that separated him from the younger generations was growing with the years. This did not merely worry him, it terrified him. He realized that there was no longer an immediate sympathy and understanding between himself and the new artist—that intimate friendship that had always existed between himself and his contemporaries. Then, in agreement with them, he knew what he wished to do and he did it, and was pleased with the result. Now, not to be behind the times, he was continually in the position of asking himself what it was he should do and what it was he ought to like.

In order to be in touch with youth and new ideas he needed an intermediary, and that intermediary he found in Boris Kochno, who became for him the spokesman for all that was new, and it is for this reason that during his final years Kochno possessed almost a greater influence over him than anyone had had during his whole career. It was not that Diaghileff accepted every project without criticism, but he allowed himself to be influenced, often against his own better judgement, because he felt in the long run youth must be right. He began to suspect his own opinions as well as those of people of his own generation, and often he hated the results, though he was loath to admit it. Kochno as well as his librettist became his absolute adviser in *décor*, costumes, choreography, and even music.

One such plunge into modernism brought a scandal that was dear to him, and convinced him that he was on the right track. Through London friends he had discovered a young English composer, Constant Lambert, from whom he commissioned the music of *Romeo and Juliet*, and Nijinska returned to do the choreography of this one ballet, Karsavina to take the leading rôle. For a long time the Russian Ballet had been considered "bourgeois" by the *surréaliste* group, and the term was as painful to him as it would have been to any Soviet commissar. The obvious thing was to commission *décor* from some of the group and win them over in that way. He selected two of their leaders, Max Ernst and Joan Mirò. Then, when the first night came, there was an uproar : whistles, rattles, catcalls, and some fighting even, that needed the intervention of the police. The other members of the group had felt themselves betrayed, and were seeking vengeance. It was a poor scandal, a sectional affair in which the general public was not in the slightest interested, but nevertheless it was a scandal and highly gratifying.

In London that same year (1926) he produced a work that gave him real pleasure, *The Triumph of Neptune*, with music by Lord Berners, whom he had long admired, and a book by Sacheverell Sitwell, one of the few Englishmen with a Russian Ballet outlook. Since the production of *Boris Godounov*, nearly twenty years before, matters had not altered. Once again the scenery was actually being completed during the playing of the overture and all was confusion. Only Grigorieff remained perfectly calm and detached. "There is plenty of time—of course it will be ready." And it was.

For a long time now Diaghileff had wished to show his modernism by putting on a ballet in the Soviet manner—not that this style of production particularly appealed to him, but again with the desire of going one better. He approached Prokofiev, realizing fully that the Soviet would not have a better composer at their disposition. It was obvious that the scenery would have to be *constructiviste*, and in order to have the real thing he sent to the Caucasus for a stage artist, Iakouloff, who had been an exhibitor in the last *Mir Isskustva* exhibition. Massine, who had never been back to Russia since the new régime, was entrusted with the choreography, and the work was called *Le Pas d'Acier*, a name as mystifying to Russians as to the French. At the same time he also put on another work with the fashionable *constructiviste* scenery, *La Chatte*, in which, according to the legend, a cat fell in love with a young man and asked Venus to transform her into a human. Since the leading rôle was to be for Lifar, Kochno reversed the legend with the somewhat ridiculous result that the young man fell in love with the cat. Notwithstanding, no one noticed the anomaly, and the ballet was a notable success, thanks to Balanchine's choreography and a very remarkable interpretation by Lifar.

In spite of these adventures into the ultra-modern Diaghileff's favourite dancer still remained the purely classical Spessivtseva, who had returned to Russia after the disaster of *The Sleeping Princess*, and when she came back some years later he did his utmost to engage her, but the Opéra, Paris, succeeded where he failed, and she remained there for some time, after which he was able to take her back into the company, just before an engagement at the Scala, Milan—also an old ambition of his. There she danced marvellously in *Le Lac des Cygnes*, and he wished her to create the Cat. It was contrary to her ideas, however; she was enamoured of classicism to the exclusion of everything else. She was finally persuaded, but after the *première* in Monte Carlo injured her foot and did not dance it again, Nikitina creating the part in Paris. It was his ambition to present Spessivtseva in Paris, and *Le Lac des Cygnes* was selected. He even

314

broke a fixed rule and wrote an enthusiastic article in *Camoedia* to prepare the ground, but once again she had trouble with her foot and the ambition remained unfulfilled.

Few of the remaining ballets directly interested him in the old way. *Ode* he gave over entirely to Kochno, who selected Nabokoff for the music and Tchelitcheff for the *décors*. He intervened, however, at the last moment, to suppress a series of cinematographic projections that horrified him. For one other novelty he revealed himself again as the old Diaghileff. It was his greatest desire to have another work by Stravinsky, whom he always considered to be the greatest living composer, and this desire was further strengthened by the fact that Stravinsky was now contemplating a ballet for Ida Rubinstein, *Le Baiser de la Fée*, which had naturally made him fiercely jealous. He was overjoyed when Stravinsky undertook to write him a ballet on a subject the composer himself had selected—*Apollon Musagètes*. Never since *The Sleeping Princess* had he revealed such energy in his search for the perfect realization. In order to avoid the banalities of a false Hellenism he skilfully entrusted the *décors* to a naïve painter, André Bauchant, criticizing the results in detail, even assisting at every rehearsal and guiding Balanchine with care, while previously, in the case of *La Chatte* and *Ode*, he had only inspected and criticized the final result. The ballet was an immense and deserved success. Lifar shone as he had never done before. It was the last manifestation of the Diaghileff touch.

For the other ballets that still remained, *Le Fils Prodigue* interested him the most, owing to the immense admiration that he had for Prokofiev. When he commissioned a work, it was always his habit to play a very considerable part in its creation. Not only did he lay down the general idea, but he always gave the most precise and detailed indications, often suppressing entire passages, carefully specifying the timing, indicating the position for a variation or a *pas de deux*. This was very much the case with *Le Fils Prodigue*.

The other ballet of that season, *Le Bal*, interested him very much less. He was growing heartily tired by now of being *dans le mouvement* and creating works that were purely of passing interest. He had *assez de la musiquette*, and was turning to Hindemith for a new ballet. After his last Paris season (1929), and a triumphant success with *Le Bal* and *Le Fils Prodigue*, he confessed to Nouvel, *"C'est tout ce que je déteste"*; all that he had truly enjoyed was Prokofiev's music, Rouault's *décor*, and Lifar's dancing.

His last production was Stravinsky's *Le Renard*, which he had conceived as a study in the grotesque, doubling the rôles between acrobats and dancers. It was Lifar's début as choreographer, and, as in the case of the young Massine, Larionov was entrusted with the task of guiding him. It was an amusing experiment, far less subtle than Nijinska's previous interpretation, and it could hardly reveal the great gifts that Lifar was subsequently to develop in that direction. *Le Renard* was to mark the end of a restless, unhappy phase in which Diaghileff himself had little faith. His plans for the future were very different.

These last years he had developed a new passion—the collecting of a library of rare Russian books of the eighteenth and early nineteenth centuries. In every town he visited he made a round of the antiquaries and sale-rooms, and only a year before his death made a special journey to Warsaw and Vilna, deeply moved after fifteen years at seeing land that had once been Russia. He even intended a visit to Mount Athos to visit the libraries there.

All the material possessions that he left behind him were those precious books and manuscripts. Never had he spent much money on himself. From 1922 onwards he lived in modest rooms, often without a bathroom, and after "Beppe's" departure he never took another valet. His wardrobe was often in a lamentable state, and from time to time his friends had to urge him to replenish it. When he bought pictures or jewellery it was always to give away. Never did he save a penny. He had brought with him from Russia the lavish sense of hospitality, and it was his greatest pleasure to act as host. How many people, I wonder, lived continually at his expense? He never refused a friend or relation, and never under any circumstances spoke about it.

§ 6 [1]

"Diaghileff had always had an iron strength. His powers of resistance were incredible, and till the final years I never saw him rest. Inactivity was a torment to him and gave him dark thoughts. Even during his holidays he was always in movement, which was a hard burden for his friends, from whom he expected the same activity. I often told him that in work he tired others as well as himself, while at rest he only tired others. Confident in his Herculean strength, he greatly spent himself, and even at fifty refused to alter his mode of life in the slightest degree. Yet he was frightened at the very thought of illness, and even a cold made him miserable.

"Finally this mode of life and the many worries he had gone through in 1921–22 began to tell their tale, and a doctor diagnosed the beginning of diabetes, and warned him that he was no longer a young man. He looked after himself with care, but refused to give up any of his activities. He knew what to expect, but action was life itself to him.

"Sometimes now I found him stretched out on his bed during the daytime, a thing that he had never done before. He com-

[1] From Walter Nouvel.

plained of heaviness in the legs, and often went to consult his friend and doctor, but, although he took the remedies prescribed, never would he rest or give up his annual holiday in Venice for a serious cure at Vichy. Four years ago in Berlin he had had a large carbuncle, disquieting in a diabetic, and this had happened several times since.

"My good friend was full of superstitions, and, added to his Russian ones, he had learned many new ones in Italy and from his valet 'Beppe.' Two months before he died, during the Paris season, there occurred an event which would have caused him intense anxiety. He had left the theatre, and Lifar and I were to rejoin him in a restaurant. Reaching for a package, a huge mirror crashed at our feet. Carefully we gathered the fragments together, and Lifar and I solemnly threw them into the Seine, since flowing water is supposed to avert the evil. We never told him.

"I remained behind in Paris, where I learnt that Diaghileff had been seriously ill almost the whole London season. However, he recovered, and when I met him at the station in Paris I was shocked to notice the change in him. He was years older, and dragged his feet as he walked. From the hotel he telephoned his doctor, who came immediately. After the consultation I found him sunk in a chair. The doctor had just told him that he had had a very narrow escape in London, that it was essential for him to give up his immediate plans, his Venetian holiday, in order to go to Vichy. He was not prepared to do this. As he had been told to be in the open, we went to dine in the Bois. That year I had decided not to go to Venice at all, but to take a complete rest and forget for a time the Russian Ballet. I went up to his room to say good-bye to him. He was lying on his bed. 'You'll leave me your address, just the same, in case I needed you urgently,' he said. 'Perhaps'—I smiled, and wanted him to understand that I would very much like to remain in peace. 'When shall we meet again?' 'Never,' I replied—'never'—for some reason I cannot clearly understand, perhaps as a joke. It was the last time I saw him."

CHAPTER XVIII

DIAGHILEFF AND THE BALLET
1914–1921–1929

THE STORY OF AN EVOLUTION: PART III

Reasons for the change of æsthetic—Direction of the change —The new dancers—Diaghileff's influence on choreography.

After 1914 there were many reasons for a change of direction —reasons both practical and æsthetic. All contact between Diaghileff and his friends of the *Mir Isskustva* in Russia was cut off, as was also the supply of new dancers from the Maryinsky Theatre. These factors, however, may merely have hastened on a change that was already foreshadowed by the employment of Nijinsky as choreographer, and by the use of more complex music—such as *Daphnis and Chloe* and *Sacre du Printemps*— than had previously been employed. In colour, too, the vogue of Bakst had spread so amazingly that it was necessary in self-defence to seek an entirely new direction. This second period is the one of which Diaghileff himself was proudest, since he was acting more fully on his own initiative, and without his original advisers, but in actual fact it was during the first period that his artistic influence on the artists themselves, was at its highest.

Bakst and Benois not only taught the French painters their *métier*, but turned their thoughts to theatrical work. In this second phase the ballet introduced the new schools of painting to a very wide public, but without eliciting anything new from the painters themselves.

The second phase, decoratively, was Moscow-Paris, as the first had been St. Petersburg-Versailles. Larionov influenced ballet

320

Diaghileff at the Lido, 1929

Diaghileff with Nouvel and Lifar. The Lido. 1927

Vera Nemchinova in *Les Biches*

into more burlesque channels, Picasso, in *Parade*, used it for an important cubist manifesto, and it was thereafter diverted into a variety of directions—a highly sensitive instrument, picking up the waves of artistic movements, rather than inaugurating them, as it had done previously. Diaghileff, for his part, never let himself be carried along by the stream, his consistent practice being to alternate classicism with modernism, exhibiting them side by side for the education of his public. There was always a didactic idea at the back of his mind. He did not believe in giving the public what it wanted, but in making it want precisely what it was his pleasure at the moment to show, and with very few exceptions he succeeded in this, while all the time remaining perfectly true to himself. The Ballet was an instrument that he played on for his own pleasure, and the path it followed was the path of his own artistic development. The future was always the thing that counted with him, but it is erroneous to say that he despised the past—what he sometimes wearied of was only the immediate past. If in this period there was a larger proportion of failures than previously, it is not to be wondered at—it was frankly an experimental period—but for him there were always categories of failure—glorious failures and just simple failures.

Clearly, if ballet had any relation to life at all, any contact with a wide public, a repetition of the formula of *Les Sylphides*, *Le Spectre de la Rose*, and *Sheherazade* no longer had any meaning. These works themselves were classics because they had represented so perfectly the mood of their period—undoubtedly they had even helped to make that period, as no later ballets could ever do—but war and revolution called for other feelings. It was impossible to remain unconscious of the dawn of cubism, to ignore *les Six*, to carry on as if Guillaume Apollinaire did not exist, especially when the artistic headquarters were in Paris. Throughout history France has been in the habit of taking tendencies and turning them into schools that embrace all the arts at once, and ballet, being a union of the arts, is the most rapidly and thoroughly affected.

The tendency of this second phase can best be noticed in the gradual change of subject from the romantic poem to the satirical commentary on contemporary life, a phase that is at its strongest after *The Sleeping Princess* (1921), in *Les Biches* (1924), *Le Train Bleu* (1924), *Barabau* (1925), *La Pastorale* (1925), *The Triumph of Neptune* (1926), *Romeo and Juliet* (1926), *Le Pas d'Acier* (1927), but that was foreshadowed by *Parade* (1917). So essentially topical are these ballets that their place on a programme can only be temporary, while the first group of transition ballets—*Soleil de Nuit* (1915), *Contes Russes* (1917), *La Boutique Fantasque* (1919), *Le Chapeau Tricorne* (1919), and *Pulcinella* (1920)—whose inspiration is more plastic and musical than literary, and whose subjects are simple, popular, and universal, have now become classics.[1] The sharp dividing line is 1921, and in this very last phase those fewer ballets with the universal and "non-dated" theme,[2] such as *Les Noces* (1923), *Les Matelots* (1925), *La Chatte* (1927), and *Les Dieux Mendiants* (1928), *Apollon Musagètes* (1928), are the most successful in retrospect. The theme, though often vague and unsubstantial, has an importance that is scarcely noticed at the time.

Ballet cannot be in deadly earnest the whole time, and these *tableaux de mœurs* are others of its aspects that Diaghileff was the first to explore. He did so with intention, if now and then a

[1] *Les Biches:* the modern woman; *Le Train Bleu:* gigolos, golf, tennis, the Riviera; *La Pastorale:* the cinema star; *Le Pas d'Acier:* Russia before and after; *Barabau:* the suburbs; *The Triumph of Neptune:* the current joke on Victorian England; *Romeo and Juliet:* surréaliste manifesto, aviator; a very temporary joke; *Soleil de Nuit:* popular Russian dances and folklore; *La Boutique Fantasque:* universal theme of childhood and toys; *Contes Russes:* popular Russian "twopenny coloured" pictures and folklore; *Le Chapeau Tricorne:* popular Spanish dancing; *Pulcinella:* a Harlequinade.

[2] *Les Noces:* universal theme of marriage; *Les Matelots:* knockabout farce; *La Chatte:* a fable; *Les Dieux Mendiants:* pastoral; *Apollon Musagètes:* mythology.

little feverishly, as though to assure himself that he was young and *dans le mouvement*. He knew well the comparative value of his works, but opposition to any particular ballet only made him more earnest in its defence, and it was especially to his intimates of former days that he revealed his true opinion. The comparative failure of *The Sleeping Princess* dictated the policy of the next few years, till the public, a little wearied by trivialities, applauded *Le Lac des Cygnes* and *Aurora's Wedding*, and came at last at any rate—grudgingly however—a part of the way to applauding Diaghileff's first idol, Tchaikovsky. The old and the new always hand in hand; experiment, then selection, and then experiment again—that was the general pattern of Diaghileff's direction of the Russian Ballet.

§ 2

The accident of war and revolution had its greatest effect upon the actual dancing. It was never Diaghileff's object to modify anything in the classical technique, as his retention of Cecchetti so clearly shows. He would have been well content to continue to draw upon the Maryinsky for his dancers, forming and developing them after his own manner. When obliged to look about him for additions to the company, his choice naturally fell upon England. Many years before, Pavlova had made the same choice, though in her case it seems to have been a question of discipline—the English being easier to handle.

"After the Russians," said Diaghileff, "the English have by far the greatest aptitude, and some day in the future they will form their own school." This policy of Diaghileff's, continued by Colonel de Basil to-day, has brought that time appreciably nearer. These English dancers, and the Russians who had not been trained in the old manner, developed with the company, and did not attain their full powers until after his death,[1] when the original members were no longer in their prime. It was a transition period in dancing, and the excellent schools of the great *ballerinas* had not yet been started.

This factor also dictated artistic policy to a certain extent. Dancing gradually lost its position as an equal partner with music and *décor*, and the dancers were assigned more positive rôles, that left less to their own powers of interpretation. The weakness of the dancing in *Les Sylphides* and *Aurora's Wedding* in the last years was very evident.

§3

War and revolution did not interfere with the fact that each one of Diaghileff's choreographers received his training as a dancer at the Imperial Schools. "Choreography is the most difficult problem in ballet. I have been singularly fortunate," he said; but he always did a good deal himself to help his good fortune. Massine, as we have seen, was entirely his discovery and creation, and it was Massine who carried the Ballet through its most difficult period. Without him, it might have perished in 1915. He was young, pliant, and highly sensitive to atmosphere. He was developing as a dancer at the same time—a point that has an important bearing on the detail of his work; and much of the early Massine choreography is built around Massine the dancer, however subconsciously this may have been done. Where Nijinsky proceeded by instinct, groping here and there, Massine, perhaps the first man in history to receive so complete a choreographic education, was guided by reason, with the museums of Europe at his back, and Bakst, Picasso, Stravinsky, Larionov, and Diaghileff himself as his professors.

[1] Nemchinova, Lifar, Danilova, and Markova have all shown their finest work in the last two or three years; Sokolova's rapid artistic development was quite exceptional, but she joined the Ballet in the days of Fokine.—A. L. H.

The next two choreographers, Nijinska and Balanchine, both persons of exceptional gifts, were far less under Diaghileff's direct control, their characters having been already formed.

If Massine [1] succeeded in producing more enduring works than they did, it does not necessarily mean that he had greater talent, but that he was creating at a time when Diaghileff was in the mood for serious productions, from 1915–21, up to the time of *The Sleeping Princess*, and before that frantic search for lost youth.

The whole of this second period, when Diaghileff was working alone, is an intimate reflection of his own artistic needs of the moment. Each of his choreographers had ability and marked individuality, and the detail was theirs, but the general aspect and the tendency of the work remained his and his alone. It is this essential fact that not one of his choreographers is prepared to admit or can possibly realize, because they were too close to him, too much a part of the actual machinery of creation.

[1] The work that Massine has accomplished to-day as an independent worker is the outstanding proof of his greatness as a choreographer. As a dancer, too, he has but recently come to his fullest development. Both these facts are also a tribute to Diaghileff as a "discoverer"—his own especial source of pride.—A. L. H.

───CHAPTER XIX───

DEATH IN VENICE

1929

"A fortune-teller had once told him that he would meet death by the sea."

"Par la mort de Serge de Diaghileff et la dispersion des aériens génies, la main du sort vient d'effacer les fresques étincelantes qui recouvraient le morne univers."

COMTESSE DE NOAILLES

"Venise, mausolée prédestiné à cet évocateur de magnificences, conserve le secret de sa dernière pensée. Peut-être a-t-il vu dans un ultime éclaire de sa conscience la trace légère, mais brillante et ineffacable, qu'il laissera sur cet terre d'ingratitude et d'oubli."

ROBERT BRUSSEL

One night, dining in the Bois, he told an old friend who had remarked upon his unaccustomed abstinence, "I have too much sugar—diabetes, you know"; and then, as if to reassure himself more than his friend, "It is nothing—very slight. It is almost cured already." He helped himself to saccharin from a little box given him by Stravinsky.

All his life he had enjoyed a robust Russian appetite, a health able to bear any tension. How he feared old age, death, and especially pain! One day in the Savoy he had had a violent toothache, and had reluctantly called in a dentist to lance the gum. But it was no use. He had screamed so loudly that the dentist had had to abandon the attempt. Infection, too, he had avoided, both real and imaginary, and he had always wrapped himself up against draughts with the greatest care. "That mania for fresh air and open windows in England is positively dangerous, and, oh, those windswept theatres of theirs!" Once at the Alhambra, during a rehearsal, he had mislaid his hat. It was a tragedy.

No one else's would fit, and he could not buy one ready-made. So he sat it through, his head muffled in a scarf, no one daring to be amused, as he shouted out his orders.

Now that there was actual danger he could not believe it—tried to conceal it even from himself. He had said, "At fifty"—long ago it had been "thirty"—"a man has passed his prime, and is no more good for creation. He can only repeat himself." He had now passed this self-appointed limit by seven years. He was still a young man, in touch with youth, surrounded by youth. The total ages of his last three collaborators had been sixty-three! His latest productions continued to cause a sensation, and for the first time his enterprise was really secure financially. He had bookings for two years ahead—an unaccustomed state of affairs, since usually everything had to be decided at the very last moment. This was no time to die. There were so many plans to be realized—a new ballet by Hindemith, further collaboration with Massine, Lifar to develop. He had succeeded in engaging his beloved Spessivtseva for further seasons. He had discovered a new "genius" too—Igor Markevitch, a young seventeen-year-old composer, whom he would soon present to the public. In that way he could renew his own youth—he *must* be young again! He had chosen this moment to make an attempt at getting thin. However young his mind, the middle-aged spread told its tale, and he hated it. Yes, he *would* be young. The year 1929 seemed rich for plans in the future, it would mark a date of new development.

But Sergei Pavlovitch, who was frightened of catching "glanders" from a carriage horse, scared at the prospect of an hour's Channel crossing, who would walk round a whole block rather than cross the path of a black cat, neglected the orders of his physician, simple though they were: "Avoid sweet things, avoid alcohol." Like a naughty child he ate chocolates greedily at times, or drank a bottle of champagne defiantly, to show off to the youth around him that he understood how to live. When he should have been resting and under treatment he journeyed to Berlin and Munich, enjoying himself hugely, and went to Salzburg for the festival.

Towards the end of the Covent Garden season, the most brilliant since the War, he was a desperately sick man. The last performances that he saw showed him the return of Karsavina in *Petrouchka*, Spessivtseva in *Lac des Cygnes*, with a brilliant Lifar performing the male variation, the successful launching of his latest choreographer, Serge Lifar, in Stravinsky's *Le Renard*, the return of Anton Dolin in *Le Bal*, and a favourite artist, very much a creation of his, Lydia Sokolova, secure the triumph of her career in Massine's *Sacre du Printemps*.[1] Covent Garden was so full that many of his oldest supporters were forced to stand at the back of the boxes. Twenty years before he had told the admiring group that flocked round him, "Wait, my friends, I will do much more." He had fulfilled his promise, and now for the last time he heard the applause of a packed house. In twenty years it had not abated.

He said good-bye to the company, and gave them a rendezvous in Paris for after the holidays. His final appearance in London was a fleeting visit to a party given by Anton Dolin to celebrate the success of *Le Bal*. He walked heavily, the expression in his eyes was strained, and many friends felt that they had seen him for the last time.

In Venice, where he was joined by Serge Lifar and Boris Kochno, for a few days after his arrival he was well and in excellent spirits, sitting in the sun and talking to his friends, among them his greatest, Madame Sert. He was thinking of the future, pointing out things to Lifar as he had done to Massine: "Look at those peasants, see exactly how they are walking," and

[1] She was dangerously ill herself, collapsing at the end of the longest solo in ballet.

nothing gave him greater pleasure than to impart his vision to the receptive boy.

Then suddenly he became very ill, with a temperature that mounted steadily, and he sank into a coma. The devoted and terrified Lifar immediately warned the Baroness d'Erlanger, one of his most faithful friends. For a few moments he recovered consciousness, but at first did not recognize her, then she took off her hat—"Ah, Catherine. . . . How beautiful you look. . . . I am ill—very ill indeed. . . . I feel so hot . . . light-headed." Those were his last words. The temperature increased, and he sank into a coma again. The doctor in attendance said that if he passed the night he stood an excellent chance of recovery. Lifar and Kochno watched by his side the whole night through, then becoming apprehensive they sent for Madame Sert, his dearest friend, to share their watch. Towards dawn his breathing ceased; there was no struggle, and he never knew that this dreaded thing had come, or how easy it was. He went off into a deep and peaceful sleep. At that moment the sun rose, and lit up his tranquil face. He had died on the water—in Venice, his favoured resting-place. The following night, as he lay in his room, surrounded by flowers, a violent thunderstorm came over the lagoon —grandiose and dramatic, as he himself would have chosen.

In the morning, after the storm, he was taken over the water to his last resting-place on the island of San Michele, amidst the bending cypress-trees. The storm had made a carpet of green leaves from the hotel to the gondola; worthy setting of his last great spectacle.

APPENDIX I

DIAGHILEFF CHRONOLOGY WITH COMPLETE LIST OF PRODUCTIONS

Those ballets with an asterisk are in the current repertoire of Colonel de Basil's Russian Ballet.

1872 Born at Perm.

1890 Went to St. Petersburg. Entered the University.

1893 Came of age. Entered into his mother's inheritance. Made a "grand tour."

1897 Organized first exhibition at the Stieglitz Museum, St. Petersburg. Works by Lavery, Guthrie, Brangwyn, Liebermann, Bartels, and others.
Scandinavian Exhibition.

1898 Russian and Finnish Painters. Steigletz Museum. Founded the *Mir Isskustva (World of Art)*. Attached to the Imperial Theatres, and edited their year-book.

1899 International Exhibition at the Academy of Fine Arts. Exhibitions yearly till 1903.

1902 Publication of Diaghileff's monograph on Levitsky.

1904 The *Mir Isskustva* ceases publication.

1905 The Historic Portrait Exhibition at the Palais Tauride.

1906 The Russian Exhibition at the Salon d'Automne, Grand Palais, Paris.

1907 Series of Russian Historical Concerts, Opéra, Paris.

1908 BORIS GODOUNOV: Opéra, Paris.
Chaliapine: Boris; M. Smirnov: Le Faux Dmitri. *Chef d'orchestre:* M. Felix Blumenfeld. *Producer:* M. Sanine.
Décors after Golovin, by MM. Yuon, Anisfeld, Lanceray, Jaremitsch, Plekhanov. Act IV by Alexandre Benois.
Costumes: M. Bilibine.

331

1909 Season of Ballet and Opera. Théâtre du Châtelet, Paris.

*LES SYLPHIDES

Ballet in one act by M. Fokine. *Music:* Chopin; Valse No. 1, op. 70; Mazurka No. 2, op. 32; Mazurka No. 3, op. 67; Prelude No. 7, op. 28; Valse No. 2, op. 64; Valse No. 1, op. 18. (*Orchestrated by* Stravinsky and others.)
Décors and costumes: A. Benois. *Choreography:* M. Fokine.
Pavlova; Nijinsky; Karsavina.
Produced in Russia as *Chopiniana.*
(Retained in repertoire throughout)

CLÉOPÂTRE

Music by Arensky. (Prelude: Tanéieff; Arrival of Cleopatra: Rimsky-Korsakov; Veil Dance: Glinka (*Mlada*); Bacchanal: Glazounov (*The Seasons*); Persian Dance: Moussorgsky.
Décors and costumes: Bakst. *Choreography:* Fokine.
Ida Rubinstein; Pavlova; Karsavina.
In revivals, Seraphine Astafieva and Lubov Tchernicheva as Cleopatra.
Produced in Russia as *Nuits d'Egypte.*

LE FESTIN

A divertissement to music by Tchaikovsky.
(Blue Bird from *Belle au bois dormant* and finale of 2nd Symphony), Moussorgsky (*Hopak*), Ghuka, and Glazounov.
Setting: C. Korovin's Act I, *Rousslan and Ludmila.*
(Not given after this season)

LE PAVILLON D'ARMIDE

Ballet in three scenes by Benois, after Théophile Gautier.
Music: Tcherepnin.
Costumes and décors: Benois. *Choreography:* Fokine.
Karalli and Mordkin.
First presented at Maryinsky in 1907 with Pavlova and Nijinsky.

*PRINCE IGOR

The Polovetsian dances from Borodin's opera.
Décors and costumes: Roerich. *Choreography:* Fokine.
Bolm as chief warrior.
(Revivals with Massine, Woizikovski.)
First produced in St. Petersburg.

IVAN THE TERRIBLE
Opera by Rimsky-Korsakov *(La Pskovitaine).*
Décor: Golovin. (2nd Scene, Roerich.)
Chaliapine as Ivan.

1909   ROUSSLAN AND LUDMILA (Act I)
Opera by Glinka.
Décors: Korovin.

1910   Baron Gunsbourg became co-director.
Season of Ballet at the Opéra, Paris.

*SHEHERAZADE
Ballet in one act by Bakst, Benois, and Fokine. *Music:* Rimsky-Korsakov (Parts I, II, and IV of symphonic poem, *Mille et une nuits).*
Décors and costumes: Bakst. *A curtain by* Serov. *Choreography:* Fokine.
Ida Rubinstein (revived with Karsavina, Tchernicheva, and Massine); Nijinsky.

*L'OISEAU DE FEU
Ballet in two scenes by M. Fokine. *Music:* Stravinsky.
Costumes and décor: Golovin. *Choreography:* Fokine.
Karsavina, the Firebird; Bolm, the Prince.
(Afterwards revived, with *décor and costumes,* by Gontcharova, with Lopokova, Tchernicheva, and Lifar.)

*CARNAVAL
Ballet in one act by Fokine. *Music:* Schumann. *(Orchestrated by* Rimsky-Korsakov, Glazounov, Liadov, and Tcherepnin.)
Costumes and décors: Bakst. *Choreography:* Fokine.
Lydia Lopokova, Columbine; Nijinsky, Harlequin.
(Revived with Kchesinska, Karsavina, Sokolova, Danilova, and Fokine, Idzikovski.)
First produced St. Petersburg.

GISELLE
Ballet in two scenes by Théophile Gautier. *Music:* A. Adam.
Costumes and décor: Benois. *Choreography:* Coralli.
Karsavina, Giselle; Nijinsky, the Prince.
Only time produced by Diaghileff. Created 1841.

Lydia Lopokova first joins the company.
Catherina Gheltzer, Moscow *prima ballerina,* dances this season.

1911   Season in Costanzi, Rome. At Monte Carlo. Châtelet, Paris. Coronation Gala, Covent Garden, London, June 21st. Formation of Diaghileff's own company. Season at Covent Garden, London, October–December.

1911 *PETROUCHKA
Ballet in four scenes by Stravinsky and Benois. *Music:* Stravinsky.
Costumes and décor: Benois. *Choreography:* Fokine.
Karsavina, the Dancer; Bolm, the Moor; Nijinsky, Petrouchka.

*LE SPECTRE DE LA ROSE
Ballet in one act by J. L. Vaudoyer, from the poem by Théophile Gautier. *Music:* Weber (Berlioz *orchestration*).
Costumes and décor: Bakst. *Choreography:* Fokine.
Karsavina, the Girl; Nijinsky, the Rose.
    (Revived with Nemchinova and Dolin)

LE DIEU BLEU
Ballet in one act by Jean Cocteau and F. Madrazo. *Music:* Reynaldo Hahn.
Costumes and décor: Bakst. *Choreography:* Fokine.
Karsavina; Nijinska; Nijinsky.
    (Subsequently Fokina and Fokine)

NARCISSE
Ballet by Bakst. *Music:* Tcherepnin.
Costumes and décor: Bakst. *Choreography:* Fokine.
Karsavina, Echo; Nijinsky, Narcisse.
    (Revival: Sokolova and Slavinsky, 1925)

SADKO
The under-sea scene from Rimsky-Korsakov's opera.
Décor: B. Anisfeld.

*LAC DES CYGNES (in London)
Ballet in two acts and three scenes. Music: Tchaikovsky.
Costumes and décor for Act II, Golovin; *décor, Act I,* Korovin.
Choreography: Petipa.
Kchesinska and Nijinsky.

AURORE ET LE PRINCE (London)
From *The Sleeping Princess.*
Kchesinska and Nijinsky.

1912   Season at the Châtelet, Paris. Covent Garden, London. Also at Berlin, Vienna, and Budapest.

*L'Après-midi d'un Faune
Ballet in one act by Leon Bakst, after Mallarmé's *Eclogue*.
Costumes and décor: Bakst. *Choreography:* Nijinsky. Piltz, the
Nymph; Nijinsky, the Faun.
(Revivals with Massine, Woizikovski, Lifar)

1912 **Daphnis and Chloe**
Ballet in three scenes by Fokine. *Music:* Ravel.
Décor and costumes: Bakst. *Choreography:* Fokine.
Karsavina and Nijinsky.
(Revived with Fokina and Fokine, and Tchernicheva and Dolin
in 1925)

*Thamar
Ballet in one act by Bakst, after Lermontov's poem.
Music: Balakirev.
Décor and costumes: Bakst. *Choreography:* Fokine.
Karsavina and Bolm.
(Revived with Tchernicheva, Doubrovska, and Woizikovski,
1925)

Lydia Sokolova and Nicolas Zverev join the company.

1913 Seasons in Monte Carlo; Paris, Opening of the Champs Élysées
Theatre; London, Covent Garden and Drury Lane.
First South American Tour under Baron Gunsbourg's direction.
Nijinsky's marriage. Fokine leaves the troupe.

Le Sacre du Printemps
Ballet in two acts by Roerich and Stravinsky.
Music: Stravinsky.
Décor and costumes: Roerich. *Choreography:* Nijinsky.
Piltz, the Chosen Virgin.

Jeux
Ballet in one act by Nijinsky. *Music:* Debussy.
Décors and costumes: Bakst. *Choreography:* Nijinsky.
Karsavina; Schollar; Nijinsky.
(Never revived)

La Tragédie de Salomé
Music: Florent Schmitt.
Costumes and décor: Soudeikine. *Choreography:* Boris Ro-
manov.
(Never revived)

LE ROSSIGNOL
Three-act opera by Stravinsky (after Andersen).
Produced by Benois and Sanine.
Décors and costumes: Benois. *Choreography:* Romanov.
Le Rossignol, Aurelia Dobrowolska, also in Paris, revivals of:

1913 BORIS GODOUNOV
KHOVANTCHINA. *Décor:* Fedorovsky.
and
LA NUIT DE MAI. Rimsky-Korsakov. *Décor:* Fedorovsky.

1914 Fokine returns. Paris, Opéra. London, Drury Lane.
(Friday, July 25th, 100th performance in London.)

LE COQ D'OR
Three-act opera by Rimsky-Korsakov (sung and danced simultaneously). *Book by* Bielsky.
Costumes and décor: N. Gontcharova.
Choreography and production: Fokine. Karsavina (dancing); Dobrowolska (singing).

LA LÉGENDE DE JOSEPH
By Hugo von Hoffmansthal and Count Harry Kessler.
Music: Strauss. *Scenery:* Sert.
Costumes: Bakst. *Choreography:* Fokine.
Marie Kouznetzoff, Potiphar's Wife (in London, Karsavina and Maria Carmi); Massine (début), Joseph.
(Never revived)

PAPILLONS
Ballet in one act by Fokine. *Music:* Schumann.
(*Orchestrated by* Tcherepnin.) *Scenery:* Doboujinsky.
Costumes: Bakst. *Choreography:* Fokine.
Karsavina; Will; Tchernicheva; Schollar.

MIDAS
Music: Steinberg.
Costumes and décors: Doboujinsky. *Choreography:* Fokine.
Karsavina; Bolm; Frohman.
(Never revived)

1915 In Italy, Switzerland, and one charity gala, Opéra, Paris. First American tour.

* SOLEIL DE NUIT
  Music. Rimsky-Korsakov (*Snegouroutchka*).
  Costumes and décor. Larionov. *Choreography:* Massine.
  (Revived with Nemchinova and Zverev)

SADKO
  The under-sea act. Costumes: Gontcharova. *Choreography:*
  A. Bolm.
  U.S.A. (January–May), Madrid, San Sebastian, Bilbao, San
  Sebastian.

Vera Nemchinova, Stanislas Idzikovski, Leon Woizikovski join
the company.

1916 TRIANA
        Music: Ravel. *Décor:* Gontcharova (in Rome).

      ESPAÑA
        Music: Albeniz. *Décor:* Gontcharova (in Rome).

      HISTOIRES NATURELLES
        Music: Ravel. *Décor:* Larionov (in Lausanne).

      KIKIMORA
      (Afterwards, a part of *Contes Russes.*) (San Sebastian.)

      *LAS MENINAS [1]
        Music: Fauré. *Décor and costumes:* Sert.
        Choreography: Massine. At San Sebastian.
                (Revived Monte Carlo, 1925)
        (*In America under Nijinsky*)

      TYL EULENSPIEGEL
        Music. Strauss. *Costumes and décors:* Robert Edmund Jones.
        Choreography: Nijinsky.

      Olga Spessivtseva first dances with the company.

1917 At Rome, Naples, Florence, Paris, Madrid, Barcelona, South
      America, Barcelona, Madrid, Lisbon.

      *LES FEMMES DE BONNE HUMEUR
        One-act ballet by V. Tommasini after Goldoni. *Music:* Scar-
        latti (arr. Tommasini)
        Décor and costumes: Bakst. *Choreography:* Massine.

[1] Debussy wrote to Diaghileff of this work, May 26th, 1917: "*Il vous a plu, mon
cher Diaghileff, que le charme si nettement français de la Pavane de Fauré se
revête de gravité espagnole; et c'est un tour de force dont il faut vous féliciter;
vous et la prodigieux Massine.*"

*Contes Russes
Ballet by Massine. *Music:* Liadov.
Décor and costumes: Larionov. *Choreography:* Massine.
Kikimora, Sokolova; Princess Cygne, Tchernicheva; Baba
Yaga, Kremneff.

Parade
Ballet in one act by Jean Cocteau. *Music:* Satie.
Costumes, décor, and curtain: Picasso. *Choreography:* Massine.

Feu d'Artifice
Music: Stravinsky. *Décor:* Balla.
(Without choreography.)
Tour of sixteen towns in Spain.

1918   London Coliseum (September).

Cléopâtre
Revival with new first act, *décor*, and two costumes by R.
Delaunay. (Tchernicheva as Cleopatra.)

Les Jardins d'Aranjuez
Music: Fauré; Ravel-Chabrier (Madrid only).
Costumes and décor: Sert. *Choreography:* Massine.

1919   London: Coliseum (January) ; Alhambra (April) ; Empire (September). Paris: Opéra.

*La Boutique Fantasque [1]
Ballet in one act. Music by Rossini. (*Orchestrated by* Respighi.)
Curtain, costume, and décor: Derain.
Lopokova and Massine, the Can-Can Dancers; Cecchetti, the
Shopkeeper; Idzikovski, the Snob; Sokolova and Woizikovski,
Tarantella.
(Subsequently Lopokova, Nemchinova, Danilova, and Woizi-
kovski.)
(*Première* in London)

*Le Chapeau Tricorne
One-act ballet by Martinez Sierra after Alarcón. *Music:* Da
Falla.
Costumes, scenery, and curtain: Picasso. *Choreography:* Mas-
sine.

[1] For an admirable graphic description of this, as well as Fokine's *Sylphides,
Carnaval, Firebird,* and *Prince Igor,* see Adrian Stokes's *Russian Ballets.* His description could not be bettered.—A. L. H.

Karsavina and Massine.
(Subsequently Sokolova, Tchernicheva and Woizikovski.)
(*Première* in London)

L'OISEAU ET LE PRINCE
Pas de deux from *The Sleeping Princess*.
Décor and costumes. Bakst.
(Only in London)

CHOUT
Ballet in four scenes. Music: Prokofiev.
Décor and costumes: Larionov. *Choreography:* Slavinsky and Larionov.

1920   London, Covent Garden. Paris, Opéra (May), Champs Élysées (December).

CHANT DU ROSSIGNOL
Ballet in one act, after Andersen's story, by Stravinsky and Massine. *Music:* Stravinsky.
Décor and costumes: Matisse. *Choreography:* Massine.

1920   PULCINELLA
Ballet with singing, in one act. Music: Stravinsky, after Pergolesi.
Scenery and costumes: Picasso. *Choreography:* Massine.

LE ASTUZZIE FEMINILI
Opera ballet in three scenes. Music: Cimarosa. (*Orchestrated by* Respighi.)
Décor and costumes: Sert. *Choreography:* Massine.

LE SACRE DU PRINTEMPS
Revival, with choreography by Massine.

1921   At Prince's, London (June). Paris: Gaieté-Lyrique.
At the Alhambra, London (November).

THE SLEEPING PRINCESS
Ballet in five scenes after Perrault. *Music:* Tchaikovsky.
(Prelude, scene 3 and Aurora's variation re-orchestrated by Stravinsky.)
Décor and costumes: Bakst. *Choreography:* Petipa, with additions (*The Three Ivans*) by Nijinska.
Princess Aurora, V. Trefilova, L. Egorova, O. Spessivtseva; Prince Charming, P. Vladimiroff; Lilac Fairy, L. Lopokova.

CUADRO FLAMENCO
Troupe of Spanish Gipsy dancers in setting by Picasso.
Music arranged by Da Falla.

Anton Dolin first dances with the company under the name of Patrikieff.

1922 *Paris: Opéra, Mogador. Tours in France and Belgium.

*LE MARIAGE D'AURORE
One act from *The Sleeping Princess.*
Costumes: Benois (from *Pavillon d'Armide*). *New Costumes:* Gontcharova. *Décor:* Bakst.
(Retained in the repertoire till the end)

LE RENARD
Ballet in one act by Stravinsky.
Décor and costumes: Larionov. *Choreography:* Nijinska.
Nijinska as Le Renard.

MAVRA
Opera by Stravinsky.
Costumes and décor: Survage.
(Paris only.)

Boris Kochno joins the company.

1923 Paris: Gaieté-Lyrique. Great fête at Versailles. Becomes "Les Ballets Russes de Monte Carlo."

LES NOCES
In four tableaux. Words and music: Stravinsky (for four pianos).
Scenery and décor: Gontcharova. *Choreography:* Nijinska.
Doubrovska, the Bride.

1924 Paris: Théâtre des Champs Élysées. London: The Coliseum.

LES BICHES (at Monte Carlo)
Music: Poulenc.
Décor, costumes, and curtain: Laurencin. *Choreography:* Nijinska.
Vera Nemchinova, Adagietto.
(Subsequently Nikitina and Petrova.)
Nijinska: the Rag Mazurka.
(Subsequently Sokolova)

Tchernicheva ⎫
Sokolova   ⎬ Chanson dansée.
(Subsequently Danilova.)

Les Facheux
Ballet in one act by Kochno, after Molière. *Music:* Auric.
Décor and costumes: Braque. *Choreography:* Nijinska.
Tchernicheva; Nijinska; Dolin; Woizikovski; Lifar; Wilzak.

Mercure
Music: Satie.
Décors and costumes: Picasso. *Choreography:* Massine.
(Taken over from Comte Étienne de Beaumont)

Les Tentations de la Bergère
Music: Monteclair. (*Orchestrated by* Casadesus.)
Scenery and costumes: Juan Gris. *Choreography:* Nijinska
Lubov; Tchernicheva; Dolin.

Cimarosiana
Arrangement of *Le Astuzzie Feminili.*
Nemchinova; Lifar (first rôle).

Le Train Bleu
Ballet in one act by Jean Cocteau. *Music:* Milhaud.
Costumes: Chanel. *Scenery:* Laurens. *Curtain:* Picasso. *Choreography:* Nijinska.
Nijinska, the Tennis Champion.
(Subsequently Gevergeva and Sokolova.)
Woizikovski, the Golfer; Dolin, Le Beau Gosse.
(Never revived)

1924   ### Le Médecin malgré Lui
Opera by Gounod.
Costumes and décor: Benois.
(At Monte Carlo)

Philémon et Baucis
Opera by Gounod.
Costumes and décor: Benois.
(At Monte Carlo)

Serge Lifar and Anton Dolin join the company.

1925   London: The Coliseum. Paris: Gaieté-Lyrique.

*LES MATELOTS

Five-scene ballet by Kochno. *Music:* Auric.
Curtain, décor, and costumes: Pruna. *Choreography:* Massine
Nemchinova (afterwards Danilova); Sokolova; Lifar; Slavin
sky; Woizikovski.

ZEPHYR AND FLORA

Ballet by Kochno. *Music:* Dukelsky.
Décor and costumes: Braque. *Masks:* O. Messel. *Choreography.*
Massine.
Nikitina (then Danilova); Dolin (then Tcherkas); Serge Lifar.
(Never revived)

BARABAU

Ballet with singing. Book and Music: Rieti.
Décor and costumes: Utrillo. *Choreography:* Balanchine.
Sokolova; Lifar.
(*Première* in London)

LA PASTORALE

Ballet by Boris Kochno. *Music:* Auric.
Décor and costumes: Pruna. *Choreography:* Balanchine.
Doubrovska; Serge Lifar.

Danilova, Gevergeva, Efimov, Balanchine join the company, having first appeared as the Russian State dancers.
Alicia Markova joins the company.

1926   London: His Majesty's, Lyceum (December). Paris: Sarah Bernhardt. Kunstlar Theater, Berlin—Turin—Scala, Milan.

JACK IN THE BOX [1]

Music: Satie. (*Orchestrated* by Milhaud.)
Décor and costumes: Derain. *Choreography:* Balanchine.
Danilova and Idzikovski.

1926   **ROMEO AND JULIET**

In two parts. Rehearsal without scenery. *Music:* Lambert.
Paintings by Miró and Ernst. *Choreography.* Nijinska
Karsavina and Lifar.

THE TRIUMPH OF NEPTUNE

Pantomime in twelve pictures. Music: Berners. *Subject:* S. Sitwell.

[1] This is the MS. that Satie thought he had lost in a taxi and that was afterwards found in an old coat.—A. L. H.

Costumes from collection of B Pollock, arranged **by Prince** Shervachidzé. *Choreography*. Balanchine.
Danilova; Sokolova; Lifar; Idzikovski; Balanchine.

LE ROSSIGNOL
New choreography by Balanchine.
Markova as the Nightingale.

NUIT SUR LE MONT CHAUVE
Music: Moussorgsky.
Décor and costumes: Gontcharova.

LA COLOMBE
Opera by Gounod.
Décor: Juan Gris.
(Monte Carlo)

L'EDUCATION MANQUÉE
Opera by Chabrier. *Décor:* Juan Gris.
(Monte Carlo)

1927   London: Prince's. Paris: Sarah Bernhardt, Opéra. Tour compris
ing towns in Germany, Austria; Budapest, Prague, and Geneva.

LE PAS D'ACIER
Ballet in two scenes by Prokofiev and Iakouloff. *Music:* Prokofiev.
Constructions and costumes after designs by Iakouloff. *Choreography:* Massine.
Tchernicheva; Danilova; Petrova; Lifar; Woizikovski; Massine.

LA CHATTE
Ballet in one act by Sobeka, after the fable by Æsop. *Music:* Sauguet.
Architectural constructions: Gabo and Pevsner. *Choreography.* Balanchine.
Olga Spessivtseva (subsequently Nikitina and Markova); Serge Lifar.

1928   London: His Majesty's. Paris: Sarah Bernhardt, Opéra. Brussels:
Inauguration of the Palais des Beaux Arts.

ODE
Ballet by Boris Kochno *in two acts. Music:* Nabokoff.
Décor and costumes: Tchelitcheff and Charbonner. *Choreog raphy:* Massine.
Lifar.

343

APOLLON MUSAGÈTES
Ballet in two scenes. Music: Stravinsky.
Décor and costumes: Bauchant. *Choreography:* Balanchine.

LES DIEUX MENDIANTS
Ballet in one act by Handel (arranged Beecham).
Scenery after Bakst. *Costumes:* J. Gris (those of *Tentations de
la Bergère*). *Choreography:* Balanchine.
Danilova; Tchernicheva; Doubrovska; Woizikovski.
(Première in London)

LES FÂCHEUX
Revival with choreography by Massine.

1929   Paris: Sarah Bernhardt. Berlin and Cologne. London: Covent
Garden.

LE FILS PRODIGUE
Ballet in three scenes by Kochno. *Music:* Prokofiev.
Décor and costumes: Rouault. *Choreography:* Balanchine.
Doubrovska; Lifar; Dolin; Woizikovski.

*LE BAL
Ballet in two scenes by Boris Kochno. *Music:* Rieti.
Décor and costumes: Chirico. *Choreography:* Balanchine.
Danilova and Dolin.

LE RENARD
New version by S. Lifar.
Double cast of acrobats and dancers.

Diaghileff dies in Venice.

APPENDIX II

COMPOSITION OF THE COMPANY AT
VARIOUS PERIODS

(I). In 1909 (55 members):

Anna Pavlova
Thamar Karsavina; Vera Karalli;
Sophie Fedorova; Alexandra Baldina

Helene Smirnova; Alexandra Féodorova;
Ida Rubinstein
Michel Mordkin; Vaslav Nijinsky;
Theodore Kosloff; Adolf Bolm;
Boulgakov; Alexandre Monakov.
Maître de Ballet: Fokine
Stage Director: O. Allegri
Stage Manager: Serge Grigorieff.

(From St. Petersburg: 25 women, 17 men; from Moscow: 5 women,
8 men.)

(II). In 1911 (83 members) [1]:

FIRST LONDON PROGRAMME
Covent Garden, Wednesday, June 21st.

LE PAVILLON D'ARMIDE, with:
Karsavina, Bolm, Cecchetti,
Nijinsky, Grigorieff. Will, Schollar,
Nijinska, Vassilevska, Kussov.

This year the troupe in Monte Carlo was composed as follows: Women: from
the Maryinsky, 7; Imperial Schools, 2: Moscow, 2; Warsaw, 11. Men: Maryinsky,
7; Moscow, 2; Warsaw, 2; Molodstoff's company (touring), 10. Additions for
Rome, Paris, and London: Women: Petersburg, 13; Moscow, 13. Men: Petersburg,
8; Moscow, 6.

Le Carnaval
  Columbine. Will   *Pierrot,* Bolm
  Chiavina, Fokina   *Harlequin,* Nijinsky
  Estrella, Schollar   *Pantalon,* Cecchetti
  Papillon, Nijinska   *Eusebius,* Kussov
            Florestan, Semenov

Prince Igor (with singing)
  Adolf Bolm.

Conductor: N. Tcherepnin
Stage Manager: Serge Grigorieff (and mime).

(III). In 1912:
  Directeur chorégraphique: M. Fokine.
  Directeur artistique: Leon Bakst.
   Nijinsky   Thamar Karsavina
   Mmes Bronislava Nijinska MM. Adolf Bolm
    Sophie Fedorova   Nicolas Kremneff
    Marie Piltz   Alexandre Kotchetovsky
    Lydie Nelidova   Pierre Vladimiroff
    Alexandra Vassilevska Enrico Cecchetti
    Marguerite Frohman   Nicolas Semenov
    Seraphine Astafieva
 et le Corps de Ballet comprenant 85 danseurs et danseuses.
  Régisseur général: Serge Grigorieff.

In 1918:
  During the last months of the war:
  Massine   Lopokova
  Gavrilov   Tchernicheva

  Sokolova; Joséphine Cecchetti; Radina; Vassilevska; Zaleska; Cecchetti; Kremneff; Idzikovski; Woizikovski; Jasvinsky.

    Serge Grigorieff.

(IV). In 1919:
     Thamar Karsavina
  Vera Karalli   Lubov Tchernicheva
     Leonide Massine
  Veceslas Svoboda   Stanislas Idzikovski

Leon Woizikovski—Nicolas Kremneff—Nicolas Zverev

et

le Maestro Enrico Cecchetti

Lydia Sokolova	Joséphine Cecchetti
Vera Nemchinova	Alexandra Vassilevska
Felia Radina	Hilda Bewicke
Leocadia Klementovicz	Jean Jasvinsky

et

le Corps de Ballet

Régisseur général: Serge Grigorieff.

(V). 1929. Programme of last performance given by the Diaghileff Ballet:

Covent Garden—Friday, July 26th.

The Ball. The Prodigal Son. Aurora's Wedding (with Markova and Dolin, Blue Bird; Danilova and Lifar, Aurora and the Prince).

The company consisted of:

Thamar Karsavina (guest in *Petrouchka*)

Olga Spessivtseva.

Alexandra Danilova	Serge Lifar
Lydia Sokolova	Leon Woizikovski
Selia Doubrovska	Anton Dolin

Stage Manager: Serge Grigorieff.

1935—*Present activities of various members of the company:*

BALANCHINE	New York. Founder and *maître de ballet*, American Ballet.
BOLM	Chicago. Teaching and producing.
BRANITSKA	De Basil Russian Ballet.
CHAMIE	De Basil Russian Ballet.
DANILOVA	*Prima ballerina.* De Basil Russian Ballet.
DEVALOIS	*Maître de ballet.* "Vic Wells" Ballet, London.
FOKINE	New York. Teaching and producing.
GRIGORIEFF	Stage director, De Basil Russian Ballet.
HOYER, J.	De Basil Russian Ballet.
IDZIKOVSKI	Teaching in London.
LADRE	De Basil Russian Ballet.

LIFAR	*Premier danseur et maître de ballet*, Opéra, **Paris.**
MARKOVA	*Prima ballerina*, "Vic Wells," London
MASSINE	*Maître de ballet, collaborateur artistique*, and *premier danseur*, De Basil Russian Ballet.
NEMCHINOVA	*Prima ballerina*. Opera. Kovno, Lithuania.
NIJINSKA	Choreographer. De Basil Russian Ballet.
OBIDENNIA	De Basil Russian Ballet.
SHABELSKA	De Basil Russian Ballet.
SOKOLOVA	Teaching in London.
TCHERKAS	*Premier danseur*, Opéra Comique, Paris.
TCHERNICHEVA	*Maître de ballet*, De Basil Russian Ballet, and member of company.
VLADIMIROFF	New York. Teaching.
ZVEREV	Choreographer and *maître de ballet*, Opera, Kovno, Lithuania.

Members of the former Imperial Ballet associated with Diaghileff as guest artists, etc.:

EGOROVA	Paris. Teaching.
KCHESINSKA	Paris. Teaching.
LEGAT	London. Teaching.
TREFILOVA	Paris. Teaching. *Maître de ballet*, Châtelet

INDEX

INDEX

BALLETS, OPERAS, ETC.

Fâcheux, Les, 305
Farucca, The, 283
Fée des Poupées, La, 120
Femmes de Bonne Humeur, Les, 275, 283
Festin, 181
Fils Prodigue, Le, 316
Firebird, The (See Oiseau de Feu, L')
Fisherman and the Naiad, The, 105

Giselle, 201, 211, 216, 233

PERSONS

Empress Dowager of Russia, 211 et seq., 232
Erlanger, Baroness d', 329
Ernst, Max, 313
Eugène of Sweden, Prince, 64
Evans, Edwin, 279 et seq., 298
Evreinova, —, Diaghileff's mother, 10

FALLA, MANUEL DA, 282, 283
Fazer, Edouard, 175
Fedorov, 227
Felix "Loco," 282 et seq.
Filosofova, Anna Pavlovna, 7, 9, 20-21 et seq.
Filosofov, Dmitri, 17 et seq., 36, 38, 57, 64, 68, 81 et seq., 85, 90, 91, 92, 94, 95, 99, 101, 102, 142, 165
Filosofov, the family, 17 et seq., 30
Fokine, Michael, xxxi, 42 et seq., 109, 122, 126, 161, 165, 166 et seq., 168 et seq., 170, 176, 177, 178, 179, 180 et seq., 185, 189, 199, 201, 202, 203, 208, 217, 218 et seq., 222, 226, 236, 237, 251, 261, 262, 263, 272, 299, 324
Franck, César, 98, 152
Fredericks, Baron, 116, 119, 212 et seq.

GALTIER, JOSEPH, 186
Gautier, Théophile, 160, 208
Genée, Adeline, 210
George, Waldemar, 301
Gert, 109
Gevergeva, Tamara, 309
Gheltzer, K., 122
Ghéon, Henri, 187
Glazounov, 121, 149, 152, 164, 179, 259, 261
Golovin, 94, 118, 119, 154, 201
Gontcharova, Natalia, 244, 269 et seq., 274, 303, 304
Gorki, 125
Gorsky, 119
Gounod, 40, 305 et seq.
Grahn, 43
Greffulhe, Comtesse de, 147, 173, 238
Grigorieff, Serge, xviii, xxv, xxvi, xxvii, 59, 122, 181, 216, 237, 239, 242, 244, 252 et seq., 261, 262, 299, 313
Grigorieff, Vsevolod, xxvii

INDEX

THE AUTHORS

ARNOLD L. HASKELL

Arnold L. Haskell was born in 1900 in London and educated at Cambridge. He has been successful as publisher, literary agent, impresario, picture dealer and journalist but he would prefer to characterize himself as a balletomaniac. For years he has followed every performance of ballet in England, Paris and Monte Carlo —sometimes attending over 250 in a single year. He organized the Diaghileff Memorial Exhibition in London, founded the Camargo Society and is the Director of the Ballet Club. On occasions he has acted as impresario, presenting Tamara Karsavina and Lydia Lopokova. Recently he was appointed dance critic of the London DAILY TELEGRAPH. *He is the friend and confident of all the distinguished dancers of our time and specializes in acting as peace-maker in emergency situations. He himself learned dancing in order to obtain a sound technical background but he is* not *a disappointed dancer turned critic. His books include* SOME STUDIES IN BALLET *(1928),* THE SCULPTOR SPEAKS *(1931),* BLACK ON WHITE *(1933), and* BALLETOMANIA *which recently appeared under the present publisher's imprint, winning wide critical acclaim.*

WALTER NOUVEL

Walter Nouvel was a close friend of Diaghileff from his university days and collaborated with him until his death. His specialty has been music and he did much to discover both Stravinsky and Prokofiev.

083723